The High Priests of American Politics

The High Priests

OF AMERICAN POLITICS

The Role of Lawyers in
American Political Institutions

Mark C. Miller

The University of Tennessee Press • Knoxville

❖❖❖

Parts of this book have previously appeared as "Courts, Agencies, and Congressional Committees: A Neo-Institutional Perspective" in *Review of Politics 55*, no. 3; "Lawyers in Congress: What Difference Does It Make?" in *Congress and the Presidency* 20, no. 1; "Congressional Committees and the Federal Courts: A Neo-Institutional Perspective" in *Western Political Quarterly* 45, no. 4; "Lawmaker Attitudes toward Court Reform in Massachusetts" in *Judicature 77*, no. 1; and "Congress and the Constitution: A Tale of Two Committees" in *Constitutional Law Journal* 3, no. 2.

Library of Congress Cataloging in Publication Data

Miller, Mark C. (Mark Carlton), 1958–
    The high priests of American politics: the role of lawyers in American political institutions/Mark C. Miller.—1st ed.
      p.   cm.
Includes bibliographical references and index.
ISBN 0-87049-902-5 (cloth: alk. paper)
1. Lawyers in politics—United States.
2. Legislators—United States.
I. Title.
KF299.L4M55   1995
328.73'092'2—dc20
                                           95-4360
                                            CIP

To my students, past, present, and future

Contents

Tables

Acknowledgments

I would like to thank former U.S. Representative John F. Seiberling (Democrat-Ohio), Ohio representative Mike Stinziano, and Professor Samuel (Pat) Patterson for their assistance in setting up the interviews upon which much of this project is based. I would also like to thank the Brookings Institution and U.S. Representative Tom Sawyer (Democrat-Ohio) for use of office space, telephones, etc. during the Washington, D.C., phase of the interviews. A special thanks to Professor Thom Little for sharing the Maryland, North Carolina, and supplemental Ohio data with me. Stephen Euper also deserves thanks for alerting me to various issues.

The Massachusetts interviews were completed with the help of a Faculty Development Grant from Clark University in Worcester, Massachusetts. Much of the Ohio data was processed with assistance from the Department of Political Science at the Ohio State University, as part of the Ohio Legislative Research Project under the supervision of Professor Samuel (Pat) Patterson. Professors Randall Ripley, Lawrence Baum, and Herb Weisberg at Ohio State University deserve special thanks for their many helpful comments on various versions of this project. Professors Christine Harrington and Robert Kaufman, and other anonymous reviewers, also made very useful suggestions for improvements on the manuscript. Meredith Morris-Babb at the University of Tennessee Press deserves special thanks for all her help.

I also want to thank Professors Brian Cook and Cynthia Enloe of Clark University for their help and guidance. Sharon Krefetz, Dean of the College at Clark and a member of the Government Department, provided invaluable assistance and encouragement. I also want to thank Patricia Miles of Clark University for all her help. Thanks also go to former Clark students Jonathan Burton, Rachel Larkin, and Zoe Laasko for their assistance with the Massachusetts interviews and data preparation. I would also like to thank various reference librarians at Clark University, at George Washington University, at the Ohio State University, at the Library of Congress in Washington, D.C., and at the National Center for the Study of State Courts in Williamsburg, Virginia. Finally, I would like to thank the students in my seminars on lawyers and politics at Clark University for all their helpful comments and suggestions.

CHAPTER ONE

The Study of Politics and of Lawyers

The profession I chose was politics; the profession I entered was the law. I entered one because I thought it would lead to the other.
—*Woodrow Wilson*

It is as natural to find lawyers in legislatures as it is to find chefs in a kitchen. Lawyers make law, after all. That's what they do.
—*A law student*

The first thing we do, let's kill all the lawyers.
—*Shakespeare, Henry VI, Part Two*

Lawyers are, and always have been, omnipresent in American political institutions and in the American public-policy-making process. Since the time of Tocqueville, students of American government have often noted the overrepresentation of lawyers in American political positions (see, especially, Tocqueville 1969, 263–70). And it seems that the more important the political office, the more lawyers occupy that office. Although lawyers can be found serving in a large variety of roles in almost all American governmental institutions, the importance of lawyers in American politics has received very little attention from contemporary scholars. This disjuncture between the omnipresence of lawyers in American politics and the lack of scholarly attention to their impact is puzzling. This book will attempt to correct this oversight by examining how and why lawyers play such important roles in American political institutions and how this lawyer-dominated environment affects the broader American system of government.

Often described as the "High Priests of American Politics" (see Matthews 1954; Eulau and Sprague 1964, 11), lawyers have long dominated our political decision making, held various elected offices, and played key roles in the American policy-making process (see, e.g., Hurst 1950; Matthews 1954, 1960; Mills 1956; Schlesinger 1957; Derge 1959; Hyneman 1959; Eulau and Sprague 1964; Keefe and Ogul 1989, 117–18). Unlike most other industrialized democracies, in the United States law and politics often merge. Lawyers, in various political, public, and private roles, make many key public-policy decisions. As Sugarman reminds us, we must recognize "the role of lawyers in creating and transmitting some of our most important political discourses" (Sugarman 1994, 106). Thus in order to have a fuller understanding of how the American political system operates, we must understand how and why lawyers and lawyers' ways dominate our political institutions.

In the United States, the legal profession has often been a stepping stone to elected or appointed political office and therefore to political power. It is surprising that the role of lawyers in gaining and exercising political power in the United States has been so neglected, because politics is often defined as the exercise of power in society (see, e.g., Isaak 1985, 15–21). According to one student of the professions, "Of all the professions, the legal profession is most likely to participate in the exercise of power in *any* modern society" (Rueschemeyer 1973, 68; emphasis added). And according to Vanderbilt, Americans must understand "the leading roles lawyers play in the community, the state, and the nation," and students of American politics must acknowledge legal education as "the gateway to politics, business, or other forms of power in an increasingly complex society of laws" (Vanderbilt 1979, 8). Becoming a lawyer is a major step in the political career of many ambitious American politicians.

Lawyers are certainly an important and powerful force in American society (see, e.g., Zemans and Rosenbloom 1981). The American legal profession is one of the largest and most powerful professions in the world. About a third of the world's lawyers are Americans, and the United States has one of the highest numbers of lawyers per capita, behind only Pakistan and Singapore (see Legal Profession 1992). Since 1960, the number of lawyers worldwide has almost doubled, but in the United States the number has tripled (see Legal Profession 1992).

The United States also has more lawyer-politicians than any other industrialized democracy in the world. In effect, the legal profession has colonized the political domain in this country.[1] Lawyers play a nearly ubiquitous part in American political life, and the legal profession has come to dominate American political decision making. Thus, at the intersection of the studies of law, power, politics, and political institutions is the study of lawyer-politicians.

Although scholars have generally overlooked this lawyer-politician phenomenon, popular culture often discusses lawyers and politics in the same breath. Many political columnists complain about the overabundance of lawyers in legislative bodies and the ability of lawyers to prevent needed changes in public policy (see, e.g., McKeen 1992, C3; Magee 1992a). The former governor of New York, Herbert Lehman, has been quoted as complaining about "the conspiracy of lawyer-legislators to perpetrate for their profession the obstructions to justice by which it prospers" (Allen 1949, xxxvii). And who can forget Gilbert and Sullivan's singing lawyer, the Right Honorable Sir Joseph Porter, who in "H.M.S. Pinafore" sang at length about how his career as an attorney qualified him to become First Lord of the Admiralty and concluded with this lawyerly advice: "Stick close to your desk and never go to sea / And you all may be rulers of the Queen's Navy."

Although lawyers dominate most American political institutions, this book will focus primarily on the effects of having so many lawyer-politicians elected to legislatures, which have long been dominated by lawyers. As one scholar has so eloquently stated, "A glut of lawyers seems to afflict legislative bodies generally" (Ross 1955, 434). Even the Supreme Court has recognized the importance of lawyers in Congress, noting that "Congress is, after all, not a body of laymen unfamiliar with the commonplaces of our law. . . . Congress is predominately a lawyers' body" (*Callanan v. United States,* 364 U.S. 587, at 594 [1961]). Scholars of women in politics have also stated that the scarcity of women in Congress is due in part to the historically low number of women who traditionally entered the legal profession (see Darcy, Welch, and Clark 1987, 94–97, 133–34; Menkel-Meadow 1989, 216). This omnipresence of American lawyer-legislators has lead Eulau and Sprague, in one of the few political science works that has studied this topic, to conclude that "no occupational group stands in more regular and intimate relation to American politics than the legal profession" (Eulau and Sprague 1964, 11).

Examining the impact of lawyer-legislators will allow us to revisit and revise previous understandings of how Congress and state legislatures operate. In order to understand fully how political institutions function in our society, it is important to reexamine how the legislators' social backgrounds affect those institutions. Just as Silbey and Sarat argue that "legal institutions cannot be understood without seeing the entire social environment" (Silbey and Sarat 1987, 165), I will argue that legislative bodies cannot be understood without examining their internal political environments, including the effects caused by their members' professional training and backgrounds.

This book joins a growing set of recent works that examine the effects on the legislative process of legislators' social-background variables: race (see, e.g., Swain 1993), gender (see, e.g., Gertzog 1984, Thomas 1994), lack of prior political experience (Canon 1990), longevity in Congress (Hibbing 1991), and legal training (see, e.g., Miller 1993a). In many ways this study is the flip side of Canon's (1990) study on the role of political amateurs in Congress. I will examine the role of political professionals in our legislatures, concentrating on those who are lawyers. Later chapters will provide a typology of lawyer-legislators, many of whom obtained a law degree simply to further their political ambitions.

In the past, scholars argued that legislators' similar social backgrounds produced similar world views (see, e.g., Edinger and Searing 1967, Kim 1973), assuming, therefore, that lawyer-politicians acted differently than nonlawyer-politicians.[2] But until recently this line of scholarly inquiry had fallen out of vogue in political science, in large part because quantitative analysis did not reveal demonstrable differences in voting patterns in American legislatures or on American courts due to differences in social background (see, e.g., Derge 1959, 1962; Gold 1961; Eulau and Sprague 1964; Schmidhauser et al. 1971; Green et al. 1973; Berg et al. 1974; Ulmer 1986; Spohn 1990).

Political scientists are beginning to realize that social-background variables can fundamentally shape an institution's political environment. Recently, several prominent political scientists, such as Nelson Polsby and Roger Davidson, have argued that social scientists generally have missed some of the important effects on the American legislative process caused by politicians' legal training (see, e.g., Davidson 1988, 1990; Polsby 1990). And Philip Duncan, a leading commentator on American politics, is certainly right when he reminds us that the behavior of many legislators is probably most affected by their prior experiences in the working world (Duncan 1991a, 87). As one Massachusetts state legislator concluded in an interview for this project, "The difference between lawyer- and nonlawyer-legislators is very real, but very abstract and very complex."

In response to Levine's (1990) and Abel's (1980) calls for more interdisciplinary sociolegal research on American political institutions, this study draws on the disciplines of political science, sociology, history, and legal studies to explore some of the effects on the American political system caused by the presence of so many lawyer-legislators. An interdisciplinary approach avoids some of the pitfalls found in any one academic discipline, although my academic training is from a political science perspective. As both a lawyer and a political scientist, I think we need a better understanding of how lawyer-politicians shape our American political institutions.

A Neo-institutional Perspective

In order somewhat to demystify the effects that the presence of so many lawyer-legislators has on Congress and on state legislatures, this book will take a decidedly institutional point of view. Just as John Brigham (1987) has encouraged a more institutional approach to the study of the Supreme Court, this book will bring an institutional approach in order to help refine our understanding of American legislative bodies. As Brigham argues, "Institutions are not simply robes and marble, nor are they contained in codes or documents" (Brigham 1987, 21). Or as Rawls conceptualizes institutions, they are "an abstract object" realized in "thought and conduct" (Rawls 1971, 11). Thus an institution's internal political environment, as well as its larger organizational context, is important in shaping how it operates and behaves in the larger governmental system.

The reexamination of the effects of institutional context on political behavior has given rise to the so-called neo-institutional approach to political questions (see, especially, March and Olsen 1984, 1989). Although the neo-institutional school may include a great many different approaches and methodologies (see, e.g., McCubbins and Sullivan 1987, Gates 1991, and Rockman 1994), this book clearly belongs in the emerging "post-behavioralist" neo-institutional tradition, found now in many of the social sciences. The institutional approach to be taken by this book is similar to much of the neo-institutional school now becoming more popular in the study of legislative and judicial politics in the United States.[3] My perspective is also similar to much of the recent neo-institutional work in sociology (see, e.g., Powell and DiMaggio 1991, Sutton 1994, Boyle and Ventresca 1994) and a close cousin to the interpretist approach used by many mainstream sociolegal researchers (see, e.g., Hunt 1985, Silbey and Sarat 1985, Silbey 1985, Harrington 1985, Harrington and Merry 1988, Greenhouse 1988, Cain and Harrington 1994, Suchman and Edelman 1994). It resembles somewhat the less-radical elements of the postbehavioralist approach advocated by some in the political science discipline (see, e.g., Easton 1992, Bay 1992) and embraces the interdisciplinary approach used by many political scientists today (see Shapiro 1993, 371–74).

As used by Epstein, Walker, and Dixon (1989), among others, the neo-institutional approach in political science combines the traditionalist scholar's interest in understanding governmental bodies as institutions with the behavioralist's emphasis on empirical, individual-level research. In other words, the neo-institutionalist perspective combines the microlevel study of individual behavior with the macrolevel sensitivity to the institutional factors that help shape that behavior (such as the internal political culture). As Fiorina has stated, "To a greater degree than behavioral political scientists have acknowledged, institutional arrangements shape individual incentives, which in turn affect behavior. Both formal institutions and informal ones, such as custom or practice, are important" (Fiorina 1990, 444).[4]

Various scholars have recently argued that political scientists and other scholars need to combine the best of the "behavioralist" and "traditionalist" approaches in order to reexamine the effects of institutional context on political behavior (see, e.g., March and Olsen 1984, 1989; Brigham 1987; Epstein, Walker, and Dixon 1989; Hall and Brace 1989, 1992; Gates 1991; Miller 1992, 1993c). As Rogers Smith concludes, "Ideally, a full account of an important political event would consider both the ways the context of 'background' institutions influenced the political actions in question, and the ways in which those actions altered relevant contextual structures or institutions" (Smith 1988, 91). Thus, as March and Olsen argue, "Much of the behavior we observe in political institutions reflects the routine way in which people do what they are supposed to do. Simple stimuli trigger complex, standardized patterns of action without extensive analysis, problem solving, or use of discretionary power" (March and Olsen 1989, 21). In other words, we need to understand the institutional context of American politics in order to understand better how our political institutions actually function in our larger political system.

This neo-institutional approach is willing to "embrace the premise that the meanings of cultural and social forms are constituted in their use" (Greenhouse 1988, 687, citing Skinner 1985, 7). And an institution's political culture is greatly shaped by the social backgrounds of the political actors who comprise the institution. The institutional approach seems especially appropriate for studying the impact of lawyers in political institutions because "lawyers have an especially *creative* role in the . . . establishing of institutions and in formulating agreements of all kinds. No other occupational group has claimed this skill. . . . Lawyers are *par excellence* institutional inventors" (Cain 1994, 31). My thesis is that we must improve our understanding of how political institutions actually operate by exploring the political culture and environments within the institutions (see Baker 1990; Almond 1990, 138–56).

The Behavioral Revolution and Postbehavioralism

In order to understand why many political scientists have missed the importance of American political institutions being dominated by lawyers' ways and lawyers' views, it is important to trace briefly some of the history of political science as a discipline. This section will also help explain why a shift to the neo-institutional perspective is productive for the purposes of this particular study.

Until the late 1950s and early 1960s, most political scholars used what is now called the "traditionalist" approach to understanding political institutions and phenomena. This approach relied heavily on the techniques of historical, legalistic, and institutional analysis (see Isaak 1985, 33–38; see also Davidson 1991, 19–23). Political scientists were concerned with how political institutions functioned and how they were structured, often with a legalistic or normative bias in their approach to these questions. The traditionalists tended to employ logical reasoning to analyze politics and to make normative statements about how politics and political institutions should operate in this country (Isaak 1985, 13). They also relied on the description of political realities and institutions as their main tool of analysis. Their works were closely related to the scholarly approaches found in the disciplines of history, philosophy, literature, and law. In other words, traditionalists often saw the study of politics as a branch of the "softer" humanities.

A key component in understanding institutional context is seeing how social-background variables, such as the legal training of the institution's members, affect the behavior of the institution. Earlier, scholars who felt that social-background variables were important components in understanding political institutions were often traditionalist political scientists. When the traditionalist approach lost favor in political science, the concern for the effects of social background also lost favor. For a period, many political scientists explored the important question of how politicians' social backgrounds affected their official duties (see, e.g., Matthews 1954, Searing 1969). Of particular interest was the importance of legislators' social backgrounds in explaining the functioning of legislative bodies (see Sisson 1973, 27). Social background was once considered an important factor in explaining the behavior and attitudes of politicians in this country. As Schlesinger notes in his landmark work on political ambition in the United States, "A politician's biography is, after all, the story of one man's political ambitions. It may not tell us all of his aspirations, when they emerged or when they changed. But it does tell us what overt moves he has made toward gaining public office" (Schlesinger 1966, 14). In more recent research, however, these important lessons tended to be lost in the shuffle because "behavioralist" roll-call vote analysis could show no differences due to social-background variables. In fact, most of the classic behavioralist works on voting behavior in Congress did not even consider the social backgrounds of the legislators (see, e.g., Clausen 1973, Mayhew 1974, Fiorina 1989, and Kingdon 1989).

Most contemporary political scientists, especially those who specialize in American politics, have adopted a decidedly behavioralist perspective. Beginning in the late 1950s, a "behavioral revolution" occurred in political science. The new view said that political phenomena must be studied using a more "scientific" approach with more "scientific" methods.[5] Eventually, the behavioralists' approach dominated political science, especially in the subfield of American politics (see Freeman 1991, 25–34; see also Davidson 1991, 27). Having developed ever more "objective" and statistically oriented techniques, the behavioralists felt that the job of political scientists is not merely to describe political realities but also to predict political behavior. Thus "its objectives are the development of empirical generalizations and systematic theory, and the use of these in the explanations of political phenomena" (Isaak 1985, 42).

The tools of the behavioralists are generally high-level quantitative statistical methods, because "quantification of data is a significant goal of every science, and no science will develop beyond a fairly primitive level unless it employs quantitative techniques of various sorts" (Isaak 1985, 42).

Behavioralists urged scholars to study individuals' political activity and behavior, not just institutional structures, rules, and cultures. They stressed "the significance of individual behavior as the basic building block of political science." "The institutionalist," they argued, "studies structures, powers, and responsibilities; the behavioralist studies attitudes, personalities, and physical activity (voting, lobbying). . . . If the characteristic feature of behavioralism is its emphasis on behavior, then the kind of behavior that should be emphasized is that of the individual" (Isaak 1985, 41). After the Behavioral Revolution, political scientists sought as closely as possible to emulate physics, chemistry, and the other "hard" sciences, and abandoned any links to the approaches of the softer humanities. As the behaviorists would often proclaim, "It is becoming increasingly evident that there exists a distinction between normative and analytic activities on the one hand, and scientific activities on the other, with the former constituting political philosophy and the latter political science" (Isaak 1985, 7).

The adherents of a more scientific approach to political science, who generally won the behavioral revolution in the discipline, generally felt that only quantitative indicators of individual political behavior, such as the legislative roll-call vote, were worthy of study. Thus they often ignored less-quantifiable factors that also help shape the behavior of actors within political institutions. In order for the behavioralist scientific statistical techniques to be successful, many data points are needed; the legislative roll call provides a great deal of "objective" data that lends itself nicely to quantitative analysis. Thus the discipline generally adopted a narrow understanding of legislative behavior, with the roll-call vote being the only acceptable scientific indicator of the behavior of legislators. Political attitudes were important only if they produced certain political behavior. This definition of legislative behavior is much too restrictive, however, and it oversimplifies how American political institutions actually operate. As Rockman concludes, "The behavioral focus in political science tended to microanalyze individual members of institutions qua individuals. A consequence of this was to treat institutions as arenas for the behavioral predilections of members" (Rockman 1994, 144). Thus an exclusively behavioral approach ignores the important institutional constraints, such as the political culture of the institution, that help shape the behavior of the actors within the institution. It also ignores the social backgrounds of the political actors unless these background variables produce quantifiable differences in things such as legislative voting behavior.

By focusing almost exclusively on floor votes in Congress and other legislative bodies, many behavioralist researchers missed many important but subtle differences between how lawyer- and nonlawyer-politicians make decisions. At the floor-vote stage in Congress and in the state legislatures, these differences are masked by many other forces that affect the floor voting decision (see Hall and Grofman 1990; Henschen 1983; Jewell and Patterson 1986, 220–21). As Jewell and Patterson, two leading scholars of legislative behavior, conclude, "The roll call is a significant, but not always decisive, step in the decision-making process. At one of the earlier stages in the legislative process, negative decisions may have precluded a roll call vote, or a positive decision . . . may have ensured consensus and unanimity in the vote. . . . [Thus,] roll call statistics can reveal *how* legislators vote, . . . [but] the roll calls cannot explain *why* legislators vote that way" (Jewell and Patterson 1986, 220–21). The reliance solely on statistical techniques acceptable to the behavioralists has therefore restricted our ability to understand how lawyers' ways and lawyers' views affect American legislatures and other political institutions. It has also prevented us from examining how the social backgrounds of the actors within the institution shape the political culture of the institution, which in turn constrains the decision-making process of those actors.

At the height of the behavioral revolution in political science, during the late 1960s and 1970s, the conventional wisdom was that no effects could be traced to the omnipresence of lawyer-politicians in American political institutions. This belief arose because much of the empirical work conducted in the 1960s and 1970s found few differences between the roll-call voting behavior of lawyers and nonlawyers in American legislatures (see, e.g., Derge 1959, 1962; Gold 1961; Schmidhauser et al. 1971; Green et al. 1973; Berg et al. 1974). In 1964 Eulau and Sprague, publishing one of the only major studies of lawyers in American politics, confirmed the conventional wisdom. Their work was based on statistical analysis of interviews conducted in the late 1950s with the members of four state legislatures (New Jersey, Ohio, Tennessee, and California). According to these scholars, "Though lawyers are clearly a distinct occupational group that is more visible, more ubiquitous, more prominent, and even more dominant in American political life than in any other, their private profession does not seem to affect a great deal of their political behavior. To put this somewhat differently, though he is a lawyer, the lawyer-politician does not differ appreciably from other politicians" (Eulau and Sprague 1964, 3).

Because it is one of the only major examinations of the question of how lawyer-politicians differ from their nonlawyer colleagues, Eulau and Sprague's work has set the tone for what little research has recently been done in this area. It should be noted that both the legal profession and American state legislatures have changed a great deal since Eulau and Sprague's research (see, e.g., Abel 1989, Cooper and Brady 1981, Rosenthal 1981), yet their work continues to be the foundation for the widespread belief among political scientists and other scholars that the effects of so many lawyer-politicians in American political institutions is not an interesting or important question. Thus one of the outcomes of the behavioral revolution was the fact that few studied the impact of the dominance of lawyer-politicians on American political institutions.

Today an emerging group of political scientists do not accept behavioralism as the only true approach to the study of political phenomena (see Moon 1991; Davidson 1991, 27). As Cooper and Brady note, "Institutional analysis has lagged behind behavioral analysis since the advent of the behavioral revolution in the early 1950s. Our ability to handle questions that posit individuals, whether in small numbers or large aggregates, as the units of analysis is far greater than our ability to handle questions that posit institutionalized collectivities in complex environments as the units of analysis" (Cooper and Brady 1981, 994). Even a strong proponent of the behavioral approach, Robert Dahl, has written, "The incompleteness of purely external, physical descriptions of human activity, combined with the difficulty of arriving at an adequate understanding of the subjective features that give human action so much of its meaning, have led some scholars to the pessimistic view that a 'scientific' understanding of human action is impossible" (Dahl 1984, 6).

According to Gabriel A. Almond, a leading advocate of a more diverse and pluralistic approach to the study of politics, "There is a long-standing polemic in political science between those who view the discipline as a hard science—formal, mathematical, statistical, experimental—dedicated to the cumulation of tested 'covering laws'; and those who are less sanguine and more eclectic, who view all scholarly methods, the scientific ones as well as the softer historical, philosophical, and legal ones, as appropriate and useful" (Almond 1990, 7). Almond continues, "This second school—to which I adhere—takes the position that relationships in the social sciences are less predictable than in the hard sciences, since the data of the social sciences—human actions and events—are governed by memory, learning, aspiration, and goal seeking. These qualities of human culture and behavior tend to limit us to the discovery of soft and 'erodible' regularities" (Almond 1990, 7). I agree with Almond's analysis, and I believe that the study of lawyers in American politics can gain a great deal from the mixing of both "hard" and "soft" (i.e., both quantitative and qualitative) methodological techniques. In discovering the effects of the dominant lawyer culture on American political institutions, behavioralist statistical analysis alone is not sufficient. Instead a neo-institutional perspective, combining the best of both the behavioralist and traditionalist approaches, is needed.

This book will challenge the conventional wisdom that the study of lawyer-politicians is unimportant by focusing on a larger definition of political behavior than that used by the behavioralists. One must look beyond mere roll-call vote analysis to see how the political culture of American legislative bodies is shaped by the presence of so many lawyer-legislators. The preoccupation with legislative results instead of fine-tuning our understanding of the subtleties of the legislative process has masked a great many of the important differences between lawyer- and nonlawyer-politicians. It has also masked the fact that lawyers' ways and lawyers' perspectives dominate the entire legislative process in this country. It is impossible to separate lawyer-politicians from the larger legislative process.

In addition to combining the best approaches of both the traditionalist and behavioralist schools, the neo-institutional perspective also allows shifts in the level of analysis (see Gates 1991, Rockman 1994, Strine 1994). Traditionalists were only concerned with the macroinstitutional level of analysis, whereas the behavioralists concentrated on the individual political actor as the unit of analysis. However, the neo-institutional perspective examines political activity from a variety of levels of analysis in order to enhance our understanding of how the institutional context affects political decisions. Therefore, the focus of analysis in this book will shift, variously, from the congressional committee to the individual legislator to the entire institution.

The American political system's preoccupation with procedures and processes instead of with the substance of public-policy decisions may be the direct result of the fact that political institutions are dominated both internally and externally by lawyers and their approach to the world. In other words, American political institutions are creatures of the broader American legal-political culture, which helps to explain some of the differences between how the American political system operates and how political institutions in other Western industrialized democracies function. Lawyers are the largest occupational group in the U.S. Congress, and, therefore, the American legal ideology dominates and shapes our legislative decision-making processes. One cannot study the American legislative process without considering the effects of having lawyer-legislators constantly molding that process.

The Data

The data for this study come primarily from semistructured interviews with more than 75 members and staff in the U.S. House of Representatives conducted during the summer of 1989; from more formally structured interviews with 129 of the 132 members of both houses of the Ohio General Assembly conducted during the spring of 1988; and from interviews with 64 members of both houses of the Massachusetts state legislature (32 percent of the total membership) during the spring of 1991.[6] At times, this study also draws on interviews conducted in 1990 with 45 of the 47 members of the Maryland senate and with 46 of the 50 members of the North Carolina senate.[7]

The following chapters combine interview data from several different interview projects. The congressional interviews focused on members' attitudes toward the courts and toward federal agencies (see also Miller 1992, 1993c, 1993d); the Ohio legislator interviews included questions on many topics and issues, including legislators' attitudes toward the Ohio state courts (see also Felice and Kilwein 1993); and the Massachusetts interviews dealt primarily with legislators' attitudes and reactions to state court decisions (see Miller 1993b). The Massachusetts and Ohio legislatures were chosen for this study in part because both resemble their congressional counterpart in many ways, as will be discussed in more detail below. In addition, some supplementary data are drawn from studies of the Maryland and North Carolina senates, where the interviews focused on a variety of subjects.

The congressional interviews focused primarily on members of three committees in the U.S. House of Representatives: the Judiciary Committee, the Interior and Insular Affairs Committee (later renamed the Natural Resources Committee and recently renamed the Resources Committee), and the Energy and Commerce Committee (recently returning to its original name of the Commerce Committee). This study includes responses reflecting the attitudes of about two-thirds of the members of these committees (see Miller 1992).[8]

Many of the tables in this book report two statistical measures of relationship, gamma and tau-b, which give the reader a sense of the strength of the relationships between the variables in the tables. Both gamma and tau-b vary from -1 to +1. The closer each statistic is to zero, the less important is the relationship. The closer each statistic is to the extremes of +1 or -1, the stronger is the relationship between the variables. The values of gamma normally tend to be higher than the values of tau-b. The reader who is unfamiliar with these statistics should feel free to ignore these numbers or to consult a social-statistics text (e.g., Blalock 1979) for further information. These statistics are reported primarily for those who would like to be able to draw some very rough comparisons across tables.[9]

A quick outline of what is to come may be helpful at this point. Chapter 2 will examine how legal training and professionalization into the legal profession help shape the world view of lawyers, and how this legal ideology stays with individuals after they become politicians. The third chapter will explore the various roles that lawyers play in the public-policy process in this country. These roles include lawyers serving as legislators, lobbyists, state executives, judges, local government officials, heads of administrative agencies, government employees, academics, and in private practice. Chapter 4 will examine some of the theories about why there are so many lawyer-politicians in elected office.

Not only must we understand more about the internal political culture of American political institutions, we must also understand how various political institutions interact with other institutions. In order to appreciate more fully the institutional context that shapes governmental decisions in this country, we must understand how various American political institutions are perceived by the other governmental units with which they interact. Because court-legislative interactions are vitally important in shaping the ultimate outcome of the public-policy process in this country (see, e.g., Katzmann 1988), several chapters in the latter part of this book will explore attitudes of legislators toward the courts and court decisions.

Realizing the need to revise the conventional wisdom in political science and other social sciences, this project presents strong evidence that the attitudes and behavior of lawyer-legislators and nonlawyer-legislators can be quite different, especially when using a broad definition of legislative behavior. Chapter 5 will explore various differences between individual lawyer- and nonlawyer-legislators in this country, including their career paths and their positions in the legislatures. Chapter 6, continuing with the individual legislator as the unit of analysis, will explore in greater detail how lawyer-legislators differ from nonlawyer-politicians in their attitudes toward the courts. Chapter 7 will develop a typology of lawyer-legislators and then examine how legislators who continued to practice law affected court-reform efforts in the Massachusetts legislature. Chapter 8 will shift the level of analysis to explore how congressional committees dominated by lawyer members differ from those dominated by nonlawyers. This chapter will also examine how the decision-making processes of congressional committees differ according to the proportion of lawyer-legislators serving on the committees. Finally, chapter 8 will explore how various types of lawyers on congressional committees affect how those committees approach constitutional questions.

After exploring various differences between lawyer- and nonlawyer-politicians, this book again shifts the level of analysis, concluding with a macroinstitutional examination in chapter 9. This final chapter will explore two very different aspects of how Congress as an institution is affected by the social-background characteristics of its dominant lawyer members. First, it will examine how the lawyerly approach to decision making affects the substantive policy choices of Congress. Then it will explore how the internal political culture of Congress is shaped by having so many lawyers serve in the body.

In many ways, our political institutions are shaped by the background characteristics of their dominant members. Because lawyers so dominate the legislative process in this country, the Congress takes on a decidedly lawyerlike approach to decision making. Even nonlawyer members must adapt to the lawyerly political culture of Congress. The lawyers' legal ideology also restricts the substantive choices available to the institution because lawyers prefer an incrementalist approach to decision making, and they abhor radical change in society.

Chapter 9 concludes that the major difference between lawyer- and nonlawyer-politicians may be in the decision-making style each group uses. Lawyer-politicians are more concerned than their nonlawyer colleagues with using proper procedures and processes. Because lawyers' dominate the internal political culture in our legislative bodies, Congress and many state legislatures have adopted lawyers' practices, lawyers' habits, and lawyers' procedures and processes. Thus the American political system's preoccupation with procedural rights at the expense of substantive policy may be the direct result of the fact that American political offices are dominated by lawyers. This domination is a large part of the reason that American political institutions operate very differently from those in other democratic societies.

CHAPTER TWO

Socialization into the Legal Profession

In order to understand fully the impact of having so many lawyer-politicians in the United States, it is necessary to examine the long-term effects of legal training on individuals. It is important to understand how lawyers view the world, because this lawyerly world view is the dominant influence on the American legislative process. As Zemans and Rosenblum note, "The enormous influence that lawyers wield in both the public and the private sectors makes their professional development of particular concern in a democratic society" (Zemans and Rosenblum 1981, 1). Or as Scheingold puts it, "An investigation of the socializing experiences of American lawyers is therefore an essential precondition to understanding the policy roles that they will be inclined to play and the strategic counsel that they will provide to political organizations" (Scheingold 1974, 151). This chapter will explore how legal training and socialization into the legal profession can produce a uniform lawyerly world view or legal ideology that stays with the individual throughout his or her professional life.

Professional Socialization

Various scholars have examined the general effects of professional socialization and training on individuals (see, e.g., Hall 1948; Vollmer and Mills 1966; Moore and Rosenblum 1970; Larson 1977; Nelson, Trubek, and Solomon 1992). Many researchers talk of professionals taking on a "professional ideology and rhetoric" that shapes the way members of the profession understand the world around them (see, e.g., Geison 1983).[1] For example, Nelson and Trubek define the professional ideology of lawyers as "the set of norms, traditions, and practices that lawyers have constructed to establish and maintain their identities as professionals and their jurisdiction over legal work" (Nelson and Trubek 1992, 5).

For most professionals, professional socialization involves acquiring specialized knowledge and skills, but it also involves learning the norms and jargon of the profession (see Moore and Rosenblum 1970). Professional socialization involves learning how to act like a professional and to think like a professional in that specific field. The process creates noticeable changes in the individual, and these changes enable the person to become a part of the closed professional fraternity. According to a leading sociologist of the professions, "The development of a professional self-conception involves a complicated chain of perceptions, skills, values, and interactions. In this process, a professional identity is forged which is believable both to the individual and to others" (Lortie 1959, 363). The stress here is on changes in individuals that allow them to perceive themselves as a member of the profession, and that allow others to identify them as a member of that profession (see also Moore and Rosenblum 1970, 78–79).

Part of professional socialization involves developing shared perspectives on how to solve various problems. These group perspectives help the individual identify with the profession, and they affect how the individual approaches various situations. During professional socialization, shared professional perspectives combine to produce a shared culture to which the individual must adapt (Becker et al. 1961). The shared professional culture greatly affects how individuals see the world and react to various situations (see Larson 1977; Hughes 1958, 33–36). Two scholars who have studied professional socialization into the legal profession conclude: "Value transmissions is especially important for the professions, since part of the justification for their special prerogatives is a presumed commitment to 'higher ideals' such as public service. Socialization to professional attitudes is therefore thought to have an important influence on subsequent careers of practitioners" (Erlanger and Klegon 1978, 12).

In acquiring a professional culture and values, individuals must adjust their self-presentation and, eventually, their self-image. For an individual, adopting a professional identity can be a wrenching experience. These changes often occur during professional training, where students are gathered together and are jointly trying to adopt a professional self-identity. In other words, professional training produces changes in an individual that stay with them throughout their career. Nelson, Trubek, and Solomon (1992) have produced an entire volume dedicated to the study of lawyer professionalism. As they conclude in one of their essays, "Ideal visions of lawyering and the lawyers' role—'professional ideology'—are important. These visions affect the way lawyers organize their practices and understand their everyday life" (178). This professional vision also affects how lawyer-politicians approach decision making.

Almost all professional training in the United States occurs in professional schools attached to major universities, and this is certainly true for the legal profession. Generally, these professional schools attempt to redirect the thinking skills of the students by forcing them to accept the professional ideology and world view of their faculty (Larson 1977, 229–30). As two legal scholars note, "Professional schools are highly invasive institutions which exert intense control by purposely influencing beliefs, values and personality characteristics of students; and law schools appear to be the most invasive among all graduate education" (Shanfield and Benjamin 1985, 65).

The Law School Experience

Law school is, of course, the first step in legal training and socialization into the legal profession in this country. American lawyer-politicians share a common approach to the world in part because American legal training, regardless of the law school one attends, is virtually invariable (see Thorne 1973, 152; Stevens 1983; Abel 1989b, 212–14). As Hegland notes, "A striking aspect of American legal education is its uniformity. No matter where you go to law school you will learn much the same thing" (Hegland 1983, 3). Or as one prominent guide to law schools states, "The choice of law school can seem next to impossible, because they all look so much alike. They all teach the law, and most of them teach the law the same way. If you could ask first-year law students at a hundred law schools to describe their experiences, you'd hear the same things over and over" (Goldfarb and Adams 1991, 13).

Because the law school experience is amazingly uniform for all law students throughout the country,[2] the experience of learning how to "think like a lawyer" is one of the key elements in shaping how American lawyers share a common approach to decision making and problem solving. This uniform approach to learning to think like a lawyer helps produce a similar world view among lawyers, regardless of their eventual career paths (see Shklar 1964). As Scheingold explains it, "A distinctive approach to problem solving is imparted in law school, and that approach influences the way lawyers think about societal issues more generally. A world view is implicit in legal analysis and tends to come along as a kind of silent partner in legal education" (Scheingold 1974, 152).

Many commentators stress the importance for the individual of the common socialization experiences of the first year of law school (see, e.g., Seligman 1978; Bonsignore 1979, 215–17; Provine 1986, 89; Wice 1991). According to one scholar, "The first year at law school is the year with the greatest effect on the professional life of a young lawyer. It is then that he [or she] should acquire the lawyer's ability to absorb facts and rules accurately and quickly, to search for the controlling reasons for a rule of law, to employ these rules in hypothetical situations, to acquire the capacity for hard, prolonged intellectual labor, and to develop a genuine interest in the law as an important aspect of life" (Vanderbilt 1979, 9). Thus law students in every American law school are introduced to law school with the same old adage: The first year of law school scares you to death; the second year of law school works you to death; and the third year of law school bores you to death.

The law-student culture prevalent at most law schools is another important factor influencing socialization into the profession. Based on interviews with law students at two large midwestern law schools, a sociologist has concluded:

> A "law student consciousness" develops among students as they interpret messages from faculty and other students about the law and the legal profession. The law student community for the most part acts as a conscious interpreter of the messages of law school, although many assumptions go unquestioned because students recognize these as crucial to their own socialization into law. Creation of a set of norms and beliefs about the law promotes professional identify for law students, as they begin "thinking like lawyers" and projecting themselves into legal careers. (Schleef 1992, 1)

In their very first class in law school, law students are immediately told that the goal of the faculty is to teach them to think like lawyers (see Bell 1989, Moll 1990, Wice 1991, Schleef 1992). As explained by one law professor, "Of all the verities of the faculty lounge, none is more plausible, or more widely believed, than the idea that law professors teach students how to think like lawyers" (Bryden 1984, 479). Of course, teaching students to think like a lawyer is really an attempt to impart a certain professional ideology (see, e.g., Shklar 1964, Scheingold 1974, Provine 1986, Kennedy 1990). And various studies report that, when asked, lawyers agree that the most important part of law school was learning to think like a lawyer (see, e.g., Stevens 1973, Gee and Jackson 1977, Zemans and Rosenblum 1981).

Learning how to think like a lawyer requires enormous and sometimes wrenching changes in how an individual sees and understands the world around them. Inherent in the teaching of a professional ideology is the view that law school must mold and reshape the mushy minds of law students. According to one law professor, "Teaching is an attempt to change the student's mind. The best teaching challenges and alters the mental pathways, connections, and 'censors' within the student's brain. But there is no doubt that teaching, totally unlike advertising, is a deliberate form of interference with how the student thinks. The student is likely to resist" (D'Amato 1987, 462).

Almost all law students experience enormous periods of stress and self-doubt while in law school (see, e.g., Elkins 1985, Carrington and Conley 1977). Because the law school experience can be so stressful, most lawyers remember it as a turning point in their lives, an experience that stays with them throughout their professional careers.[3] In some ways, learning to think like a lawyer is analogous to giving birth to a new person with a new personality, or at least it feels as painful as childbirth for most law students.

Turow's now classic book, *One L,* gives a detailed explanation of the many changes that occur in an individual during the first year of law school. Turow recounts a conversation with another law student about the changes in thinking that law school was forcing on the often unwilling students, a change that is familiar to those who have attended law school: "'They're turning me into someone else,' she said, referring to our professors. 'They're making me different.' I told her that was called education and she told me, quite rightly, that I was being flip. 'It's someone I don't want to be,' she said. 'Don't you get the feeling all the time that you're being indoctrinated?'" (Turow 1977, 83).

Turow continues his contemplations on thinking like a lawyer by saying, "[This friend] was not the only classmate making remarks like that. About the same time, from three or four others, people I respected,

I heard similar comments, all to the effect that they were being limited, harmed, by the education, forced to substitute dry reason for emotion, to cultivate opinions which were 'rational' but which had no roots in the experience, the life, they'd had before. They were being cut away from themselves" (Turow 1977, 86–87).

From their study of law students' attitudes at the beginning and at the end of their law school educations, Erlanger and Klegon believe that all successful law students eventually internalize what it means to think like a lawyer. They conclude, "All of the students interviewed felt that the biggest change they had undergone was in learning to 'think like a lawyer,' i.e. to distinguish a legal from a nonlegal issue, to see the various sides of a problem, to reason formally and logically, and to express themselves clearly, concisely, and unemotionally" (Erlanger and Klegon 1978, 30).

A severe critic of the legal profession, Auerbach writes about his own law school experiences: "It was the proudest boast of law schools to train students to think like lawyers. This process entailed a highly stylized mode of intellectual activity that rewarded inductive reasoning, analytical precision, and verbal felicity. . . . Craft was rewarded over choice and process over purpose" (Auerbach 1976, 276). Auerbach concludes, however, that "there was something quite compelling in legal education. . . . The substance was a disappointment but the process, at best, was analytically rigorous and its corrosive skepticism was not without its virtues. After so many years spent learning what to think it was a relief to be told that I was learning how to think" (Auerbach 1976, viii–ix). Thus, notes Stevens, "In addition to imparting the elements of a formal legal education, law schools shape the legal profession through more subtle influences on lawyers as individuals" (Stevens 1973, 671).

Various scholars have examined attitudinal changes in individuals that occur during law school (see, e.g., Warkow and Zelan 1965, Rathjen 1976, Carrington and Conley 1977, Erlanger and Klegon 1978, Himmelstein 1978, Hedegaard 1979, Auerbach 1984, Elkins 1985). Some scholars have even argued that law school and professional socialization produces a certain personality type among lawyers (see Wice 1991, 50–52).[4] Bonsignore claims that legal education has "encompassing tendencies," which tend to crowd out the competing values and approaches law students bring with them to law school (Bonsignore 1979, 215; see also Provine 1986, 89). And Scheingold (1974) suggests that these attitudinal changes can be very subtle.[5] But most commentators accept the reality known to all lawyers that law school has changed them. According to one sociologist, "Popular belief suggests that people change in law school, becoming more cynical or 'lawyerlike.' More scholarly accounts may also imply that a 'legal consciousness' is acquired by law students as they take on new beliefs about law and the legal system" (Schleef 1992, 1). In training students in how to "think like a lawyer," law schools can produce dramatic changes in the ways individuals think and view the world around them. As one scholar notes, "You cannot really unfrock a priest, unmake a doctor, or disbar a lawyer" (Larson 1977, 229).

What Are the Effects of Thinking Like a Lawyer?

Various observers of legal education have offered their evaluations of what thinking like a lawyer means. Almost everyone agrees that it involves developing keen analytical skills that promote a rationalistic approach to problem solving (see, e.g., Van Loon 1970, 337; Provine 1986, 87–91). As a leading guide to law schools argues, lawyers have "a zest for problem solving. Most lawyers' work has to be approached like a puzzle" (Goldfarb and Adams 1991, 7). According to Lief Carter, legal thinking "requires the ability to see specifics and to avoid premature generalizing and jumping to conclusions" (Carter 1988, 6). As one law student explained, "Law school teaches you how to take a vast amount of material, break it down, decipher it and make a logical decision and argument" (Schleef 1992, 7).

Many stress the ability to manipulate facts and rules accurately and quickly, especially in hypothetical situations, as a key to thinking like a lawyer (see Shklar 1964; Vanderbilt 1979, 9; Provine 1986, 89). Vanderbilt discusses the four foundations of legal training: abstract rules, specific facts, complex personalities, and an appreciation of the social order (Vanderbilt 1979, 19). According to Provine, "The approach law school promotes centers around respect for the value of rules in organizing social life and solving public problems, the view that 'for each dispute there is either a rule or else a rule can be derived'" (Provine 1986, 89, quoting Scheingold 1974, 159). Because of this rule orientation, lawyers are often preoccupied with procedures and processes: "Law students tend to become more concerned with matters of proper procedure and exhibit an increased tendency to reason by analogy" (Moll 1990, 27). As a legal historian explains, "The lasting influence of the case method [used almost universally in American law schools] was to transfer the basis of American legal education from substance to procedure and to make the focus of American legal scholarship—or at least legal theory—increasingly one of process rather than of doctrine" (Stevens 1983, 56).

The professional ideology of the law is thus rooted in positivist rationality and objectivity (see, e.g., Silbey 1985, Kennedy 1990, Sarat and Kearns 1991, Harrington 1994). American law schools are especially skillful at this task of imparting analytic skills in their students and extolling rationality (Van Loon 1970, 337). According to one sociologist, "Academic knowledge legitimizes professional work by clarifying its foundations and tracing them to major cultural values. In most modern professions, these have been the values of rationality, logic, and science" (Abbott 1988, 54). Schleef has identified four aspects of the legal ideology taught by law schools: that law is a science, meaning that law can be studied in an objective and value-free manner; that legal problems always involve a simple solution with a clear winner and a clear loser; that lawyers should be the strongest possible advocate for their clients' interests; and that law has a mysterious nature unavailable to the layperson (Schleef 1992, 8). Schleef concludes, "These strategies suggest that law is a neutral, formal philosophy, capable of separating fact from fiction, and only highly trained professionals are capable of handling it" (Schleef 1992, 9).

Another aspect of thinking like a lawyer involves believing in the so-called myth of rights, which means a belief that all social change in society can come through changes in the law (see Scheingold 1974, 5–9; Olson 1984, 21–24; see also McCann 1986). According to Scheingold, the legal ideology teaches "a social perspective which perceives and explains human interaction largely in terms of rules and of the rights and obligations inherent in rules" (Scheingold 1974, 13). In her work on changes in the law to aid persons with disabilities, Olson also argues that legal ideology forces lawyers to accept the myth of rights. According to Olson, "This myth of rights deeply penetrates American political culture. The formal constitutional basis of our government puts politics within a framework of rules about who has which capacities and rights and how the rules can be changed" (Olson 1984, 22).

Therefore, thinking like a lawyer encompasses a very narrow, rights-focused view of solutions to broad social problems, which tends to ignore other, broader alternatives (see McCann 1986; Olson 1984, 30; Shklar 1964; Brill 1973; Scheingold 1974, esp. chap. 10; Bell 1976; Sorauf

1976, 86–88). The *Pre-Law Handbook* for Duke University students reportedly states that "there seems to be substantial validity to the well-known saying that a legal education sharpens a mind by narrowing it. . . . Hence, the legal mind is a disciplined one and the range of actions that a lawyer can take is often quite limited" (Moll 1990, 27). From her perspective as a female law professor in a male-dominated field, Minow tends to agree with this analysis. She argues that "the basic method of legal analysis requires simplifying the problem to focus on a few traits rather than the full complexity of the situation" (Minow 1990, 2). The legal ideology produces decision makers with a narrow conception of problem-solving alternatives. According to Scheingold, "The legalist is someone who is lost among the trees and cannot *or will not* consider the overall shape of the forest" (Scheingold 1974, 153).

Because of the strength of the legal ideology, lawyers tend to avoid calls for massive or radical social change because the legal profession tends to favor stability and predictability in the society at large and particularly in the political sphere (see Ehrmann 1976; Friedman 1989, 18). As one scholar notes, "Stability in law is important, of course, so that people may plan their affairs and expect that their plans will not be unduly disrupted by changing legal rules" (Epp 1992b, 704). Scheingold (1974) argues that lawyers are taught to worship continuity and to seek ways to modify the status quo only incrementally.[6] Hacker (1964) complains that lawyers in Congress are often more parochial than nonlawyers, and that they prevent the use of imaginative solutions to our nation's problems. As McCann notes, "Given lawyers' specialized training and socialization, they tend to find mobilization politics somewhat distasteful and ordinarily try to steer away from militant confrontations" (McCann 1986, 204). Or as Scheingold puts it, "It is, then, the quest for continuity that characterizes legal analysis—not the ad hoc solution but the general outline. What the [law] student must learn are the secrets of harmony and consistency; these are the rules of the law game. . . . The rules that endure tend to be those that allow the game to proceed as smoothly as possible" (Scheingold 1974, 156).

The American legal ideology includes a belief in liberal procedural democracy, built on the foundation that democracy is inherently intertwined with the notion of the "government of laws and not of men" (see, e.g., Hurst 1956; Bickel 1962; Lowi 1979; Minow 1991, 36–40; Epp 1992b, 704). As Greenhouse explains it, the American legal view "assumes that all people are equals, agents of the law by their very actions in relation to other people, through the media of their respective social roles" (Greenhouse 1989, 265, citing Schneider 1968). Again according to Scheingold, "Traditional views about the law in America see it as beneficent and tend to reinforce legitimacy and stabilize the polity" (Scheingold 1974, 3). In a more recent work, Scheingold summarizes this aspect of the dominant world view of American lawyers: "The law is seen as a timeless but evolving social institution that is the cornerstone of organized social life, particularly in complex and heterogeneous modern societies. At the heart of the matter is the law's procedural structure, which guarantees such cherished values as predictability, impartiality, fairness, justice, and common sense. Part and parcel of the law's beneficence is its capacity for reform" (Scheingold 1994, 266).

Some critics argue that legal education produces a certain individualistic mind-set that crowds out a consideration of the broader social good and thus prevents true reform. As one sociologist argues:

> Both in law and in popular culture the individual's interest is clearly preferred to the collective well-being. Lawyers reinforce this tendency; in some ways, they are its perfect embodiment. By their very presence they suggest that all social relations should be regarded as potentially adversarial in character; that a rigorous calculation of self-interest is the most orderly way to conduct social life; that any appeal to the collective good which requires selflessness or altruism is suspect. The more committed to this combative view we become, the less able we are to bear any other standards for organizing public life. (Spangler 1986, 2–3)

Thinking like a lawyer may also manifest itself in the fact that lawyers often tend to attempt to dominate groups in which they participate (see Goldstein 1968; Murrin 1971, 442–43; Scheingold 1974; Seligman 1978; Thielens 1980, 427–29). In her work on nonlawyer judges in New York State, Provine (1986) explores why lawyers have come to dominate most judicial posts in this country. According to this scholar, "Legal education, perhaps even more than other professional programs, gives students a sense of mastery over their environment that extends well beyond technical problems" (Provine 1986, 90). Olson and McCann both discuss how lawyers came to dominate the social reform movements of the 1960s and 1970s (Olson 1984, 8–11, 21–39; McCann 1986, 34; see also Berry 1977, 85, 88, 94). In addition, Kluger (1977) discusses how NAACP lawyers dominated that organization's agenda, Handler (1978, 5–14, 25–

33) cites lawyer domination of various causes, and Sorauf (1976, 150, 154) points out how lawyers dominated First Amendment litigation sponsored by national groups.

Lawyerlike Thinking for Politicians

Thinking like a lawyer involves accepting a legal ideology, and this professional ideology begins in law school and stays with the individual throughout his or her professional career (see Harrington 1994). Rathjen concludes, "The law school experience is the single most notable part of the socialization process that distinguishes lawyers from other participants in the political process. Many believe that the practice of law itself has a long term impact on shaping and developing legal and political beliefs, attitudes and values" (Rathjen 1976, 86).

Thus, thinking like a lawyer can mean a preoccupation with procedural rationality at the expense of substance. This rule and rationality orientation seems to be especially important for understanding how thinking like a lawyer affects the decision-making processes of lawyer-politicians. Lawyer-politicians learn how to manipulate abstract rules and complex personalities without harming the existing social order. They therefore tend to seek incrementalist solutions to society's problems. As Melone concludes, we need to recognize lawyers as "makers of social institutions and carriers of social tradition" (Melone 1979, 1).

Because lawyers are so prevalent in American political institutions, some scholars have argued that law schools should consciously train them for public service. For example, Lasswell and McDougal state that "if legal education in the contemporary world is adequately to serve the needs of a free and productive commonwealth, it must be conscious, efficient, and systematic training for policy-making. The proper function of our law schools is, in short, to contribute to the training of policy-makers for the ever more complete achievement of the democratic values that constitute the professed ends of American polity" (Lasswell and McDougal 1948, 24). After discussing threats to democracy around the world, these scholars continue: "What is needed now is to implement ancient insights by reorienting every phase of law school curricula and skill training toward the achievement of clearly defined democratic values in all the areas of social life where lawyers have or can assert responsibility" (Lasswell and McDougal 1948, 25).

Many lawyers think more politicians should adopt the lawyer's world view. As the dean of the George Washington University Law School put it, "From the standpoint of an educator, the more people who are trained in legal methodology, the better it is for our society. . . . There is no substitute for the analytic tools with which American law schools provide their students. . . . There is no substitute for an ability to ascertain the issues, recognize competing policies, understand the risks and potential consequences of alternative actions, and ponder ethical considerations before deciding on a course to follow" (Friedenthal 1991, 2).

In response, many law schools actively attempt to encourage more lawyers to get into politics. According to a former dean of the Harvard Law School, to be an American lawyer "is to pursue a learned art as a common calling in the spirit of public service—no less a public service because it may incidentally be a means of livelihood" (Legal Profession 1992, 3). The relationship between politics and the law seems to be a natural match in American society, or in Eulau and Sprague's terms, the two professions have converged, not merely because the lawyer's skills are valued in American politics, but because the lawyer's world view has come to dominate American political institutions.

CHAPTER THREE

Lawyers, Lawyers Everywhere

Lawyers play a vital part in American politics. Through a variety of positions, official and unofficial, public and private, the legal profession has effectively colonized the political realm in this country. Lawyers dominate the judicial, legislative, and executive branches of our government, and when they are not part of the government, they are often in position to influence their fellow lawyers who do hold official governmental positions. Even in private practice, lawyers serve a "linking function" in American politics, because they connect with other lawyers, judges, government officials, and their clients (see Agger 1956, McCann 1986).

Sometimes lawyers affect the American public-policy process because they hold official elected, appointed, or other governmental posts, but often lawyers are influential in American politics through their unofficial roles. This chapter will first discuss some of the general attributes of the American legal profession and then outline the various ways that lawyers are key players in American political institutions.

The American Legal Profession

In order to understand fully how lawyers affect the decision-making process in American political institutions, it is helpful to view the American legal profession from a comparative perspective. First, the legal profession is much larger in the United States than in most other countries (see Lewis 1986, Legal Profession 1992). Second, the nature of the American legal profession is quite diverse (see Heinz and Laumann 1978, 1982; Curran 1986; Kelly 1994), whereas the profession in other countries tends to be much more homogeneous (see Lewis 1986). Many lawyers in the United States leave the practice of law per se, many for law enforcement, judicial, or other political careers (see Arron 1991, Moll 1990); fewer non-American lawyers leave the profession. Finally, the American legal profession enjoys greater wealth and more political influence than the national legal professions of any other country (Abel 1988b, 186).

In addition, the American legal profession is different from other national bars because of the type of work American lawyers perform (see Spangler 1986). The overwhelming number of American lawyers prefer to work in private practice, whereas lawyers in other countries are often drawn to civil service positions (Abel 1988b, 228). The huge law firms found in New York, Washington, D.C., Chicago, Boston, Los Angeles, and other major metropolitan areas are a uniquely American phenomenon (see Galanter and Palay 1991; Abel 1988b, 229). Lawyers in other countries are much more likely to work in small firms or as civil servants. As a survey of the legal profession notes, "Large law firms devoted to serving business clients have always been an Anglo-American oddity. In other places restrictions have kept law firms relatively small" (Legal Profession 1992, 5).

Not only does the United States have many more lawyers, but also the boundaries of the legal profession here are not always clear. As part of the historical evolution of the American legal profession, the American bar expanded its work wherever it could in order to exploit any promising, lucrative business and was careless about the precise location of its outer boundaries. According to Friedman, "The American lawyer has always been a jack-of-all-trades. It is not true of the British barrister and certainly not of the Soviet or Cuban lawyer. . . . Nobody in the United States knows where 'law' begins and ends. Every major social development turns into an opportunity for lawyers" (Friedman 1989, 6, 8). American lawyers are therefore also more closely associated with politics than are lawyers in other countries. The American legal profession has expanded into a variety of areas, including many political ones, differentiating it from the profession as practiced in other societies.

American lawyers are also more likely to represent their clients before courts, administrative bodies, and legislatures; lawyers in many other societies have a more limited venue. Thus, American lawyers are different from lawyers in other countries because the American legal profession is large and diverse (see Kelly 1994), because aspects of the American legal system such as the power of judicial review give U.S. lawyers roles and tasks they do not have in most societies (see Friedman 1989,

6), and because American lawyers have such a large role in shaping the dimensions of the American public-policy process (see, e.g., Irons 1982).

Lawyers as Chief Executives

American lawyers have long dominated many political offices. For example, 25 of the 52 signers of the Declaration of Independence were lawyers, as were 31 of the 55 members of the Continental Congress. Lawyers also dominated the state conventions called to ratify the Constitution and the conventions called to write the state constitutions (Brown 1948, 17). At the 1872 Pennsylvania constitutional convention, 103 of the 133 delegates were lawyers. In Ohio, 43 of the 108 delegates to the 1850–51 constitutional convention were lawyers; at the 1872–74 convention, 62 out of 105 were lawyers (Friedman 1985, 647).

In the United States, heads of the executive branch at both the state and the federal level have often been lawyers. After 1850, between one-half to two-thirds of states' governors were lawyers (Friedman 1985, 647). From 1930 to 1940, 52 percent of the nation's governors were lawyers (Matthews 1954, 30). In the 1980s, the percentage of state governors who were lawyers ranged from a low of 48 percent in 1989 to a high of 66 percent in 1983. In 1991, 54 percent of the nation's governors were lawyers (see Ehrenhalt 1983; Barone and Ujifusa 1985; Duncan 1989, 1991b). That figure was also true in 1993, when twenty-seven of the nation's fifty governors (54 percent) were lawyers (Duncan 1993).

Lawyers have also dominated the executive branch of the federal government. Recent presidents who were lawyers include Franklin Roosevelt, Gerald Ford, Richard Nixon, and Bill Clinton. Harry Truman attended law classes at night in Kansas City before becoming president. In fact, twenty-five of the forty-one individuals who have served as president were lawyers (see Watson and Thomas 1988, 516–19; Thomas, Pika, and Thomas 1993, 458–60). Between 1877 and 1934, more than 70 percent of the presidents, vice-presidents, and cabinet members combined were lawyers (Matthews 1954, 30).

Recently, lawyers have also been commonplace among presidential candidates. In 1988, nine of the thirteen prominent major party candidates for president were lawyers. Only George Bush, Paul Simon, Jack Kemp, and Jesse Jackson were nonlawyers. On the Democratic ticket in 1988, both Governor Dukakis and Senator Bentsen were lawyers. And, of course, Vice-President Dan Quayle is also a lawyer, as is his wife. Thus, in 1988 three of the four major party candidates on the ballot for president and vice-president were lawyers.

In 1992 the prevalence of lawyers aspiring for the nation's top offices continued because both Bill Clinton and Dan Quayle were prominent lawyer-politicians on the presidential tickets. In addition, of the seven major Democratic candidates for president during the primary season in 1992, six were lawyers (Cuomo, Harkin, Wilder, Clinton, Brown, and Tsongas). Also, three of the 1992 Democratic candidates (Clinton, Harkin, and Tsongas) were married to prominent lawyers (see Quindlen 1992, Goodman 1992). Three of the Democratic candidates (Brown, Clinton, and Tsongas) were Yale Law School grads, as were other prominent political figures, including Gary Hart, Clarence Thomas, Anita Hill, and Hillary Clinton (see Margolick 1992, Stark 1992). In the 1992 general election, on both sides of the political aisle two-lawyer couples squared off, with the Clintons facing the Quayles for the lawyer trifecta.

The legal training of many lawyer-politicians appears to influence how they present themselves on the campaign trail. Many of Bill Clinton's television advertisements for the 1992 New Hampshire primary prominently mentioned his Yale law degree, making the fact that he was a lawyer very important in the campaign. But various critics of Clinton's campaign style complained about his lawyerlike answers and "his too clever legalisms" in response to difficult questions concerning the issue of his character (see, e.g., Alter 1992, 36). For example, when asked about illegal drug use in his past, Clinton responded with the notorious but incredibly lawyerlike answer, "I did not inhale." Among the 1992 major Democratic candidates, only Senator Bob Kerrey of Nebraska was a nonlawyer, and Kerrey often attacked Paul Tsongas, especially in the Midwest, for being merely a "corporate lawyer and a Washington lobbyist" (see Stanley 1992, Frisby 1992).

Hillary Rodham Clinton's law career also became a political issue in the 1992 campaign. For example, just before the Republican National Convention in August of 1992, Hillary Clinton lavishly praised Anita Hill at the American Bar Association convention for her courage in coming forward with her sexual harassment accusations against then Supreme Court nominee Clarence Thomas (see Torry 1992). During the campaign, the Republicans continuously attacked Hillary Clinton for her positions on such matters as her support for expanding legal rights for children and for married women, and her arguments for independent counsel for children in child abuse cases (see Marcus 1992). Apparently, the Republicans were not comfortable with the image of a successful female attorney serving as the First Lady, although they did not complain about Marilyn Quayle's role as the Second Lady.

In addition to attacking the Clintons because they were lawyers, the Republicans also attacked their ties to the legal community. At the 1992 Republican National Convention, both President Bush and Vice-President Quayle tried to make legal reform and the legal profession an issue for the 1992 campaign. President Bush blamed the legal profession for blocking attempts to limit the number of law suits filed and to reduce the monetary costs of large awards in civil suits. The Republicans also attacked Bill Clinton because of his endorsement by the Trial Lawyers Association, and thus indirectly attacked Clinton for his legal training and background. The Bush/Quayle campaign added attorneys to the members of the "cultural elite" who, they said, were attempting to destroy American society (see Sack 1992; Fineman and McDaniel 1992, 29).

The Bush/Quayle campaign also repeated general attacks against the legal profession by several academics who variously claimed that each new law graduate costs the U.S. economy $2.5 million per year (Magee 1992a, 25), that lawyers collectively indirectly cost the U.S. economy $300 billion per year (President's Council on Competitiveness 1991, 1), that our national health-care crisis is due to too many medical malpractice suits, and that the legal profession impedes economic growth in this country (see, e.g., Magee, Brock, and Young 1989; Laband and Sophocleus 1988; Murphy, Schleifer, and Vishny 1991). Epp (1992a and 1992b), Sander (1992), and Cross (1992), among others, have offered rebuttals of these claims.[1]

Even when a public official's legal training is not necessarily relevant for the issue at hand, the press often highlights the legal backgrounds of many lawyer-politicians. For example, in an article discussing one senator's visit to Cuba for discussions with Fidel Castro, the journalist repeatedly referred to the senator as a farmer and a lawyer, although his legal background seemed to have no bearing on his discussions with the Cuban leader (see Crossette 1991).

Sometimes, however, the fact that a politician is a lawyer seems relevant. For example, it appears that former New York governor Mario Cuomo's lawyer background has been important in shaping his political persona. In an article profiling the then-possible presidential candidacy of Cuomo, Jonathan Alter highlighted Cuomo's legal training and background as an important part of what defines the very essence of the governor (Alter 1991, 33). Alter's observations were a result of the fact that Cuomo himself emphasized his lawyer background as a major influence on how he sees the world. Alter reported that after he asked the governor about how his alleged "thin skin" would affect his possible presidential campaign, Cuomo was quoted as replying, "If by thin-skinned you mean very, very quick to respond—that's what I've done for a lifetime. I'd been a lawyer for more than 20 years. You can't let the comment from the witness pass. If there's a jury, *everything* is important" (Alter 1991, 33). Therefore, Alter concluded, "[Cuomo experiences] life as a courtroom: reporters are witnesses to be cross-examined; voters are juries. This much is irreducibly part of his nature" (Alter 1991, 33). Thus, at least for Cuomo, the fact that he is a lawyer-politician seems to be a very important component of his approach to politics.

During the Clinton presidency, it has become even more apparent how Bill Clinton's legal training has affected how he performs his duties of office. For example, Clinton's misunderstanding of the potential backlash against his campaign promise to allow gays and lesbians to serve openly in the military reveals that he approached this issue from a highly legalistic viewpoint, instead of looking at the issue politically. From a legal and constitutional point of view, most observers assume that the courts will eventually force the military to admit gays on equal protection grounds (see, e.g., Towell 1993, 1971; Labaton 1993, A21), much like the Canadian courts forced the integration of gays into their military (see Swardson 1993, A8). Clinton saw discrimination against gays as a clear legal and constitutional issue. When he announced that he was going to force the military to accept openly gay and lesbian soldiers, he greatly underestimated the reaction of Congress and of the American people. He viewed this issue through the eyes of a lawyer, instead of through the eyes of a politician sensitive to the political fallout from such a bold move.

Another example of Clinton's legal training affecting his actions comes from the difficulties he had finding an acceptable nominee for the post of attorney general. He first nominated Zoe Baird for the position, but later had to withdraw her nomination after it was discovered that she had knowingly and illegally hired illegal aliens as household help and had failed to pay the required social security taxes (see Idelson 1993a, 179–81). Word then circulated that Clinton would nominate Judge Kimba M. Wood for the post. But Wood's chances for the position evaporated when it became public that she too had hired illegal aliens, although at a time when it was not illegal for employers to do so (see Idelson 1993b, 271). Stung by his problems over the Baird nomination, Clinton reportedly asked Wood if she had any "Zoe Baird problems." Wood responded with the narrow, technically correct, lawyerly answer that no, she had never broken the law. But she failed to reveal that politically her situation might be perceived as very similar to Baird's, even though technically the situations were very different. Clinton, angered at her "lawyer-speak" response, instead of the "political-speak" response that he had wanted, decided not to nominate Wood. After being hurt by his own lapses into "lawyer speak" during the campaign and during the gays-in-the-military controversy, he would not tolerate such narrow legalistic statements from potential cabinet members (see Dowd 1993, 8). After yet a second fiasco with his nominee for attorney general, Clinton nominated Janet Reno, who was single and childless and of course had no child-care problems.

Critics of Clinton and of lawyers in general have had a field day with Clinton's lawyerlike approach to certain issues. After the Kimba Wood problem, one columnist wrote, "Even by the standards of a capital accustomed to a glut of lawyers, this President has surrounded himself with a lot of lawyers, many in top jobs that require no legal training. He has also conducted the opening weeks of his Presidency in a lawyerly way, getting bogged down in technicalities, loopholes, caveats and flyspecking" (Dowd 1993, 8). Concerning the Zoe Baird and Kimba Wood episodes, the editor of the *Washington Monthly* has said, "In both instances, you had a tremendous number of lawyers who fooled around and missed the main point. Isn't that a symbol of what happens when you've got all these lawyers running things?" (Dowd 1993, 8).

Federal Government Lawyers

In addition to lawyers in the Oval Office, attorneys have also been prominent as heads of executive-branch agencies. As of the fall of 1993, thirteen of the eighteen members of President Clinton's cabinet were trained in the law (see Dowd 1993, 8), a higher percentage than in any other modern presidential administration.[2] As Dye has complained, "If the Clinton administration 'looks like America,' then we have become a nation of lawyers and lobbyists" (Dye 1993, 693).

Traditionally, many of the members of federal regulatory boards and commissions have been lawyers. Lawyers have long dominated top positions in the following federal regulatory agencies: the Civil Aeronautics Board, the Equal Employment Opportunity Commission, the Environmental Protection Agency, the Federal Communications Commission, the Federal Trade Commission, the Interstate Commerce Commission, the National Labor Relations Board, and the Securities and Exchange Commission (Kemp 1986). Noting the large number of lawyers on federal regulatory commissions in the 1970s, a political pundit has said, "We might think of regulation as employment programs for lawyers" (Kemp 1986, 267).

At times, it is difficult to classify the role of federal government lawyers as purely legal or purely political (see Seymour 1975, Meador 1980, Palmer 1984, Clayton 1992, Salokar 1994). For example, as head of the Justice Department, the U.S. attorney general is both a political figure and a lawyer for the government. In her work entitled *Conflicting Loyalties: Law and Politics in the Attorney General's Office,* Baker notes, "The attorney general serves both as a presidential appointee and as an officer of the court. Many of the responsibilities are quasi-judicial, including the long-standing role as the president's legal adviser. The attorney general has a foot in both the political and legal worlds" (Baker 1992, vii). Other recent studies of the attorney general include Meador (1980), Palmer (1984), and Clayton (1992), and several works on state attorneys general have appeared recently (see Heiser 1982, Morris 1987). Another important work on specialized federal government attorneys is Harringer's careful examination of the federal special prosecutor (Harringer 1992).

The U.S. solicitor general is another government lawyer with responsibilities for both politics and the law (see Salokar 1992, Caplan 1987). The solicitor general is the federal government's chief lawyer, presenting the government's position in cases before the Supreme Court and sometimes referred to as "the tenth justice" (Caplan 1987) or "the nation's lawyer" (Salokar 1992, 1). In her recent work on the solicitor general, Salokar concludes, "As both a presidential appointee and an officer of the Supreme Court, the solicitor general serves two institutions as the nation's lawyer. This lawyer's statutory responsibilities include protecting the interests of the executive branch before the highest court in the land. But in carrying out this task, the solicitor general is also a respected advisor to the justices and a gatekeeper, controlling a large portion of the litigation that reaches the Court's docket" (Salokar 1992, 1). At times the solicitor general is seen as an arm of the Supreme Court; at other times the president demands his or her loyalties. Thus attorneys fill a variety of crucial positions in the upper echelons of the federal government, and as such they have a lasting effect on public policy in this country.

Lawyers who are lesser employees of the federal government are also key players in shaping American public policy. Almost all federal agencies employ lawyers in various capacities (see Spangler 1986). Federal lawyers, of course, litigate suits by and against the government. But they are also involved in drafting proposed legislation, drafting proposed regulations, writing speeches, issuing press releases, and interpreting statutes, court decisions, and administrative regulations (see Brown 1948, 71–90). In her work comparing the various types of law practice in the United States, Spangler notes that "all government programs, whether of the service-providing or the regulatory variety, have legal dimensions that require the participation of lawyers" (Spangler 1986, 108).

The number of lawyers employed by the federal government has grown rapidly over the years and appears to be continuing to increase. Between 1954 and 1970, the number of self-employed lawyers in the United States increased by only 19 percent while the number of lawyers employed by the federal government increased by 108 percent and the number of lawyers employed by state governments increased by 167 percent (Abel 1989a, 103). Today, governmental attorneys comprise about 15 percent of all American lawyers (Wice 1991, 78). Lawyers were also the heart and soul of the New Deal (see Auerbach 1976; Irons 1982; Stevens 1983, 160). As Spangler notes, "Regulatory activities produce employment for lawyers, both in the private enterprises being regulated and in the government agencies doing the regulating" (Spangler 1986, 107). In fact, when President Reagan attempted to drastically curtail many of the federal government's regulatory practices, he replaced many agency lawyers with economists (McCann 1986, 236).

Although salaries are generally lower for federal government employees than for lawyers in comparable positions in private practice (see Abel 1989b, 167), there are many reasons why some lawyers prefer to work as employees for the federal government. In part because of historical discrimination in private law firms, female and minority lawyers are over-represented in government agencies (see Abel 1989b; Wice 1991, 78). Some lawyers prefer to work for the federal government because working hours are often shorter than in private practice and because there is a great deal of job security in the government. According to one scholar,

"Public agencies . . . provide job security without the intense competitive pressure found in larger firms as associates battle one another for the select few partnership positions" (Wice 1991, 78). Also, some attorneys come to the federal government because they have a strong ideological commitment to the agency's political goals (see Spangler 1986, 114).

Other attorneys use federal jobs as stepping stones to more lucrative employment in the private sector (see Spector 1972, 1973; Spangler 1986, 111–13; Abel 1989b, 168; Wice 1991, 78). These jobs include normal private practice law firms, and some former government attorneys become the famous Washington lawyer-lobbyists discussed in more detail below. Federal government attorneys often gain skills and experience not available in the private sector. They are given much greater responsibility more quickly than one could achieve in private law firms (see Wice 1991, 78). Government attorneys are also able to establish invaluable networks of contacts that stay with them throughout their legal, or possibly political, careers (see Spangler 1986). Thus many young attorneys see the government as a convenient first job in a long legal career. But some express concern about the larger political ramifications of the so-called revolving door, with federal regulators moving to work as lawyers and lobbyists for the regulated (see, e.g., Kolko 1963, Quirk 1981).

Lawyers are at the heart of many federal government activities, and various scholars have examined the effects of having so many lawyers working in federal agencies (see, e.g., Weaver 1977, Horowitz 1977a, Wollan 1978, Katzmann 1981, Plumlee 1981, Kemp 1986, Spangler 1986, Baker 1992, Harringer 1992). Some scholars draw a careful distinction between those agency lawyers who handle the government's litigation and those who counsel the agency about various questions (see Horowitz 1977a, Spangler 1986). Generally, the Justice Department handles most important litigation for all the federal agencies, but many other agencies maintain litigation staffs of their own as well (see Spangler 1986, 11). The functions of federal government attorneys are generally divided between litigation and negotiation. In his study of how lawyers' ways and lawyers' world views dominate the federal regulatory process, Horowitz concludes, "Exactly where a lawyer sits in government may be an important determinant of the accommodation that he reaches between his professional calling and his bureaucratic employment. The lawyer who serves in a substantive department may develop one orientation toward his work; the lawyer who serves the Justice Department may develop another" (Horowitz 1977a, 1).

Other scholars have also studied how lawyers function when employed by the federal government. In her study of government lawyers who perform both negotiation and litigation functions, Suzanne Weaver has examined the work of lawyers in the Antitrust Division of the Justice Department (Weaver 1977). This scholar describes the lawyers' approach to their work in this division as very detached, nonideological, analytical, professional, aggressive but not moralistic, and without a broad vision or passion for the long-range effects of their work.[3] Weaver concludes, "Because the antitrust laws are enforced in the courts, the division's task calls for the skills of lawyers. It does not [however] necessarily call for lawyers in the high proportion in which they are present" (Weaver 1977, 36).

The question then arises: Do government employees who are lawyers approach their jobs differently? Various studies have approached this question, and the results are somewhat mixed. For example, one study discusses the differences between the approaches of lawyers and nonlawyers who work in various federal agencies but finds no significant differences in policy making between the two groups (Plumlee 1981). On the other hand, another study found clear conflicts between the professional goals of lawyers and economists in the Federal Trade Commission (Katzmann 1981). Other studies have also discussed conflicts between lawyers and nonlawyers in federal regulatory agencies (Weaver 1977; Bardach and Kagan 1982, 41; Quirk 1981). Although the subject remains controversial, many studies point to clear differences between lawyers and nonlawyers in the government.

Many commentators have argued that the presence of so many lawyers in government produces a concern for procedures and processes over substance. Kathleen Kemp has argued that the dominance of lawyers in federal regulatory agencies produces an "incremental, case-by-case approach to policymaking" (Kemp 1986, 267–68). Other scholars have complained that the dominance of lawyers in federal agencies produces a short-term approach to policy making (see Davis 1971, Kohlmeier 1969). In his examination of federal regulatory agencies, Kohlmeier has argued, "Lawyers in government or private practice are paid to be specialists, not generalists. But specialization inhibits informed comprehension of the total fabric, which is woven of economic and political as well as legal strands" (Kohlmeier 1966, x). Other critics have detailed the role that lawyers played in scandals such as Watergate, and have generally attacked the profession for not doing enough to bring about needed changes in American society (see, e.g., Auerbach 1976, Kennedy 1990).

Local Government Lawyers

One of the fastest growing segments of the legal profession are those attorneys who work for local and state governments (see Abel 1989b).
Lawyers are, of course, present as prosecutors and public defenders (see
McIntyre 1987). And most cities now have a legal department. According to two legal scholars, "Municipal law officers are specialists in advising municipalities of their legal rights and duties as established by state
laws and city charters and as elaborated by city ordinances and other
regulations. . . . Practically every municipal action requires study of the
city's legal authority" (Blaustein and Porter 1954, 105).

Lawyers are less prevalent in many aspects of elected local government than they are in state legislative bodies (Blaustein and Porter 1954,
104; Prewill 1970). However, local bar associations are often active in
local political affairs (see Jacob 1978, 74–76; Sheldon 1977). And local
practicing attorneys often play key roles in local political-party activities.
According to one study, "Power in local political affairs, then, tends to
be based on accessibility to sources of decision in larger institutions. . . .
The lawyer gains his paramountcy through technical knowledge and personalized nonparty contacts up the political hierarchy with other lawyers. He is the mediator between the local party and the party hierarchy,
and transforms his personalized contacts into political indispensability
in the local community" (Vidich and Bensman 1960, 102).

Lawyers in and around the Legislatures

Lawyers play key roles in Congress and in state legislatures as staffers
for the representatives and senators and for legislative committees. Although the following discussion focuses on staff lawyers for the U.S. Congress, many state legislatures also have staff attorney positions.

Most of the important day-to-day work of Congress, of course, is
done in its committees and subcommittees (see also Fenno 1966, 1973;
Goodwin 1970; Manley 1970; Price 1985; Smith and Deering 1990). As
Woodrow Wilson first observed in his 1885 classic, *Congressional Government,* "Congress in session is Congress on public exhibition, whilst
Congress in its committee-rooms is Congress at work" (Wilson 1973,
69). And almost every committee and subcommittee has at least one, and
usually several, lawyers on its staff, often known as committee or subcommittee counsel.

Subcommittee and committee counsel play an extremely important role in the U.S. legislative process (see Ripley 1969, 1975; Fox and Hammond 1977; Davidson 1988). In addition to advising committee members, they often handle many of the details of the legislation the committees consider. Lawyers have dominated committee staffs since the 1946 Legislative Reorganization Act first created permanent committee staff positions (see Keefe and Ogul 1989). One study from the early 1970s found that more than half of committee staffers were lawyers (Fox and Hammond 1977, 44). Another study of both houses from the late 1970s and early 1980s found that 41 percent of top committee staff were lawyers (Aberbach 1990, 81). The presence of so many lawyers as staff to congressional committees helps shape how the committees go about their work.

In addition to their committee staffs, many lawmakers have lawyers on their personal staffs. The members' personal staffs are hired by the individual representatives and senators; the committee and subcommittee staffs are hired by the committee and subcommittee chairs, respectively. According to one study, in the early 1970s more than 15 percent of the members of personal congressional staffs in the Senate were lawyers, and 19 percent of the personal staffers in the House were lawyers (Fox and Hammond 1977, 36, 39). Of administrative assistants (AAs) on the Hill, (i.e., generally the chief of staff on members' personal staffs), 30 percent of the Senate AAs and 18 percent of the House AAs had law degrees. Of legislative assistants (LAs) (i.e., those persons on the personal staffs who rank below the administrative assistants and who specialize in giving the members legislative advice), in the early 1970s, 52 percent of the Senate LAs and 25 percent of the House LAs had law degrees (Fox and Hammond 1977, 175).

Some lawyers work for Congress in order to gain valuable experience that can be turned into high-paying jobs in private-sector law firms, as lobbyists, or as both. Many have commented on the "revolving door" phenomenon among Washington's lawyer-lobbyists (see, e.g., Green 1975; Malbin 1980, 19–24; Salisbury et al. 1992), meaning that most lobbyists in Washington have gained a great deal of experience working for the government before they set out to lobby that same government. Many congressional staffers leave their jobs on Capitol Hill to become lobbyists, and this is especially true for the lawyers who have worked as staff attorneys (see., e.g., Bisnow 1990).

The prevalence of lawyers on congressional staffs has created a certain amount of controversy. According to one scholar, "The great danger in overemphasis of legal training for professional committee work is that lawyers are too seldom exposed in their training to social, economic, and political problems. They bring to committee work the same narrow, technical, legalistic background already characteristic of so many legislators" (Kammerer 1951, 1130). On the other hand, another student of congressional staffs argues that a legal education for congressional staff encourages the staffer "to adopt a client-counsel attitude. It equips him to be a generalist. It is helpful in preparing bill analyses, briefs, opinions, and other legal memoranda. . . . It is very useful in handling casework and other kinds of legislative oversight duties involving technical points of law" (Kofmehl 1962, 85–86). Additionally, it is an asset in dealing with other committee members, many of whom are also lawyers.

Lawyers are also found in many support offices that provide specialized services to senators and representatives. All of the professional staffers in the Legislative Counsel's Office are lawyers. This office performs most of the technical legislative drafting duties for the Congress (see Jones 1952; Fox and Hammond 1977, 140–41; Congressional Quarterly 1983, 106; Cain 1994, 28). Lawyers are needed for drafting duties because, as one study explains, "Bill-drafting is lawyer's work, not because lawyers have any special facility with words, but because mastery of existing law is called for at every stage in the performance of a drafting assignment. A statute drawn up without sufficient attention to laws already on the books, as well as to the state of relevant judge-made law, inevitably raises vexing problems of interpretation" (Blaustein and Porter 1954, 99–100). Legislative drafting can have important political consequences, as Cain reminds us: "[Bill] drafting is an influential activity in its own right, not simply a neutral application of a technical skill" (Cain 1994, 28).

Most members of Congress and their staffs use the services of the Legislative Counsel's Office. As explained in Congressional Quarterly's sourcebook on Congress, *How Congress Works,* "Members who want to introduce legislation rely on the lawyers in the Office of the Legislative Counsel to put the proposal into the appropriate legalese. The lawyers analyze and research the precedents, compare the bill with existing laws and sometimes suggest alternatives. The office works closely with committee staffs as legislation is considered and marked up. Its assistance is also called upon during House-Senate conference committee negotiations" (Congressional Quarterly 1983, 106).

Lawyers are also important players in the Senate Legal Counsel Office and in the House General Counsel's Office, which advise Congress of its legal options when conflicts arise with the courts or with other political institutions (see Craig 1988, Miller 1989). According to one scholar, Congress created these offices in the 1970s "to meet the need for a comprehensive approach to legal actions and to protect their institutional interests in judicial proceedings" (Salokar 1992a, 1).

Lawyer-Lobbyists and Washington Lawyers

After they leave their jobs as congressional staffers or as executive-branch attorneys, many lawyers become Washington lawyer-lobbyists. Lawyer-lobbyists are an important tool for interest groups in this country. Although most interest groups do their heaviest lobbying in Washington, they also lobby state capitals (see Rosenthal 1981, 1989, 1990; Dalton, Wirkkala, and Thomas 1984; Bell 1986; Sheridan 1989; Cronin 1989; Thomas and Hrebenar 1992).

Interest groups attempt to influence American public policy in a variety of ways, and Washington-based groups are especially skillful at influencing the government's decisions.[4] Washington-based interest groups thus lobby Congress, the White House, the federal agencies, and the courts. McGuire (1993a and 1993b) has shown that the vast majority of lawyers who practice before the Supreme Court are located in Washington. They also raise a great deal of money and mobilize grass-roots support for candidates and political issues (Petracca 1992, 18). Some of these activities, such as litigation, require the assistance of lawyers. Lawyers also assist interest groups with many other lobbying activities. As described by one who teaches the art of lobbying in Washington, "The city's main product—what people in Washington create, organize, manipulate, and respond to—is words: legislation, floor statements, resolutions, proclamations, speeches, legal briefs, court decisions, newsletters, reports, press releases, and so on" (Wolpe 1990, 5). Because lawyers are highly skilled "Symbol Traders" (Cain 1994), they are perfectly suited to produce the words Washington thrives on. The vast majority of Washington-based interest groups have lawyers on their staffs or hire special Washington law firms to help them with lobbying activities (see Schlozman and Tierney 1986, McCann 1986).

The number of interest groups lobbying in Washington is at a record high (see Knoke 1986, Berry 1989, Peterson 1990, Salisbury 1990, Birnbaum 1992). According to one interest-group scholar, "Explosion is a completely accurate way to describe the massive number of interest groups that have descended upon Washington, D.C. since the 1960's" (Petracca 1992, 13, 14). There are currently more than fifteen thousand registered lobbyists in Washington (Wolpe 1990, 3). The interest-group explosion has created diverse lobbying groups, including ones for lawyers and law firms, nonprofit associations, labor unions and corporations, citizens' groups, governmental entities, and foreign interests (Petracca 1992, 13, 14). Almost all of these groups use lawyers in various roles.

With the growth of the regulatory and other aspects of the federal government in the latter part of this century, the number of lawyers practicing before the federal government has grown exponentially. As one historian notes:

> In the twentieth century, the growth of business regulation and the phenomenal career of the Internal Revenue Code have meant tons of new rules and regulations that were (formally) part of the law. Lawyers were instrumental in writing these statutes and rules and were ready, willing, and able to help businesses and wealthy individuals cope, adjust, and evade. Lawyers, after all, had always been in the business of dealing with government. . . . They played a central role in the welfare-regulatory state, defending business against regulation and teaching it how to live with rules and regulations. (Friedman 1989, 9)

The number of Washington lawyer-lobbyists is certainly expanding. From 1973 to 1983, the number of lawyers who were members of the District of Columbia Bar more than tripled, from just under 11,000 to more than 37,000 (Laumann et al. 1985, Nelson et al. 1987). By 1980, there were more than 12,000 Washington lawyers who actively represented business interests before federal regulatory agencies and the federal courts (Vogel 1989, 197). The number of out-of-town law firms with branch offices in Washington, D.C., exploded from 45 in 1965 to 247 by 1983 (Petracca 1992, 14).

A special type of lawyer-lobbyists in the nation's capital are the "Washington Lawyers." Washington lawyers do not merely practice law in D.C.; they are key players in shaping the fundamental policy decisions of our federal government. According to Goulden, "The lawyer's historic role was that of advising clients how to *comply* with the law. The Washington Lawyer's present role is that of advising clients how to *make* laws, and to make the most of them" (Goulden 1971, 5–6).

Most Washington lawyers are part of the relatively small circle of the truly powerful in Washington who have personal contacts at the highest level of government. Many of these Washington lawyers have previously served in various capacities in the government. They are currently some of the most important movers and shakers. They have access to the top decision-makers in Congress and in the executive branch, and they often have a great deal of influence in shaping public-policy decisions. As Green explains, "Washington lawyers have burrowed themselves into the federal establishment. They influence a whole range of policy matters that deal with the way we live. . . . Thus what the social Philadelphia lawyer was two generations ago and the financial Wall Street lawyer one generation ago, Washington lawyers are today—as the locus of public power shifts from pedigree, to money, to politics" (Green 1978, 4).

Various authors have all discussed in some detail the powerful world of the Washington lawyer (see, e.g., Kraft 1964; Goldfarb 1968; Goulden 1971; Pike 1980; Clifford 1991; Cain 1994, 29–31). Green (1978) was so disturbed by their power that he titled his book *The Other Government: The Unseen Power of Washington Lawyers*.

Some scholars feel that the importance of Washington-based lawyer-lobbyists has been overemphasized. Nelson and Heinz examined the influence of Washington lawyers on policy making in the United States, and they found that among Washington lobbyists there was the perception that Washington lawyers "are not as prevalent, active, or influential in national policy making as the popular image suggests. Rather, the findings indicate that lawyers occupy a relatively specialized niche in the system of interest representation, one that allows them to command substantial economic rewards and to maintain a measure of independence and autonomy in their work, but that limits their influence in policy formation" (Nelson and Heinz 1988, 237). Kagan and Rosen argue that Washington lawyers do not make policy, because they merely represent the policy wishes of their clients. In other words, lawyers do not take the lead on public policy as an independent social force, they are merely hired to do a job, and they do it (Kagan and Rosen 1985).

Many Washington lawyers attempt to minimize the publicity about their influence in the nation's capital. A key advisor to several presidents and a longtime Washington lawyer, Clark Clifford, concludes, "By the sixties, I was sometimes described as a pillar of the Washington power structure, a quintessential member of the Washington establishment. I was not displeased with the compliment implicit in such a description, but at the same time it always amused me. . . . I did not consider myself an old Washington hand. In my own mind, I was what I had always been, a lawyer" (Clifford 1991, 652–53). Nevertheless, Washington lawyers are a very special type of lawyer-lobbyists.

Public Interest, Legal Aide, and Other Reform Lawyers

Not all interest groups lobby on behalf of the rich and powerful. A new variety of interest group, the self-labeled "public interest group," lobbies on behalf of various outsiders in the American political system. Today the term "public interest group" has come to mean liberal advocacy groups, such as consumer groups, environmental groups, women's groups, and groups such as the American Civil Liberties Union (ACLU), the League of Women Voters, People for the American Way, the NAACP Legal Defense Fund, and Common Cause, which lobbies for campaign finance reform and the elimination of political action committees (PACs) sponsored by other interest groups.

Usually born in the upheaval of American politics in the 1960s, these groups were shaped by the experiences gained from the civil rights movement, the welfare rights movement, and the antiwar movement. Some commentators refer to them as "citizen groups" (see Petracca 1992, 16). All of these groups were to the left of the political spectrum in the United States. As McCann writes, "Public interest liberalism was conceived in America amid the passionate promises and protests of the 1960s. Against a background of escalating economic prosperity, rising education levels, a liberal social consensus, and the explosion of popular mass media technology, the most important movement leaders began their purposive quests for public attention" (McCann 1986, 29).

Many of the leaders of this new, liberal public interest movement, such as Ralph Nader, were lawyers. In addition, more than half of the professionally trained activists were also lawyers (about 35 percent of the total rank and file members of the public interest movement) (see McCann 1986, 34; Berry 1977, 85, 88, 94; Handler et al. 1978; Olson 1984, 3–20). As McCann notes, "This striking number of lawyers in the movement further encouraged mutual intercourse built upon shared vernacular and specialized understanding of the world" (McCann 1986, 34). In other words, these groups adopted lawyers' language and lawyers' ways of seeing the world. Lawyers and other professionals also constituted one of the most stable sources of grass-roots support within the general public for the reform movement (see McCann 1986, 56). As McCann concludes, "From the outset each developing social movement enlisted the aid of professional lawyers to promote its various causes through legal action" (McCann 1986, 31). Or as Clement Vose expressed it, "There is a special appropriateness for small, organized interests to work through litigation" (Vose 1972, 330). Throughout recent American history, social reformers—the leaders of the Progressive reforms and of the New Deal, for example—have often been lawyers (see Auerbach 1976, 102–230).

The liberal reform movements of the 1960s and 1970s used a legal-rights approach to expanding democracy (McCann 1986, 26, 106–21; see also Halpern and Cunningham 1971, Selznick 1974, Horowitz 1977c, Olson 1984). According to Susan Olson, another aspect of social change through legal reform involves "the growth of collective rights consciousness—the recognition that problems previously thought to be personal are instead collective and the rising sense of entitlement to relief from those problems" (Olson 1984, 5). And lawyers, in and out of public office, are often the ones to push for the social acknowledgment of collective rights.

This lawyerly approach to social problems often paid off, because "each movement represented a consecutive wave of law reform leading to important new legislative statutes and court actions to extend and enforce their effectiveness" (McCann 1986, 31; see also Rabin 1976, 207–61). These lawyers used litigation and a variety of other political tactics to educate the public about the issues, encourage supporters inside the bureaucracy, force political adversaries to negotiate, and eventually increase the cause's bargaining power (Olson 1984, 9). Thus liberals in the 1960s and 1970s chose a legalistic, rights-oriented approach to social reform (see also McCann 1986, 25, 31).

As the liberal public interest movement matured, many lawyers set up organizations and clinics similar to law firms to promote law reform and social change through the law. In his discussion of liberal social movement lawyers, McCann notes that "if collective electoral and protest action was the focus of earlier Populist, New Deal, and even civil-rights movement building, then class-action suits, test-case litigation, legislative lobbying, and administrative rule making best exemplify the participatory commitments of the new reformers" (McCann 1986, 199). Various scholars have studied the recent explosion of public-interest lawyers and public-interest law organizations (see, e.g., Moore 1972; Halpern 1976; Erlanger 1978b; Olson 1984; O'Connor and Epstein 1984, 1989; Aron

1989; France 1991; Lopez 1992). These lawyers often worked (and continue to work) for low salaries because they believed in their cause. Today public-interest lawyers are still often ideologically committed to using the courts as a mechanism for social change.

Of course, public-interest law is not without its problems and criticisms. Many worry about whether public-interest lawyers are representing the best interests of their specific clients, or whether these ideologically committed lawyers are more concerned about their group's political agenda (see, e.g., Wexler 1970, 1053; Cahn and Cahn 1970, 1021–22; Brill 1973, 54; Denvir 1976, 1144; Bell 1976, 470; Handler 1978, 18–33; Olson 1984, 21–39). Olson raises this very real concern: "Confusion about the degree of autonomy of lawyers becomes politically significant when courts make policy at the behest of lawyers representing groups of people who are not formally part of the suit or who at least do not personally speak on their own behalf. The problem of knowing whom exactly the lawyers represent is greatest in public interest litigation, as evidenced by the endless debates over who determines the public interest" (Olson 1984, xii).

Another group of lawyers dedicated to using the courts for social change work for the federally funded Legal Services Corporation. In fact, Spangler, in her work comparing various aspects of law practice, entitled her chapter on these lawyers "Generally Contentious People: Legal Services Advocates" (Spangler 1986, 144–74). This federal agency was set up during the Great Society days of the 1960s to provide legal assistance for the poor, primarily in noncriminal cases (see Johnson 1974). In addition to providing routine legal advice and assistance to the needy, many Legal Services lawyers began using their positions to encourage the courts to create public policies favorable to the poor and the disenfranchised (see Erlanger 1978a, Katz 1982). These political activities infuriated conservatives, and the Nixon and Reagan administrations did all they could to curtail these political cases by placing severe restrictions on the activities of Legal Services Corporation attorneys when they failed to abolish the agency altogether (see Spangler 1986). Lawrence (1990) discusses the victories legal services lawyers won in the Supreme Court over the years, and Christopher Smith (1991) looks at how court policies affect the disadvantaged in our society.

Liberal interest groups have long used the courts as a vehicle for changing public policy (see Bentley 1908; Truman 1951, 1971; Vose 1957, 1958, 1966; Vose 1972; O'Connor and Epstein 1983a; Olson

1984; Baum 1989). In the conflict between politics and the law, public-interest advocates such as Ralph Nader have argued that "the struggle for legal supremacy in a society lies in the tension between raw power and just law" (Nader and Green 1976, vii). Groups such as the National Association for the Advancement of Colored People (NAACP), the NAACP Legal Defense Fund, the National Consumers' League, the Women's Rights Project, the Sierra Club Legal Defense Fund, and the ACLU repeatedly urged the courts to make decisions establishing various public policies (see, e.g., Vose 1955, 1957, 1959; Meltsner 1973; Kluger 1976; O'Connor 1980; Wenner 1982; Wasby 1984, 1986; Epstein 1985, 1991). According to one scholar, groups like the NAACP must use the courts "because they are temporarily, or even permanently, disadvantaged in terms of their ability to attain successfully their goals in the electoral process, within the elected institution or in the bureaucracy. If they are to succeed at all in the pursuit of their goals they are almost compelled to resort to litigation" (Cortner 1968, 287).

Over the years, interest groups have been quite good at exploiting the policy-making powers of American courts. According to David Truman, "The activities of judicial officers of the United States are not exempt from the processes of group politics. . . . Though myth and legend may argue to the contrary, . . . the judiciary reflects the play of interests, and few organized groups can afford to be indifferent to its activities" (Truman 1971, 479). Various recent works have chronicled the use of the courts by interest groups to achieve their public-policy goals. For example, Casper (1972) describes the activities of lawyers in helping to shape the policy initiatives that were handed down by the Warren Court. Olson's (1984) work focuses on how lawyers and nonlawyers helped make public transportation accessible to persons with physical disabilities. Horowitz's (1977b) classic work focuses on how courts shape public policy, as well as does Johnson and Canon's (1984) work on the implementation and impact of court decisions. Recently there has been increasing scholarly attention paid to interest groups and the courts (see, e.g., bibliography in Lee Epstein's [1991] work).

In reaction to the success of liberal interests groups in the courts, various conservative groups formed their own court-centered interest groups. Several studies have shown how conservative interest groups have used the federal courts to shape policy (see O'Connor and Epstein 1983b, Epstein 1985, O'Connor and Ivers 1987, O'Connor and McFall 1992). O'Connor and Epstein found that conservative interest-group involvement in Supreme Court litigation grew steadily from 1969 to 1980 (O'Connor and Epstein 1983b). According to some other students of this topic, "By the mid-1970's, myriad conservative public interest law firms and special interest litigating groups were created. Moreover, many conservatives believed that these new voices would effectively pursue the conservative agenda through litigation" (O'Connor and McFall 1992, 263). Buoyed by the election of Ronald Reagan to the presidency on a platform of appointing only conservative judges to the federal bench, these groups hoped to counter the victories won by liberal groups throughout the activist Warren Court era.

Interest groups must use the correct legal channels to lobby the courts. According to a leading scholar in this area, "The rules of the legal game simply prohibit direct encounters [between lobbyists and judges]. Hence, if interest groups wish to influence the outcomes of legal disputes, they must find alternative routes of 'lobbying,' routes that correspond to the norms of the judiciary" (Epstein 1991, 335). Interest groups that use the courts for social change are compelled to hire attorneys to help them with this task. McGuire (1993a and 1993b) has shown that the number of lawyers who argue cases before the Supreme Court is fairly small, and many of the most visible repeat players represent powerful interest groups.

Lawyers as Judges

Lawyers affect the American public-policy process in another key role: as judges. The vast majority of judges in this country are, of course, lawyers.[5] Judges, as interpreters of the law, are in a key position to affect public policy. Therefore, as Tocqueville observed, "scarcely any political question arises in the United States that is not resolved sooner or later into a judicial question" (Tocqueville 1969, 270).

Of course, much of the policy-making power of American courts stems from their power of judicial review. Judicial review is the power of the courts to declare unconstitutional acts of the legislative and executive branches. American courts are almost unique in this regard. In the United States, judges and the lawyers who argue before them can exercise an enhanced policy-making role when the courts overrule the policy decisions made by other political institutions (see Slotnick 1987). As explained by one study, "In the United States the political power of the legislature was inhibited by constitutional limitations. But if the power of the legislature is limited, who is in a better position than the lawyer to know whether the Constitution has been violated? . . . [Thus] the lawyer was on his way to political dominance" (Eulau and Sprague 1964, 15).

In addition, lawyers arguing before the courts can greatly affect American public policy. For example, Bartee (1984) looks at how lawyers have shaped many Supreme Court decisions, and Casper (1972) examines the role individual attorneys in private practice played in bringing cases to the Supreme Court during the Warren era. As powerful Washington lawyer Clark Clifford said in his memoirs, "I have always been proud of my profession. I know of no other work in the private sector that offers a greater challenge, more potential rewards, and greater variety than the practice of law" (Clifford 1991, 269). Clifford continues: "A central aspect of practicing law is the art of persuading others of one's point of view. Arguing before a judge or jury—the act of *advocacy,* of trying to convince others of the merit of your case—is, to my mind, the very essence of being a lawyer" (Clifford 1991, 269–70).

Many scholars have reminded us that the eventual determination of public policy in this country is often a result of the continuous interactions and dialogues between Congress and the federal courts (see, e.g., Bickel 1962, Agresto 1984, Johnson and Canon 1984, Katzmann 1988, Fisher 1988). As Katzmann has concluded in his now-classic collection of essays on court-legislative interactions, "How courts and Congress interact has ramifications beyond those branches. . . . The interplay of Congress and the courts has vital consequences for the administrative state itself" (Katzmann 1988, 12). And according to another scholar, "Many legal issues have inescapable policy implications. . . . This lack of a clear delineation between law and politics in our system plagues every officer who is charged with the task of legal interpretation" (Baker 1992, 4).

It is now a very familiar refrain from American political scientists that the federal courts and their judges are important components in the American policy-making process (see, e.g., Dahl 1958; Casper 1976; Horowitz 1977b; Halpern and Lamb 1982; O'Brien 1986; Brigham 1987; Slotnick 1988; Van Horn, Baumer, and Gormley 1989; Baum 1990, 1992; Adamany 1991). The Supreme Court has long been recognized as a key player in the policy-making process. As one political scientist has stated, "There can be little question that the legal system and especially its most prominent institution—the Supreme Court of the United States—plays an important role in public policy-making" (Casper 1972, 3).

Lower courts, however, can also be key policy makers in our political system. Recently there has also been increased scholarly activity regarding policy making by the often-neglected state courts (see, e.g., Porter and Tarr 1982, Fino 1987, Daniels 1988, Tarr and Porter 1988, Baum 1989, Jacob 1990, Glick 1991, Stumpf and Culver 1992, Emmert 1992, Emmert and Traut 1992). Atkins (1987) argues forcefully that trial courts in resolving even routine disputes greatly affect the public-policy choices available to other decision makers. The power of lawyers serving in the judiciary should not be underestimated. As one scholar concludes, "If the bar, therefore, is to state quite honestly the measure of its participation in public life, it must admit that law-trained persons maintain a complete monopoly over one branch of government, and considerable effective control over the other two" (Brown 1948, 20–21).

Academic Lawyers

Lawyers working in academia can also have a great deal of influence on the policy-making process. Law review articles and other legal-scholarship materials are often cited by the Supreme Court and other American courts (see Friedman et al. 1981, 810–17; Richardson 1983; Sirico and Margulies 1986; see also Baum 1991, 410). Interest groups often use law journals to argue their points of view. Of course, one of the first law review articles that helped change policy in this country was a piece on legal concepts of privacy written by Samuel Warren and future Supreme Court justice Louis Brandeis in 1890. Since then, academic lawyers have continued to play a key role in affecting the shape of American public policy.

One key forum for legal scholarship is the American Law Institute (ALI) (see Darrell and Wolkin 1980). The ALI convenes various groups under the leadership of scholars to establish "model" legal rules on various issues. Often these model rules are widely adopted by courts or state legislatures. Scholars thus have a great deal of impact in proposing innovations in numerous areas of the law (see Baum 1991, 420).

Academic lawyers can have a great influence on the shape of public policy in this country. As one student of the courts concludes:

> In the development and flow of ideas for new doctrines, legal scholarship plays a major role. Much of this scholarship is aimed at influencing doctrinal development in the courts; in a sense, law professors and other legal scholars can be viewed as doctrinal entrepreneurs. Their

influence is considerable, because scholarly writing—especially in the journals published by law schools—has high visibility and carries considerable prestige for the courts. Moreover, many law clerks on appellate courts were student editors of law journals, experience that makes them attentive to legal scholarship. (Baum 1991, 420)

Not all academic lawyers are housed in law schools; many (including this author) teach at the undergraduate level. Others teach graduate students in political science, sociology, and other disciplines outside of the law schools. About a third of the members of the American Political Science Association's section on Law and Courts hold both a Ph.D. and a law degree (see Sarat et al. 1990). Academic lawyers are very active in the sociolegal research movement and in such organizations as the Law and Society Association (see Levine 1990 and Abel 1980).

Lawyers in Private Practice

Finally, lawyers in private practice also have a great deal of influence on the shape of public policy (see, e.g., Harrington 1994). Several works have looked at the political power of various bar associations (see, e.g., Melone 1979, Halliday 1987, Powell 1988), but this section focuses on the political role of lawyers working as individuals and in firms in private practice. As Provine explains, "Where law is plentiful and disputes over its application are frequent and involve large sums of money, as in the United States, legal experts are particularly valuable" (Provine 1986, 22). Since 1960, the number of lawyers worldwide has almost doubled, but the number of lawyers in the United States has tripled during the same period (Kelly 1994, 3).

A good lawyer in the United States can represent clients before the courts, before administrative agencies, and before legislative bodies, all institutions that affect public policy. The arguments private practice attorneys make before these institutions have a great deal of ability to shape the eventual decisions of these institutions (Wice 1991, 52). Therefore, American lawyers can represent their clients using a wide variety of methods that are not available to their counterparts in other countries. According to two students of the legal profession, "The prominence of lawyers in public elective and appointive office, even considering in addition the lawyers holding numerous other government jobs or serving as important policy advisors, represents only a part of the political role of the bar. More pervasive and potentially more important is the public impact of the bar in its generally private role as counselor and advocate of private interests" (Zemans and Rosenblum 1981, 1).

In private practice, lawyers can also affect public policy by being expert advisors to decision makers. As Lasswell and McDougal explain:

> The lawyer is today . . . the one indispensable adviser of every responsible policy-maker of our society—whether we speak of the head of a government department or agency, of the executive of a corporation or labor union, of the secretary of a trade or other private association, or even of the humble independent enterpriser or professional man. As such an adviser the lawyer, when informing his policy-maker of what he can or cannot legally do, is in an unassailably strategic position to influence, if not create, policy. . . . For better or worse our decision-makers and our lawyers are bound together in a relation of dependence or of identity. (Lasswell and McDougal 1948, 27).

Even when lawyers are not attempting to shape public policy, their interactions with their clients often have political overtones. According to Sarat and Felstiner, in their now-classic work on the interactions between divorce lawyers and their clients, "As lawyers and clients together define how people behave and explain why they behave as they do, as they try to make sense of life events, they give shape and content to such behavior and events. What lawyers tell their clients about social relationships, how they respond to client questions concerning the behavior of other people, structures, at least in part, the way in which clients 'experience and perceive their relations with others'" (Sarat and Felstiner 1988, 740, quoting in part Hunt 1985, 15). In many ways, almost everything that a private-practice lawyer does can be construed as having political effects.

Private-practice lawyers often combine their law practices with the holding of local or state political offices. Many of the lawyer-legislators in state legislatures are in reality part-time politicians and full-time lawyers. In fact, Cohen (1969) has looked at politics as another specialty for private-practice lawyers. According to one scholar:

> Legal advice and advocacy form the core of the lawyer's service to the incumbents of positions of power as well as the basis of his participation in power processes. However, the lawyer's role will often broaden

beyond his sphere of immediate technical competence. Legal counsel of policy-makers is likely to acquire organizational and interpersonal knowledge and skills which enlarge his opportunities for influence. . . . If for such reasons counsel takes a particularly crucial place in the staff of policy-makers of all kinds—in corporations, trade associations, unions, government departments, and legislative bodies—he will, finally, also have a good chance to be recruited out of his staff role into the decision-making positions. (Rueschemeyer 1973, 68–69).

Thus, practicing lawyers historically have been seen as natural choices for political positions. As two leading scholars conclude, "In the formative years of the country, lawyers were considered particularly suited for careers in government . . . because their vocation was seen as one of public service and public trust" (Eulau and Sprague 1964, 16).

Americans seem to have a love-hate relationship with their lawyers. Most Americans realize that lawyers are very important in society, and one study found that roughly two-thirds of the adult population has consulted a lawyer at least once about a personal, nonbusiness legal problem (Zemans and Rosenblum 1981, 2). But we remain uneasy about our relationships with our lawyers. As Olson explains, "On the personal level individuals feel considerable ambivalence about their relationships with private lawyers. While we want our lawyer to prevent, cure, or at least shield us from our legal difficulties, we are often dissatisfied with the results" (Olson 1984, xii).

Just as various types of lawyers influence American public policy, lawyers also play various direct and indirect roles in the public-policy process. Many of the ultimate political decision makers in this country have legal training and legal backgrounds. Lawyers are the largest single professional group elected to the U.S. Congress and to many state legislatures. The heads of federal and state regulatory agencies are often lawyers, and by definition and tradition, almost all the judges in this country are lawyers. Because so many lawyers are making key decisions in our political system, the governmental institutions in which they serve often adopt very lawyerlike decision-making processes.

Lawyers also serve as crucial staff to the individual decision makers and to governmental institutions as a whole. Almost all presidents and governors hire lawyers as advisors, often giving them the title of "chief counsel" or "White House counsel." Support organizations such as the

House General Counsel's Office and some parts of the Congressional Research Service are staffed by lawyers who assist in the drafting of proposed legislation. These support organizations are becoming more common in the more professionalized state legislatures as well. Judges hire law clerks, young lawyers right out of law school, to assist them in their legal research and writing duties. Federal agencies all have law departments, which often serve as legal advisors to the heads of the agencies. Therefore, even when the ultimate decision makers are not lawyers themselves, they are often surrounded by assistants and staff who are attorneys by training. This omnipresence of lawyers causes many political institutions to adopt lawyers' ways of thinking and doing.

Lawyers also serve as lobbyists, attempting to influence the decisions made by the ultimate decision makers. They "lobby" the president and his close advisors, the Congress, the courts, the federal agencies, and the general public. Their job is to attempt to influence the choices made by the ultimate decision makers. Because both those being lobbied and the lobbyists are often lawyers, the entire process takes on the language and the ways of lawyers. In fact, groups that are often unsuccessful at influencing public policy in this country are generally those that do not approach the decision-making process from a lawyerlike perspective. As Melone reminds us, "Given the cultural milieu [in the U.S.] . . . lawyers are ideally situated to define, alter and redefine the boundaries of legitimate political argument. Ultimately, these powers may be far greater than the ability to defeat particular legislative proposals" (Melone 1979, 4).

Even when lawyers are not attempting directly to influence public-policy choices in this country, their actions can have political consequences. Prosecutors and defense attorneys, even in their most mundane cases, collectively influence the political decision-making process. If politics is defined as the exercise of power in society (see, e.g., Isaak 1985, 15–21), prosecutors and defense attorneys in their routine roles are influencing the power relationships in the United States. Whenever a lawyer in private practice discusses a case with his or her clients, there are political consequences. Whenever a government attorney writes a new draft regulation or cautions the agency against some proposed action, that lawyer is helping to shape the decisions that will ultimately be made by the public-policy process. Citing the fact that lawyers are omnipresent in American political institutions is not enough; we must also understand how the American public-policy decision-making process is dominated by lawyers' ways and lawyers' language.

CHAPTER FOUR

The Prevalence of Lawyer-Legislators in the United States

By now the reader is quite familiar with the fact that almost every elected office in the United States is dominated by lawyer-politicians. As Woodrow Wilson is quoted as saying, "The profession I chose was politics; the profession I entered was law. I entered the one because I thought it would lead to the other" (Watson and Thomas 1988, 131). Lawyers are certainly the largest professional group represented in the Congress and in many state legislatures. This chapter will provide data on the numbers of lawyer-legislators in the United States, and then focus on why lawyers so dominate our legislative bodies.

The History of Having So Many Lawyer-Legislators

The U.S. Congress has long been dominated by lawyer-politicians. During the early years of the Republic, often 75 percent of the Senate members and up to 65 percent of those in the House were lawyers (Hurst 1950, 47). According to one historian, from 1790 to 1930 the percentage of lawyers in Congress remained fairly stable, with about two-thirds of the Senate and about one-half of the House of Representatives being lawyers during the entire period (Friedman 1985, 647). As table 1 indicates, the number of lawyer members of the House has ranged from a low of 42 percent in the early part of the nineteenth century to a high of 67 percent in the mid-nineteenth century. Throughout our history lawyers have been the largest single occupational group in Congress.

Traditionally, a higher proportion of lawyer members in Congress came from the South (see Hacker 1964). In 1964 all of the members of the Alabama and Arkansas delegations in the House were lawyers, as

Table 1

Occupational Backgrounds of U.S. Representatives, by Decade of Entry into House, 1789–1960

	Lawyer (%)	Educator (%)	Other Professional (%)	Agriculture (%)	Business (%)
1789–1800	45	<1	8	13	13
1801–10	42	<1	9	18	15
1811–20	55	<1	8	11	12
1821–30	57	<1	8	11	12
1831–40	64	<1	8	10	12
1841–50	67	<1	8	9	13
1851–60	67	<1	9	5	16
1861–70	62	<1	8	5	22
1871–80	66	1	6	6	20
1881–90	61	1	8	7	22
1891–1900	60	2	8	8	24
1901–10	61	1	7	5	24
1911–20	60	2	9	3	23
1921–30	58	4	8	4	21
1931–40	51	5	10	6	24
1941–50	51	5	11	4	22
1951–60	52	5	7	6	21

Source: Bogue, Clubb, McKibbin, and Traugott 1976, 284.
Note: Percentages may not add to 100 due to rounding.

were four out of five of the representatives from Mississippi. All told, 74 of the 106 members of the House from the South (approximately 70 percent) were lawyers in 1964 (Hacker 1964, 74). According to one researcher, southerners sent lawyers to Congress in order to prevent major societal reforms from passing. Southern lawyers were seen as part of the pro–status quo establishment who could be trusted to block changes demanded by reformer politicians from outside the Old South (Hacker 1964, 14, 74–75).

Table 2

Percentage of Lawyer Members of Congress for Selected Years

Year	House (%)	Senate (%)	Total (%)
1943	58	74	61
1955	57	60	57
1965	57	67	54
1975	51	67	54
1981	45	59	47
1983	46	61	49
1985	44	61	47
1987	42	62	46
1989	42	63	46
1991	42	61	46
1993	42	58	45
1994	42	60	46
1995	39	54	42

Sources: Brown 1948, 17; Stanley and Niemi 1992, 202; Ornstein et al. 1992, 22–23, 28–29; Cranford 1992, 9; Duncan 1993.

Lawyers' domination of Congress continues today, although recently the proportion of lawyers in the House has declined somewhat while the number of lawyers in the Senate has roughly held steady. As table 2 indicates, at the beginning of the 101st Congress in 1989, 42 percent (184 members) of the House of Representatives were lawyers (47 percent of the Democrats and 35 percent of the Republicans). Sixty-three senators were lawyers, nearly equally distributed between the two parties (Ornstein, Mann, and Malbin 1990, 20–21, 26–27). At the beginning of the 102d Congress in January of 1991, 46 percent (244 of the 535 members of both houses) claimed attorney as their profession (see Characteristics of Congress 1991, 118). At the beginning of the 103d Congress in 1993, 42 percent of the House members (47 percent of the Democrats and 33 percent of the Republicans) were attorneys, and 58 percent of the senators (58 percent of both parties) were lawyers (Stanley and Niemi 1994, 204). Since the mid-1950s, the proportion of lawyer members has been somewhat higher for the Democrats than for the Republicans, especially in the House, probably because the Republican Party attracts more nonlawyers with a straight business background (see Ripley 1975). Although after the 1994 elections the Republicans took control of both houses of Congress for the first time since the early 1950s, the number of lawyers in Congress did not drop dramatically. At the beginning of the 104th Congress in January 1995, 39 percent of the House members and 54 percent of the senators were lawyers.

In order to appreciate fully how lawyers totally dominate Congress, it is important to compare the number of lawyer-legislators in the United States with the number in other democracies around the world. Although lawyers in many countries gravitate toward politics, the United States has more lawyer-politicians than most, as indicated in table 3. Historically,

Table 3

Percentage of Lawyer Members of National Legislatures for Selected Countries

Country	Percentage	Year
Columbia	66	late 1960s
United States	45	1993
India	33	1980
Canada	25	1988
Venezuela	25	1986
Australia	20	1985
Netherlands	20	1980–85
Italy	17	1976
United Kingdom	16	1945–74
Brazil	14	1980–85
Norway	10	1980–85
France	5	1981
West Germany	5	1969–83
Denmark	4	1945–74

Sources: Loewenberg and Patterson 1988, Cranford 1992, Abel 1989, Perez Perdomo 1988, Rydon 1987, DiPalma and Cotta 1986, Mellors 1978, Friedman 1989, Boigeol 1988, Pedersen 1972.

in the late nineteenth and early twentieth centuries lawyers dominated the national legislatures of Italy, France, the Netherlands, Germany, Norway, Brazil, and Venezuela (Abel 1988a, 41). Today, however, the proportion of lawyer-legislators has declined dramatically in most of these countries, and the general trend is toward fewer lawyer-legislators, especially in the civil law countries of continental Europe (Lewis 1989, 37–38). The American experience—lawyers dominating the legislative bodies—is fairly rare.

Historically, a large number of U.S. state legislators have also been attorneys. Lawyers were traditionally more prevalent in legislative bodies with smaller memberships and longer tenures (Hurst 1950, 47). Therefore, lawyer members are generally more abundant in the upper houses of state legislatures. Southern legislatures had an especially large proportion of lawyer members, whereas in the North, lawyers tended to represent large metropolitan areas (Friedman 1985, 647). Still today, lawyer-legislators tend to be most prevalent in southern states, and the fewest number of lawyers are found in the rural western and rural New England state legislatures (Patterson 1983, 154). Some scholars (see, e.g., Baker 1990) have argued that differences among the states in the occupational status of state legislators can be linked to differences in state political cultures, as defined by Elazar (1966), especially in the preprofessionalization periods of these legislatures. When state legislatures were part-time bodies, lawyer-politicians could hold legislative office and still practice law full time

Table 4

Lawyer Members in State Legislatures, by Region

Region	1976	1979	1986*
Northeast	19	17	13
North Central	18	16	13
South	32	29	24
West	14	12	12
Total states	22	20	16

SOURCES: 1976 and 1979 figures are from Insurance Information Institute; 1986 figures are from Bazar. All figures are percentages.

*In the 1986 figures, legislators with law degrees who indicated that their occupation was "full-time legislator" are not included in these figures. The 1986 figures certainly underestimate the number of lawyers in some state legislatures.

Table 5

Lawyer Members of State Senates for Selected States

State	1979 (%)	1986* (%)	1991 (%)
Virginia	67	40	43
Texas	58	55	45
California	38	25	25
Massachusetts	35	33	48
Ohio	31	33	27
North Carolina	22	34	34
Colorado	11	17	22
New Hampshire	4	4	8
Delaware	0	0	5

SOURCES: 1979 figures are from Insurance Information Institute; 1986 figures are from Bazar; 1991 figures compiled by author.
*In the 1986 figures, legislators with law degrees who indicated that their occupation was "full-time legislator" are not included in these figures. The 1986 figures could underestimate the number of lawyers in many state legislatures.

(see Cohen 1969). This practice continues today, even in some full-time legislatures such as the one in Massachusetts.

Recently, the overall number of lawyers in state legislatures has declined somewhat. According to a comprehensive study done by the Insurance Information Institute, nationwide in 1979 only 20 percent of state legislators were lawyers; in 1966 this figure was 26 percent nationwide. In 1979, Virginia had the highest percentage of lawyer members, with 53 percent; Delaware was the only state legislature in the country without a single lawyer member. In 1979, lawyers controlled more than a third of the seats in only seven legislatures; in 1977, there were eleven states in which lawyers controlled at least a third of the seats (Insurance Information Institute 1979, 8–9).

The greatest decline in the number of lawyers serving in state legislatures occurred in the 1970s (see Rosenthal 1981, 42–44). Several scholars have attributed this decline to the increasing time demands of both the legal profession and the state legislatures, and to the fact that successful attorneys can no longer financially afford to accept the low salaries that many state legislators receive (see Ehrenhalt 1991, 16–17, 171;

Table 6

Lawyer Members of State Lower Houses for Selected States

State	1979 (%)	1986* (%)	1991 (%)
Virginia	47	47	43
Texas	38	31	33
California	26	14	20
Massachusetts	22	13	23
Ohio	25	16	18
North Carolina	21	20	17
Colorado	9	18	18
New Hampshire	2	2	2
Delaware	0	0	2

SOURCES: 1979 figures are from Insurance Information Institute; 1986 figures are from Bazar; 1991 figures compiled by author.

*In the 1986 figures, legislators with law degrees who indicated that their occupation was "full-time legislator" are not included in these figures. The 1986 figures could underestimate the number of lawyers in many state legislatures.

Rosenthal 1981, 39). Today, as two commentators note, "the income disparity between successful attorneys and public officials is much greater now than it was twenty, or even ten, years ago" (Fowler and McClure 1989, 127). And as another keen political observer observes, "Nearly any successful lawyer, even in a medium-sized American town, quickly attains a standard of material life well beyond the reach of an average member of Congress, let alone a state legislator. He is very unlikely to give up that life for public office" (Ehrenhalt 1991, 16).

Also, the time demands of the legal profession have changed, and fewer lawyers today have the luxury of practicing law and holding political office simultaneously. Fowler and McClure note that "the [legal] profession has changed in the last decade; today the law is a highly competitive field with an increasingly corporate structure and mentality. It has become less feasible to serve the two masters—the client and the voter—to whom a lawyer who is an elected official must bow" (Fowler and McClure 1989, 127). And a leading scholar of state politics remarks, "A number of legislators . . . find it extremely difficult to pursue two careers simultaneously. . . . Legislative service on a sustained basis can be particularly hard for attorneys" (Rosenthal 1981, 42–43). In fact, as one lawyer-legislator described his professional life, "He sensed that his lawyer colleagues were getting way ahead of him, working full time, developing their skills, and advancing their legal careers. A person with two occupations has trouble competing with a person practicing only one" (Rosenthal 1981, 43).

Despite these important changes, today the proportion of lawyer members of state legislators is roughly the same as it was in the 1970s. Tables 4, 5, and 6 indicate the current proportion of lawyers in state legislatures by region and in selected states. Some states still have a very small number of lawyer-legislators; for example, Delaware had only one lawyer member in each chamber in 1991. In the 400-member New Hampshire house, only 5 of the members were lawyers that year. But in Texas, in 1991, there were 49 lawyers in the 150-member house and 14 lawyers in the 31-member senate. In Massachusetts, 19 of the 40 members of the state senate were lawyers in 1991. It is no wonder that lawyers have become the "High Priests of American Politics."

Why So Many Lawyer-Politicians?
Professionally Oriented Explanations

Political observers and scholars have offered various explanations as to why lawyers dominate this country's legislative bodies. The following section will outline some of these theories, beginning with those that concern various aspects of the legal profession.

The first reason offered by many scholars for the dominance of lawyers in U.S. politics is the "high status" argument. Based largely on the observations of Tocqueville, some scholars argue that because attorneys are in a high-status occupation, American voters tend naturally to choose them for political office (see, e.g., Matthews 1954, 30–32; Prewitt 1970, 90; Watson and Thomas 1988, 131). According to Provine, during the revolutionary period, "lawyers were selected for lawmaking bodies in part because they formed a significant proportion of the educated class at this time. Physicians were also overrepresented in these assemblies" (Provine 1986, 10).

To use Tocqueville's terminology, lawyers are the natural American political class. In their pathbreaking work on lawyers and politics, Eulau and Sprague explained, "[Tocqueville] implied that there must be a class of persons in a democracy to run the government. The legal profession is well qualified to fulfill this function in the United States because there is no traditional American ruling class. . . . The legal profession fills institutionally and functionally necessary governing roles that cannot be left unoccupied" (Eulau and Sprague 1964, 33).

The legal profession in the United States therefore became the new aristocracy, replacing the non-existent American hereditary nobility. As Bryce explained around the turn of the century, "The lawyers best deserve to be called the leading class, less powerful in proportion to their numbers than the capitalists, but more powerful as a whole, since more numerous and more locally active" (Bryce 1911, 303). In 1870, the *Albany Law Journal* told its readers that "in every age of civilized man, the lawyers have been an important instrument in the work of refining and elevating the race" (An Address 1870, 165). In 1853, *Livingston's Monthly Law Magazine* praised the role of lawyers "in exerting a wholesome influence on the rising generation of the American people" (Stevens 1983, 28). But it is important to remember that Tocqueville also said that "lawyers, as a body, form the most powerful, if not the only, counterpoise to the democratic element" (Tocqueville 1841, 268).

A second explanation for the dominance of lawyers in U.S. legislatures is the so-called American legal culture argument. Some scholars argue that the American political culture prefers to judge political results by legal standards,[1] thus viewing the legal profession as the legitimate source of public leadership (see Derge 1959, 408; Scheingold 1974). It has become a truisim that, as Tocqueville first told us, almost all political questions in this country eventually become legal questions (see, e.g., Tocqueville 1969, 270; Hartz 1955, 48–49, 102–6; Casper 1972; and Scheingold 1974). As one scholar notes, "Ever since Thomas Paine brandished his rhetorical sword to slay the legitimacy of monarchy and proclaimed that 'in America law is king,' many of our fundamental conflicts have been settled around the bar of legal justice" (McCann 1986, 106). And as two students of the legal profession observe, "The centrality of law in American society has contributed to the prominence and power of the legal profession" (Zemans and Rosenblum 1981, xv).

Even in their day-to-day practice of law, attorneys become involved in political issues. As a prominent political scientist has argued, "The fact that Americans maintain such a busy legal system, with frequent recourse to the legal determination of rights and responsibilities, encourages the spread of legal norms and legal personnel to areas of life where they might not otherwise be found in great numbers. This definitely includes the occupation of lawmaking" (Polsby 1990, 114).

A third explanation for the abundance of lawyer-politicians in the United States centers on the expansive historical development of the American legal profession (see Larson 1977; Halliday 1979; Harrington 1985, 46–49; Provine 1986, 1–23). Some commentators argue that lawyers as a profession were the natural group to mold a distinctly American political culture because the swiftly expanding and decentralized society of the late eighteenth century demanded laws and rules in order to prevent chaos and disorder.[2] As American society evolved, the principles of written constitutions, and the lawyers and judges who interpreted them, became key elements in the American political system. Because lawyers largely wrote and then interpreted the Constitution and the various state constitutions, "the legal profession . . . could become an ex officio interpreter of our national credo" (Haber 1991, 68). As James Bryce said, "Law is of course the business which best fits in with politics" (Bryce 1911, 306).

A fourth explanation for the prevalence of lawyer-politicians is the "special skills" argument. Various scholars have argued that attorneys bring special skills and training to politics, which give them major advantages over nonlawyers (see, e.g., Hain and Piereson 1975; Provine 1986, 18; Nelson and Heinz 1988; and Davidson and Oleszek 1990, 116). This is the mirror image of the argument that "[political] amateurs' lack of proven political skills affects their chances of winning office and may influence their effectiveness in Congress when they do win" (Canon 1990, 3).

Lawyers are trained in personal skills, such as argumentation, verbalization, advocacy, arbitration, mediation, and negotiation, which are useful in both campaigning and holding public office (see Adler and Bellush 1979, 245; Davidson 1988, 91; and Watson and Thomas 1988, 131). After winning election to office, lawyers are better able to negotiate and compromise in the legislative process because they are accustomed to procedurally oriented systems of decision making (Gold 1961, 84). As leading scholars of the legislative process state, "Like all successful politicians, the lawyer is an adroit broker of ideas as well as of interests. Legal training, if deficient and illiberal on some counts, is extraordinarily successful in assisting its recipients to master the intricacies of human relations, to excel in verbal exchange, to understand complex and technical information, and to employ varying tactics to seize advantage. These qualities of mind and makeup serve the legislator no less than the campaigner" (Keefe and Ogul 1989, 118). Lawyers were the natural choice for political positions because they combined their high social position with special knowledge and skills (see Tickamyer 1981, 22).

A fifth explanation for so many lawyer-politicians centers around the flexible time requirements of the practice of law in this country. Traditionally not only could practicing attorneys often serve in state legislatures on a part-time basis, but also lawyers could enter and leave politics without damaging their legal careers (see Weber 1946, 85; Provine 1986, 18; Polsby 1990, 116). Others argue that in general the law changes slowly in this country, and thus a lawyer-politician can keep up with the changes in the law while devoting a fair amount of time to politics (see Matthews 1954, 31; Tickamyer 1981, 230). And as the prominent political scientist, V. O. Key, has said, "The high incidence of lawyers among the politically influential provides a base of economic independence; the defeated politician can always find a few clients" (Key 1961, 540). Or as two other scholars put it, "A lawyer can leave his practice for two years or six, or for an even longer time, with some assurance that he can return to his practice with professional skills unimpaired and with the prospect of newly attracted clients to replace those he might have lost during his years in Washington" (Blaustein and Porter 1954, 98).

A sixth explanation for the abundance of lawyer-legislators is the so-called lawyer advertising argument. Some scholars argue that lawyers were and are attracted to political office as a way to advertise and gain name recognition in order to attract more clients for their law practices (see Mills 1951; Blaustein and Porter 1954, 98; Barber 1965, 67–69; Jacob 1978, 74–76; Fowler and McClure 1989, 127; Tickamyer 1981, 23). The power, knowledge, prestige, contacts, and influence that are side benefits of legislative office may greatly increase a lawyer's attractiveness to clients (Adler and Bellush 1979, 246). In the early 1950s a veteran lawyer-legislator was quoted as saying, "A seat in our state senate is worth $10,000 a year to a practicing lawyer, even if he is a man of absolute professional integrity" (Blaustein and Porter 1954, 98). As one Massachusetts senator said in an interview with this author, "Lawyers need to be more political in their profession, and they naturally gravitate toward the legislature to enhance their law careers. Practicing lawyers are more involved politically because they have a professional incentive to be involved."

The fact that legislative service may prove quite lucrative for lawyers seems to have been true throughout much of American history. A historian notes that "legislators took financial and other favors from sources that had business before their body. Lawyer-legislators were retained by clients for whom they apparently gave no service outside their influence as members of the legislature, and lucrative retainers likewise came to law firms of which legislators were partners" (Hurst 1950, 63). According to another historian, in the American West "lawyers came early to the frontier boom towns, eager to turn a quick dollar. . . . Politics was the best way to scramble up the greasy pole. In these small communities, one of the biggest businesses was government. Politics was bread and butter work" (Friedman 1985, 646). It was quite common for lawyers to mix their private practice with public legislative office, because "campaigning was one of the few means available to young attorneys to advertise themselves, and the ordinary pace of business allowed lawyers enough flexibility to hold elective office without damaging their clients' interests. Some lawyers even benefitted from the perception among their clientele that they were well-connected politically" (Fowler and McClure 1989, 127).

In a variation on this theme, several scholars have argued that lawyers seek seats in the legislature when they see their self-interests and financial needs being threatened by various rival groups (see Mills 1951). In a fascinating story, Ehrenhalt (1991) describes the decline of lawyer dominance in the Alabama state legislature in the 1970s, followed by the reversal of this trend in the mid-1980s. The traditional, conservative, business-oriented lawyers who dominated the state legislature for much of Alabama's history left it in the 1970s, when legislative service infringed too much upon their lucrative law practices. In the 1980s, a different breed of attorneys, the liberal-leaning trial lawyers, flocked to the legislature when they saw their potential incomes threatened by tort-reform proposals backed by the business community (Ehrenhalt 1991, 171–81). Thus lawyers may enter and leave legislative service depending on their broader personal financial and professional needs.

Finally, some scholars have offered the so-called "lawyers as free agent" theory of politics to explain the prevalence of lawyer-legislators. The American voters tend to prefer to send lawyers to the legislatures because lawyers are seen as independent, neutral parties, not naturally beholden to any special interests. As explained by one scholar, "As guardians of 'the law' and justice, lawyers when involved in politics tend to think of themselves as representing 'the community' or 'everyone' rather than business, agriculture, or labor" (Agger 1956, 438). Lawyers are able to represent all sides of an issue because of their legal training and reputation for impartiality (see Hyneman 1959, 569; Eulau and Sprague 1964, 16; Keefe and Ogul 1989, 118–19; Schleef 1992, 16). And as one historian has stated, "The history of the bar shows the persistent tendency of all politically effective, organized interests to take the [lawyer-legislator] as their agent" (Hurst 1950, 39). Lawyers are influential because they define and represent all sides in the American political debate (see Melone 1980, 229).

Lawyers' Access to Elected Offices

Many of the explanations, from an electoral perspective, for so many lawyer-legislators in the United States revolve around "strategic politician" arguments. It has become almost a truism in American politics that those with political ambitions naturally gravitate toward the legal profession because lawyers are much more likely than nonlawyers to achieve their political goals (see Mills 1951; Blaustein and Porter 1954, 99; Watson and Thomas 1988, 131). And American lawyers usually learn personal and verbal skills that are very useful in American-style campaigning (Davidson 1988, 91). A leading historian concludes, "It was not so much the case that public office required legal skill as that lawyers were skillful at getting and holding these offices. They were by instinct political; political animals gravitated toward the practice of law. A public career was helpful to private practice, which cannot be easily said for doctors, bankers, or farmers" (Friedman 1985, 647).

Stretching Jacobson and Kernell's (1983) concept of the strategic politician, those who desire a career in politics may use law school as a stepping stone toward becoming a professional politician (see Eulau and Sprague 1964). As Canon reminds us, "Experienced politicians respond to the structure of political opportunities and generally attempt to follow the path that will ensure their smooth advancement" (Canon 1990, xiii). Certainly law school is the first step on this path for many ambitious politicians. "A legal career appears to be such a good warm-up for politics that men and women interested in public careers often select the law as their launching point," note Adler and Bellush. "Presumably, lawyers have something of a head start with the public. Many people may assume that, since the business of legislatures is making laws, it should be entrusted to people who know how law works" (Adler and Bellush 1979, 245). In the early 1970s, a study of six major law schools found that a desire to enter politics was for many students one of the motivational factors in their decision to attend law school (Stevens 1973, 578–79). Some have even referred to law school as "The Gateway to Politics" (Vanderbilt 1979, 8).

Another explanation for lawyers' accessibility to elected office is the "political personality" argument (see, e.g., Lasswell 1954; Matthews 1954; Schlesinger 1957; Barber 1965; Browning 1968; Canon 1990, 17–18). Some scholars have argued that personality types who are attracted to politics are the same ones who are attracted to the law. As two students of political ambition indicate, "The personal characteristics and inclinations that cause [people] to seek legal training are such as will also pull them into active political affairs. This affinity is indicated by the fact that in many state university law schools there are often members of the state legislature in the student body" (Blaustein and Porter 1954, 98).

Adding to the political ambition explanation is the fact that many political offices in the United States, such as district attorney and attorney general, are exclusively the domain of politicians trained in the law (see Brown 1948, 17–18; Schlesinger 1957, 1966; Hain and Piereson 1975, 42–43). The easy access that lawyers in the United States have to a wide variety of political offices has led Cohen (1969) to talk about politics as another specialty within the legal profession, and Eulau and Sprague (1964) to refer to the convergence of the careers of law and politics. As Hain and Piereson state:

> The advantages enjoyed by lawyers in the American political opportunity structure can be easily appreciated. Lawyers are generally eligible for all offices for which their fellow politicians are eligible, but only lawyers are generally qualified to hold the large number of elective and appointive legal posts such as judge, prosecuting attorney, public attorney, and the like. They are thus advantaged in their ability to advance in their careers primarily because they are able to monopolize an important route of political advancement. (Hain and Piereson 1975, 42–43)

Another important factor in lawyers' easy access to elected office is the fact that, due in large part to the weak party system, American candidates are often self-starting political entrepreneurs who owe little allegiance to their party organizations (see Schlesinger 1966, Price 1985, Loomis 1988, Davidson and Oleszek 1990). According to one scholar, "The [political] career structure in the United States is relatively open. Compared to nations with stronger party systems, the United States requires little in the way of party or office apprenticeship, even for the highest offices" (Canon 1990, 3). American politicians run candidate-centered campaigns in which party affiliation is rarely mentioned (see Salmore and

Salmore 1989). In the vast majority of countries, the norm is for the party leaders to choose their candidates for elected office (see Ranney 1981). Due to the American system of nominating party candidates through primary elections controlled by the voters and not by the party leaders, the parties have little or no control over who their candidates are or the policies that they advocate (see Canon 1989).[3]

In such an individualistic electoral system, the skills of the lawyer can be extremely helpful during the campaign season (see, e.g., Hain and Piereson 1975; Nelson and Heinz 1988; Davidson and Oleszek 1990, 116). Because American candidates are self-starting entrepreneurs with little attachment to party organizations, they need to be comfortable discussing policy proposals, in mastering the intricacies of human relations, in understanding complex and technical information, and in strategizing for the campaign. These skills are often ones possessed by lawyers (see Keefe and Ogul 1989, 118).

Finally, American lawyer-politicians bring with them to the legislature skills that are important assets in bodies without party discipline and without a strict hierarchical structure (see Blondel 1973). In fact, Congress has the weakest party discipline and the most individualistic voting patterns among its members of any legislative body in the world (see Loewenberg and Patterson 1988). In legislatures dominated by weak party systems, the skills of verbalization, advocacy, arbitration, mediation, and negotiation are important for personal advancement (see Mezey 1979, Sinclair 1989), and these are the skills that lawyer-politicians bring to the legislature (see Davidson 1988, 91; Keefe and Ogul 1988, 118; Epp 1992a, 590).

Many scholars argue that because lawyers are accustomed to procedurally oriented systems of decision making, they are better able to negotiate and compromise in a legislative process such as the one present in the United States, where individualistic negotiating skills are so essential (see, e.g., Gold 1961, 84). Others cite the importance of verbal skills for producing so many lawyer-politicians, the same skills that have led to more and more teachers, journalists, and bureaucrats in legislative bodies (Matthews 1985, 20–21).

Thus the specific attributes of the American legal profession combine with the unique nature of American legislative bodies to produce a political system in which lawyers dominate. In other countries with smaller and more specialized legal professions, where parties and voting tend to be class-based, and where legislatures are controlled by party discipline and hierarchical norms, lawyers are much less numerous. American law-yer-politicians thus enjoy many advantages not shared by their counter-parts in other societies.

Lawyers as Middle-Class Representatives of a Middle-Class Society

The American legal profession and American political preferences reflect strongly middle-class biases. The failure of socialist or working-class po-litical parties in this country is certainly evidence that American politics remains oriented toward the vast American middle class (Friedman 1989, 9). Many have noted the middle-class nature of American political par-ties (see, e.g., Epstein 1967, 1981; Harrigan 1993, 6–9). Of course, middle-class political parties tend to choose middle-class candidates (see Epstein 1967), and lawyers are the archetypical representative of the middle class in the United States.

The American legal profession has long been viewed as the represen-tative of middle-class interests (see Stevens 1983; Irons 1982; McCann 1986; Sugarman 1994, 117). Historically, notes Friedman:

> American lawyers were . . . the sign of something new in the world: a middle-class society—that is, a society with a dominant, middle-class majority. This developed very early in America, and its basis was own-ership of land. It developed in a country with no established church, no king, no aristocracy, and few traditions that could substitute for formal norms. These two factors—widespread land ownership and the weak-ness of traditional authority—produced the need for a large, active, legal profession. (Friedman 1989, 8)

And American legal education has long attempted to create lawyers who reflect and represent fairly similar middle-class values in our society (see Carlin 1962, 1966; Stevens 1983; Granfield 1991; Kahlenberg 1992).

Lawyers serve as spokespeople for middle-class political values in the United States. Building on Gramsci's theories of the "organic intellectual" who serves as the "translator," "tongue," or "representative" of class interests, Szelenyi and Martin (1989) claim that lawyers are prevalent in political office because they are the "translators" of bourgeois class in-terests, which in the United States means middle-class interests. Accord-ing to these scholars:

[Lawyers] are the prototype of "organic intellectuals." No other profession can make as persuasive a claim that its job is representation. Indeed, for at least a century lawyers were able to convince society that they could be trusted as 'neutral' and "disinterested" representatives, which explains their pivotal role in bourgeois democratic politics. People thought it was a good idea to elect a lawyer as their senator, member of parliament, or even president. Since the lawyers' job was to represent all sorts of interests, they could be expected to perform the political role of "organic intellectual" with equal competence. (Szelenyi and Martin 1989, 280–81)

In addition to having a strong middle-class bias, some scholars argue that American lawyers, and thus lawyer-politicians, are inherently conservative in the sense that the profession tends to favor stability and predictability in the society at large, particularly in the political sphere (see Ehrmann 1976). Because the rule of law is advocated by those who value stability in society, lawyers are seen as inherently conservative or prosystem in nature. As Friedman notes, "The [legal] profession tends to defend the current state of affairs, whatever it may be; it lends legitimacy to existing governments" (Friedman 1989, 18).

Throughout their professional training and recruitment, lawyers come to share the prevailing values of their systems of government, making them unlikely to advocate radical change in society (see Ehrmann 1976, 55; Vanderbilt 1979, 19). In the American political system, which seems to prize stability and to abhor radical political change, it seems natural that lawyers would dominate elected political offices.

Of course, not all American lawyers support the policy positions of whichever administration is currently in power, but even reform-minded lawyers tend to support the established system of government. As one scholar argues, "Moderate lawyers help to fill another important social function: they form part of the loyal opposition. They fight 'the system,' but within strict limits. They are conservative rebels: their complaint is not that the system is rotten to the core, but rather that it does not follow its own principles or uphold its stated ideals. Arguably, this kind of moderate opposition helps to legitimate the political structure in general" (Friedman 1989, 19). Friedman continues: "Lawyers tend to be oriented toward the regime and toward the legal system itself. All social orders are 'conservative,' at least in the sense that they resist their own overthrow. A truly revolutionary legal system is a contradiction in terms. The legal profession takes on the colors of the regime in power" (Friedman

1989, 20). Along these lines, Abel and Lewis argue, "Law (and lawyers) have provided a means of challenging inequality in the modern era. Yet, law and lawyers also constitute a powerful legitimation for those inequalities that persist, which then are attributed to choice, effort, natural endowments, or the costliness of change" (Abel and Lewis 1989, 484).

In societies where socialist and working-class political parties compete effectively and where voting tends to be class-based, lawyers do not dominate elected offices. In these societies, lawyers tend to be seen as representatives of the upper class. In a comparison of lawyer-politicians in the United States, Canada, Great Britain, and Australia, Rueschemeyer (1973, 73) demonstrates that the two countries with the strongest social democratic parties and the highest degree of class-based voting (Great Britain and Australia) have the lowest proportion of lawyers in their legislatures. On the other hand, in Canada and the United States, which traditionally have not had strong working-class parties and where voting is often not based on class cleavages, there exists some of the highest proportions of lawyer-politicians in the world. Rueschemeyer concludes: "The chances of lawyers to attain political office seem lowest (1) where voting is strongly based on class position, (2) where leftist parties take a large part of the vote, (3) where leftist parties have a developed organizational apparatus and/or are closely linked to unions and other labor associations with such an organization, and (4) where lawyers—because of their education, profession, and clientele—are viewed as a conservative group" (Rueschemeyer 1973, 72). Of course, none of these criteria hold true in the United States. Thus it is not surprising that this country has one of the largest proportions of lawyer-politicians in the world.

But Americans remain somewhat ambivalent about the effects of so many lawyer-politicians running the country. As Ross declared, "Every lawyer in the House keeps out someone of another occupation, and many other occupations are represented quite inadequately or not at all" (Ross 1955, 434). Echoing these feelings, former congressman John Jenrette has also noted that "some people feel the legal profession has dominated Congress too long. They advocate diminishing the number of attorneys in public office. But I do not think any professional group will climb to the sheer numbers that the legal profession has enjoyed in Congress" (Jenrette 1977, 27). Two scholars have concluded that the high percentage of lawyer-legislators does not "accord well with strict democratic theory. . . . Presumably, lawyers have something of a head start with the public. Many people may assume that, since the business of legislatures is making laws, it should be entrusted to people who know how law works. It might be different if voters asked whether lawyers as such are especially skilled in understanding how society works" (Adler and Bellush 1979, 244–45). And as Riley notes, "We know the law is a precious spirit among us, and we sense that lawyers have a special connection to that spirit. We select them to write our constitutions, and elect them to run our governments. We rely on them at every step in our business dealings. Yet we also distrust lawyers. We think of the legal profession as an honored tradition, and we think of individual lawyers as shysters out to make money off our troubles" (Riley 1976, 81).

No one explanation for the large number of lawyers in American politics seems to capture exactly why lawyer-politicians seem to dominate our political system. Certainly lawyers hold a high-status position in our society, and the American political culture is undeniably legalistic. Lawyers also have the necessary skills to thrive in our peculiar political institutions. Other explanations, such as the flexibility of law practices and the need for lawyers to advertise, seem less relevant today, when legislative service demands more and more time, and when many lawyer-politicians are really full-time politicians. But there is no doubt that some strategic politicians with a certain political personality obtain law degrees for the sole purpose of making themselves more attractive to voters, because American voters seem to continue to prefer to elect lawyers.

From a comparative perspective, the explanation for the dominance of lawyers in American elected office is five-pronged. First, lawyers in the United States are in a diverse profession that includes many political aspects and many aspiring politicians. Second, American judicial and law-enforcement officials are recruited exclusively from the general bar, thus providing lawyers with a great deal of access to other elected offices. Third, lawyers in this country are more likely to recruit themselves to run for public office in the absence of party control over nominations. Fourth, lawyers are likely to get elected in this country because the legal profession is seen as a pragmatic protector of middle-class interests. Finally, the skills lawyers acquire are more useful in Congress or in the state legislatures than they are in legislative bodies with stronger party control or with a more hierarchical structure. Strategic politicians seek legal training to enhance their chances of election and to help them succeed in the legislatures after they get elected.

CHAPTER FIVE

Are Lawyers Really Different
from Nonlawyers?

Having established the fact that lawyers numerically dominate American legislatures, this chapter will begin to examine how lawyers help create and influence the political environment in the legislature. The abundance of lawyer-politicians in the United States has led to questions about whether the behavior of lawyers in American legislatures is different from the behavior of nonlawyers.

Although there is some literature examining the differences between lawyers and nonlawyers in various positions, including chief corporate executives (see, e.g., Miller 1951, Priest and Krol 1986), and in various government agencies (see Weaver 1977, Horowitz 1977a, Wollan 1978, Plumlee 1981, Katzmann 1981, Kemp 1986), Eulau and Sprague's (1964) work remains one of the few examinations of differences between law-yer- and nonlawyer-legislators. Recall that their work established what was to become the conventional wisdom in political science: that lawyer- and nonlawyer-politicians generally do not behave differently because of the convergence of the professions of law and politics. This chapter will provide evidence that the conventional wisdom is wrong, and that there are some very clear and important differences between the behavior of lawyer- and nonlawyer-legislators. These differences will help reveal exactly how the lawyer domination of our legislatures ultimately affects the public-policy process in this country.

The notion that lawyers approach the world differently from their nonlawyer colleagues is not new. Many early works, especially those in the traditionalist mode, assumed that lawyer-politicians act differently than nonlawyer-politicians (see, e.g., Schlesinger 1957, Schubert 1960, Wasby 1970, and Halper 1970). Some more recent studies have even examined biological differences between lawyers and nonlawyers, arguing, perhaps tongue in cheek, that lawyers have higher levels of testosterone than nonlawyers (see Kelton 1991).

The observed differences between lawyers and nonlawyers in legislatures have often been subtle. According to one early study, "The lawyer is more likely to concern himself with questions concerning the language of proposed bills or with the constitutionality of legislation. There is an observable tendency on the part of nonlawyer members to defer to the judgment of their lawyer colleagues on such 'legal' questions" (Blaustein and Porter 1954, 99). These scholars also found differences in the technical legislative drafting activities of the lawyer members: "In the state legislatures, particularly in states where bill-drafting services are not available, a lawyer-legislator usually does a substantial amount of actual drafting. The great usefulness of a competent lawyer in the typical state legislature is principally a matter of his ability to detect and correct 'sleepers' and technical defects in bills" (Blaustein and Porter 1954, 99–100).

Morgan's interviews with members of Congress in 1959 also found several differences between lawyer and nonlawyer members, including the fact that nonlawyer members were much more willing to pass constitutional questions on to the courts. Lawyers were also more attentive to the technical aspects of lawmaking (Morgan 1966, 156–57, 336, 343–44). These differences are subtle, but extremely important.

Some of the more recent empirical works have also discovered key differences between lawyer- and nonlawyer-politicians. For example, on the admittedly narrow issue of no-fault auto insurance, one study found clear differences in the voting records of lawyers and nonlawyers in four state legislatures (Dyer 1976). Another study found distinct differences between lawyers and nonlawyers in their support of measures to strengthen the legislature as an institution (Engstrom and O'Connor 1980). A similar group of scholars found several clear behavioral differences between lawyers and nonlawyers in the Louisiana House (O'Connor et al. 1978). These scholars conclude, "If the factor of occupation accounts for few of the differences in voting patterns that one observes in the legislature, the same cannot be said for its influence on the way that legislators go about their jobs. . . . The conclusion is inescapable from this research that several dimensions of job performance are affected by the presence or absence of legal training and practice" (O'Connor, Green, Engstrom, and Kim 1978, 79). It is important to highlight these differences in the decision-making processes, because the lawyerly approach to decision making has come to dominate the legislative process in this country.

Recently, several prominent political scientists have argued that social scientists generally have missed some of the important effects on the American legislative process caused by politicians' legal training (see, e.g., Davidson 1988, 1990; Polsby 1990). As part of a general article on the legislative process, Roger Davidson, a leading scholar on Congress and its behavior, recently hinted that he believes that the predominance of lawyers in Congress greatly affects the total legislative decision-making process (see Davidson 1988, 91–93). After citing the empirical works that found few differences between lawyers and nonlawyers in their voting behavior, Davidson nevertheless concludes, "One suspects, just the same that social scientists may have missed the more subtle effects of legal training on the legislative process" (Davidson 1988, 92).

Nelson Polsby, another preeminent scholar of American politics, seems to agree that social scientists have missed key impacts on the legislative process resulting from the members' legal training. Polsby notes: "Not only do a great many lawyers serve in Congress; the occupational culture of Congress is dominated by lawyers' ways and lawyers' jargon. Committees are organized to elicit information by "holding hearings" in which "witnesses" "testify" and are examined "on the record" by questions from members and staff. At least one high-ranking staff member, and usually more than one, is a lawyer and is known as "counsel" to the committee. Hearings make the legislative record that surrounds legislation" (Polsby 1990, 114). The legal training of the members seems to have subtle, but very important, effects on the legislative process.

The remainder of this chapter and most of the rest of this book will focus on differences between the lawyer and nonlawyer members of three American legislative bodies: the U.S. House of Representatives, the Ohio General Assembly, and the Massachusetts state legislature. The original data for this part of the project came from interviews with more than 75 members and staffers in the U.S. House conducted during the summer of 1989; from interviews with 96 percent of the 132 members of both houses of the Ohio General Assembly conducted during the spring of 1988; and from interviews with about one-third of the members of both houses of the Massachusetts legislature (64 out of 200) conducted during the spring of 1991.[1]

Lawyers-Legislators Are Seen as Different

Many lawyer-politicians see clear differences between themselves and nonlawyers in the legislature (see, e.g., Morgan 1966, 28, quoting the late senator Jacob Javits; Abourezk 1977; Kastenmeier and Remington 1988). For example, former congressman John Jenrette has said that nonlawyer-legislators "bring a fresh and different approach to the problems facing Congress" (Jenrette 1977, 27). During the interviews for this project with the Massachusetts state legislators, an impressive 78 percent of the lawyer-legislators (and a majority of the nonlawyer members) spontaneously mentioned that lawyer and nonlawyer members behave differently in Massachusetts, especially when dealing with the courts (see table 7). A majority of the lawyer members of the U.S. House also mentioned clear differences between the lawyers and nonlawyers in that body (see table 8). Lawyers often see themselves as a distinct group in the legislature, noting that their approach to decision making is not always shared by their nonlawyer colleagues.

In the Massachusetts legislature, there seems to be a certain amount of conflict between the lawyer members and the nonlawyers. One female member expressed her frustration with the legislature by saying, "The Massachusetts legislature is top-heavy with forty-five-year-old white male lawyers, who all look alike, they dress alike, and they vote alike." Along these lines, a Massachusetts senator complained, "Lawyers need to be more political in their profession, and they naturally gravitate toward the legislature to enhance their law careers. But the problem is that the lawyer-legislators spend as little time here as possible. The lawyer members resent the time they spend on legislative business. They make a lot more money in their law practices."

Table 7

Percentage of Massachusetts Legislators Who Perceive Differences between Lawyer and Nonlawyer Members

Legislators	Differences	No Differences
All lawyers (N = 18)	78%	22%
All nonlawyers (N = 46)	54%	46%

Note: gamma = .49 / tau-b = .22

It is amazing that during the Massachusetts interviews many members (both lawyers and nonlawyers) repeatedly used the phrase "lawyer-legislator" to describe their colleagues who had law degrees. As one nonlawyer member complained, "Law school seems to change people's behavior; lawyer-legislators have a superiority complex. On technical issues, clearly they know more than you do. But generally they are so vague and abstract. Some of the lawyer-legislators here are very narrow and not very bright. They use their legal training to see the world in a very restricted way, but they can't generalize to make the kind of quality decisions that legislators must make every day. They all have tunnel vision."

Another nonlawyer member expressed disgust with the lawyers in the Massachusetts legislature: "The lawyers in this place have a holier-than-thou attitude. The lawyer-legislators don't see any conflicts of interest in continuing to practice law while serving in the legislature. But I see it. I often see the conflict of interest when they vote on the floor. The lawyers here see the world through the myopic view of their law practices. They don't understand the role of a legislator." An astute nonlawyer representative said that in the Massachusetts legislature, there is a clear difference between the "old-boy lawyers-legislators" and the "new-boy lawyers." According to this representative, the old-boy lawyer-legislators are very successful in their law practices because they are part of the old Boston lawyers' network, which has controlled the courts and the legislature for years. "The old boys are making an obscene amount of money by claiming political prerogatives," he said. "The old-boy lawyer-legislators care only about increasing their incomes and their standing in the legal community; they don't understand the role of a legislator. It's hard to be both a legislator and a lawyer. Today the two jobs are too demanding."

Table 8

Members of Congress Who Perceive Differences between Lawyer and Nonlawyer Members

Members of Congress	Differences	No Differences
Lawyers (N = 37)	51%	49%
Nonlawyers (N = 26)	8%	92%

Note: gamma = -.85 / tau-b = -.46

Finally, on the differences between lawyer-legislators and nonlawyer members, one nonlawyer Massachusetts state representative noted, "Everyone here thinks I'm a lawyer. I talk like a lawyer, I think like a lawyer, and I know the details of the court system. But I enjoy being a nonlawyer. Everyone tells me to go to law school, but would that piece of paper really improve the way I think? I don't think so." It is evident that the members of the Massachusetts legislature saw clear distinctions between the attitudes and behavior of their lawyer and nonlawyer colleagues.

Outside of the Massachusetts legislature, other legislators commented on the differences between lawyer and nonlawyer members. A member of the Ohio legislature also made a clear distinction between the lawyers and nonlawyers in that body: "I pay a great deal of attention to Ohio court decisions. I pay more attention than the normal legislator because I am a lawyer. And as a lawyer, I know that I should react to the courts' decisions with respect. Any response should not be a politically vicious criticism, like you hear from my nonlawyer colleagues." One member of the U.S. House Judiciary Committee expressed his strong preference for working with other lawyer members: "[House] Judiciary is special because there are so many lawyers there." Another lawyer member certainly understated his view of the distinction between attorneys and non-attorneys in Congress when he noted that "the only real difference between the lawyers and the nonlawyers in Congress is that they [the nonlawyers] have a harder time understanding the process. Lawyers have an easier time understanding what goes on around here."

These conflicts between lawyers and nonlawyers have also been found in other studies. Barber found some clear resentment of lawyer-legislators by nonlawyers in the Connecticut legislature (Barber 1965). Eulau and Sprague's (1964) study on lawyers in the state legislatures of New Jersey, Ohio, Tennessee, and California reported some sharp complaints by nonlawyers about their lawyer colleagues. Said one nonlawyer, "Lawyers draw up laws so nobody including themselves can understand them. It makes business for them. Judges have to decide in courts what laws mean and sometimes they reverse themselves. Laws could be drafted that would be clear and simple if they wanted to" (Eulau and Sprague 1964, 22). Another nonlawyer is quoted as proclaiming, "Lawyers are lousy legislators because they have too much of a technical attitude. They can't look at it as laymen can. They can't see practical problems. They are too much interested in legal technicalities. The lawyer is good to defend you or give you legal advice, he's not good to represent all the people. The average layman is better equipped to be a legislator" (Eulau and Sprague 1964, 22).

Various commentators also complain about the high number of lawyer-politicians. One political scientist has written that the high proportion of lawyers in Congress slows down the work of that body because lawyers "have the habit of splitting hairs and worrying unduly about the possible interpretation that could be made of every word and punctuation mark" (Hacker 1964, 74). Herbert Lehman, the former governor of New York, has been quoted as complaining about "the conspiracy of lawyer-legislators to perpetrate for their profession the obstructions to justice by which it prospers" (Allen 1949, xxxvii). One nonlawyer-legislator is quoted as saying about his lawyer-legislator colleagues, "There are too many lawyers. They represent clients, try to win lawsuits in the legislature that they can't win in the courts" (Eulau and Sprague 1964, 22).

Lawyers are also accused of slowing down legislative decisions. According to Hacker, the lawyers' "concern for technicalities and niceties of language" may in reality be attempts to prevent Congress from taking action on various needed reforms (Hacker 1964). This scholar then concludes that lawyer-legislators tend to be very conservative because they represent their upper-middle-class orientation and local business interests. "The 'legal mind' of Capitol Hill," Hacker concludes, "is too much that of the local lawyer, reflecting not only a parochial training but a general professional experience that is inevitably limited in its horizons" (Hacker 1964, 75).

Some argue that lawyer-legislators deliberately confuse the average voter, who wants to understand congressional decisions. As a political columnist has stated:

> People in official capacities . . . think they can intimidate us ordinary folks by using the most highfalutin' language they can put together. One place you get a lot of this kind of stuff is in so-called lawmaking bodies, such as city councils, state legislatures and Congress. And one reason there's such a surplus of wind-baggy writing and speech there is because most such bodies are dominated by lawyers. Lawyers are constitutionally incapable of stating things in simple, straightforward English. They are the only people in the world who would put together a 20,000 word statement and call it a brief. (McKeen 1992, C3)

Most U.S. representatives interviewed for this book would not admit without prompting that there were any important differences between lawyers and nonlawyers in Congress. But a majority of the lawyer-legislators did volunteer that because they were attorneys, they treated court cases differently than did their nonlawyer colleagues. Citing another important difference between lawyers and nonlawyers, another lawyer member declared, "Lawyers in Congress have more awareness of the impact of legislative history and the dangers of ex parte communications. Lawyers are more familiar with administrative procedures. Nonlawyers tend to see unnecessary red tape in administrative and judicial procedures. Lawyers understand the necessity of proper procedures. But sometimes lawyers get caught up in the details; nonlawyers don't get so trapped in the details of legislative language."

During the congressional interviews, many representatives did not explicitly mention differences between lawyer and nonlawyer members, but their comments clearly indicated a difference in emphasis, if not in substance. For example, when one lawyer member was asked how he would react to an unfavorable federal court decision, his response sounded very much like a law school professor: "It depends on the quality of the decision and the quality of the judge. If it is a decision from a lower court, with little facts and a short opinion, then I give it less deference. But I give great deference to opinions from individuals of high quality such as Judge Green [who presided over the case that led to the breakup of AT&T]." No nonlawyers in these interviews went into such lawyerlike detail in defining their reactions to unfavorable court decisions.

Most of the committee counsels and other staffers interviewed in the U.S. House report noticing clear differences between lawyers and nonlawyers who serve on their committees. During background conversations, U.S. House Judiciary Committee staffers, all lawyers themselves, implied that they strongly preferred working with lawyer members on the committee. They all seemed to feel that nonlawyer members would have a very difficult time understanding the legalistic subject matter within that committee's jurisdiction. They also implied that nonlawyers would not give committee deliberations the special care and consideration these decisions deserved.

Although some congressional staffers could not distinguish which members on their committees were lawyers and which were not, most seemed automatically to see a clear distinction between lawyer and nonlawyer members on their committees. One congressional staffer noted, "On [the Energy and Commerce Committee], the staff knows who is a lawyer and who isn't. Naturally, the staff treats them differently." An Interior Committee staffer observed, "We have fewer lawyers on our committee than on most. But the lawyers we have aren't real lawyers like they have on Judiciary. Most of our lawyers haven't practiced for years. The ones that act like real lawyers are obvious on the committee."

Many congressional staffers, especially those with law degrees themselves, expressed a preference for working with attorney members. According to one staffer, "Because of their training and discipline, lawyer members see the importance of nuance and wording. They also ask tougher questions of witnesses." When preparing committee members for upcoming hearings or mark-up sessions, the committee counsels reported needing more time and patience when working with the nonlawyer members. One committee staffer who is a lawyer hinted that the subcommittee counsel get very frustrated with the ignorance of nonlawyer members. The staffer commented, "Nonlawyers in Congress do not understand the law like the lawyer members do. The nonlawyers react very differently without understanding all the implications." Along these same lines, a House Energy and Commerce staffer declared, "The nonlawyer members on the committee don't understand the importance of the lower federal courts. Nonlawyer members underestimate the effects of lower court decisions. Many see the lower courts as irrelevant. They only react to Supreme Court decisions. But the lower courts are setting policy in our area."

One nonlawyer staffer noted clear differences in approach between lawyer and nonlawyer members: "My boss always acts in a lawyerlike manner, and it shows with other members. The members' legal training impacts how they argue cases and how they view legislation. Bill drafting is easier for lawyer members; they understand the importance of proper drafting. But sometimes there is a better give and take with the nonlawyers. For example, the late Mickey Leland [a nonlawyer congressman and former member of the Energy and Commerce Committee] always pointed out the human side of the issue, not just the legalistic side."

In my own experience working as a staff attorney for several active members of Congress, I have observed some clear differences between lawyers and nonlawyers on Capitol Hill. Two of the representatives for whom I worked had practiced law for many years before they came to Congress. They were "real lawyers" (as will be defined in later chapters).

Lobbyists often mentioned the legal backgrounds of my bosses in discussions with me, and both gentlemen often mentioned their legal backgrounds in meetings with constituents. Both of these lawyer-legislators treated lawyers on their staffs much differently than they treated nonlawyer staffers. The members often discounted advice from their nonlawyer staff members, but they almost always followed the advice of the staffers who were lawyers. They entrusted the most sensitive political tasks to the lawyer staffers, and the more routine matters were assigned to the nonlawyers.

Nonlawyer staffers in these offices often expressed difficulties in getting the lawyer members to even read their memos and notes. The nonlawyer staffers frequently stated that they felt they were just not talking the members' language. I also observed that lawyer members in general tend to hire staff with law degrees more than do nonlawyer members, perhaps because lawyer members feel that communication with lawyer staffers is faster and easier because they share the same training and professional socialization. My former bosses also seemed to treat other lawyer members in Congress with greater respect than they did nonlawyer colleagues. When asked directly, however, neither of my former employers would pinpoint any important differences between lawyers and nonlawyers in Congress.

In my own work as a congressional staffer at committee hearings and mark-ups, I also noticed that I and other staffers would have to use different explanations and approaches for lawyer and nonlawyer members. Interactions, in both tone and substance, with lawyer and nonlawyer members were very different. During my years on Capitol Hill, I was involved in many conversations in which lawyer staffers discussed how they treated the lawyer members of their committees differently from the nonlawyers. They told stories about "watering down" their explanations for the nonlawyer members, whereas they discussed issues in highly technical, legalistic terms with the lawyer members. They stated that lawyers wanted to know all the details of legislative drafting questions, whereas the nonlawyers just wanted to know the "big picture" or the "bottom line."

In my experience, the lawyer staffers seemed to play two different roles and to speak two different languages, depending on whether they were dealing with a lawyer-legislator or a nonlawyer member. When working with nonlawyer members, they seemed to fall into a lawyer-client relationship, sharing specialized knowledge and expertise that the nonlawyers did not possess. Their job was to translate legalistic concepts and language into terms that the lay person could easily understand. With the lawyer members, however, the lawyers staffers would act more like advisors on an equal plane, merely reminding the lawyer members of things that they already knew. The staffers felt much less need to educate the lawyer members on technical questions, instead spending time on the necessary political considerations.

Differences in Legislative Positions and Careers

If lawyer-legislators are seen as somehow different from their nonlawyer colleagues, are there also differences in their positions in the legislature and in their role orientations toward their legislative work? This study finds some clear differences in this area as well. Lawyers are more likely to come to politics earlier in life than nonlawyers, and they are more likely than nonlawyers to hold key positions in the legislature once they get there. Not only do lawyers dominate legislatures numerically, but their overrepresentation in important leadership positions inflates their impact as a group.

Since the early days of the Republic, lawyers have dominated key positions in American legislatures. Throughout our early history, lawyers were highly overrepresented on the most important legislative committees, and they held most of the chairmanships on these committees. Historically, the importance of lawyer-legislators in many American legislatures has always been greater than their numbers (Hurst 1950, 47). For example, based on interviews from the late 1950s with state legislators in Ohio, New Jersey, Tennessee, and California, one study found that lawyer-legislators were more likely to serve as officers of the legislature, committee chairs, and members of important procedural committees than were nonlawyers (Eulau and Sprague 1964, 118). In the 82d Congress, another study reports that lawyers held almost all the key legislative positions of power, including the Speaker of the House, the vice-president, the president pro tem of the Senate, the House and Senate majority leaders, and twenty-four of the thirty-four chairs of standing committees (Blaustein and Porter 1954, 97). Throughout our history, lawyers have also been more prevalent in legislative bodies with smaller memberships and longer tenures, where individual legislators could amass more power than in larger bodies with higher turnover rates (Hurst 1950, 47).

Historically, lawyers were also much more likely than nonlawyers to serve on judiciary committees and other committees that deal with legalistic subject matters (Rosenthal 1981, 185). This is still certainly true today in the state legislatures in Massachusetts and Ohio, and in the U.S. House of Representatives. For example, 78 percent of the members who served on the Massachusetts joint Judiciary Committee in 1991 were lawyers, and two-thirds of the members of the Massachusetts joint Criminal Justice Committee were lawyers in that year. In the U.S. House, the Judiciary Committee has traditionally been comprised exclusively of attorney members. The judiciary committees in the Ohio legislature are also dominated by lawyer-legislators.

Lawyers may have some real advantages in the legislature, because they are seen as being experts on legislative procedures and processes (Eulau and Sprague 1964, 113). Recall that Blaustein and Porter (1954, 99) found that nonlawyers in the legislature were likely to defer to the lawyers on questions of legislative wording and the constitutionality of proposed legislation. This gives lawyers major advantages in the legislative hierarchy. Because of their assumed expertise, lawyers are therefore often called upon to assume leadership roles: "In regard to roles that are highly differentiated in terms of legislators' prepolitical occupational skills and experiences, such as the expert or leader roles, lawyers differ from nonlawyers. In these roles the lawyer dominates not as a politician but in his identity as a lawyer" (Eulau and Sprague 1964, 121). Nonlawyers in the legislatures often defer to lawyers because lawyers are thought to hold more expertise on many legislative questions and because lawyers are stereotyped as better leaders. This lawyer domination of key positions in the legislatures has important ramifications for how legislative decisions are made.

This trend for lawyers to hold key legislative leadership roles seems to hold true today. In the contemporary Massachusetts legislature, lawyers are much more likely than nonlawyers to be committee chairs. In both houses of the Massachusetts legislature, 43 percent of the total lawyer members were committee chairs in 1991, whereas only 18 percent of the nonlawyers held this position. The dominance of committee chairmanships by lawyers is especially true in the Massachusetts senate, where 82 percent of the lawyers in that body chaired a committee in 1991 and only 30 percent of the nonlawyers held that position. Just under half the members of the Massachusetts senate were lawyers in 1991, but they dominated key committee chairmanships. About one-third of the twenty-eight committee chairs in the Massachusetts house were lawyers during that period, but in the senate more than two-thirds of the twenty-one chairs were lawyers. According to one female nonlawyer member of the Massachusetts legislature, "There is a tradition here that the lawyer members get all the committee chair openings. But I don't understand why a committee chair has to be a lawyer." Not surprisingly, most of the female legislators are nonlawyers, and thus few of the committee chairs are women. This lack of female legislative leaders has been linked to the lack of women in the legal profession (see Darcy, Welch, and Clark 1987, 93–102). With male lawyers dominating key committee positions, it is no wonder that the entire legislative process takes on a lawyerly approach to decision making.

In the contemporary U.S. House, lawyers are also overrepresented among the committee chairs. In 1989 lawyers comprised 42 percent of the voting members of the House, but 52 percent of the committee chairs and 51 percent of the subcommittee chairs were lawyers. Lawyers in the House are also overrepresented among the most prestigious committees in that body. Table 9 lists the House committees according to their attractiveness to members of both parties and according to their prestige (see Parker and Parker 1985; Bullock 1973, 94; for an older ranking of congressional committees by prestige, see Goodwin 1970). The lawyer-legislators are generally found in higher proportions on the more prestigious committees and are less numerous on the less-attractive committees. In fact, as table 9 suggests, the trend is rather striking. The two most notable exceptions to this pattern are the nonlawyer-dominated and moderately prestigious House Agriculture Committee, which traditionally draws mostly rural representatives who are often farmers themselves (see Smith and Deering 1984, 105–6), and the lawyer-dominated but less-prestigious House Judiciary Committee, which has over the last several decades become a very unattractive committee due to its jurisdiction over no-win issues such as abortion, school prayer, and busing for desegregation (see Smith and Deering 1984, 102). Lawyers dominate the most prestigious committees in the U.S. House, and these committees are the ones which make the most important decisions.

Lawyers and nonlawyers also appear to take different routes to political office. One key study from the 1960s found that lawyer-legislators tended to be more likely to be self-starters than their nonlawyer colleagues. The lawyer members got into politics without much encouragement from their parties, from interest groups, or from others. The lawyers often identified themselves as "self-made politicians" (Eulau and

Table 9

House Committees Ranked by Attractiveness and Prestige, 1989 Membership

Committee	Rank	Lawyer Members (%)
Rules	1	53
Ways and Means	2	44
Appropriations	3	49
Budget	4	47
Energy and Commerce	5	61
Armed Services	6	45
Government Operations	7	41
Foreign Affairs	8	48
Agriculture	9	34
Merchant Marine and Fisheries	10	41
Public Works and Transport	11	29
Science and Technology	12	55
Interior and Insular Affairs	13	33
Judiciary	14	97
House Administration	15	32
Banking and Urban Affairs	16	35
Veterans Affairs	17	36
District of Columbia	18	20
Post Office and Civil Service	19	39
Education and Labor	20	31

SOURCE: Rankings based primarily on the rankings used by Parker and Parker (1985), as modified by Dodd and Oppenheimer (1989). In 1989, lawyers comprised 42 percent of the U.S. House.

Sprague 1964, 69). These findings continue to hold for the contemporary Ohio legislators interviewed for this study. In these interviews, almost all of the lawyer-legislators said that they had a longtime interest in politics and that is why they ran for the legislature in the first place. In Ohio, the lawyer-legislators were also more likely than their nonlawyer colleagues to say that the party organizations were weak in their districts. Thus lawyer-politicians tend to be political entrepreneurs who get into politics on their own without much support from party organizations.

Table 10

Maryland Senators' Desire to Run for Higher Office

Senators	Yes	Maybe	No
All lawyers (N = 12)	25%	42%	33%
All nonlawyers (N = 33)	12%	15%	73%

Note: gamma = .57 / tau-b = .33

Table 11

North Carolina Senators' Desire to Run for Higher Office

Senators	Yes	Maybe	No
All lawyers (N = 16)	31%	19%	50%
All nonlawyers (N = 30)	13%	10%	77%

Note: gamma = .49 / tau-b = .26

Lawyer-politicians also tend to become involved in politics at an earlier age. Eulau and Sprague found that "in general, the data suggest that lawyers come to politics at an earlier stage of their political life history than do non-lawyers" (Eulau and Sprague 1964, 62). Barber (1965) also found age differences between lawyers and nonlawyers in his study of the Connecticut legislature. In both the contemporary Maryland and North Carolina senates, lawyer members tend to have less seniority and therefore to be younger than the nonlawyer members. Currently, in the Massachusetts house, lawyers and nonlawyers have about the same levels of seniority, but lawyers in the senate are more likely to have served in that chamber for longer periods than their nonlawyer colleagues.

Lawyer members also appear to be more politically ambitious than their nonlawyer colleagues. As Eulau and Sprague note, "In general, it would seem that lawyers more than non-lawyers are looking forward to another political office—evidence of their greater professionalization as politicians. . . . Insofar as the state legislature serves as a proving ground for politicians, it appears that lawyers move on to other political offices not by predestination, but by force of forethought" (Eulau and Sprague 1964, 80). As tables 10, 11, and 12 indicate, in Maryland, North Caro-

Table 12

Ohio Legislators' Desire to Run for Higher Office

Legislators	Yes	Maybe	No
All lawyers (N = 30)	50%	23%	27%
All nonlawyers (N = 96)	29%	27%	44%

Note: gamma = -.35 / tau-b = -.18

Table 13

Massachusetts Legislators' Desire to Run for Higher Office

Legislators	Yes	Maybe	No
All lawyers (N = 16)	38%	38%	25%
All nonlawyers (N = 43)	33%	42%	25%

Note: gamma = .06 / tau-b = .03

lina, and Ohio the lawyer members were much more likely to indicate a desire to run for higher office than were their nonlawyer colleagues. Strangely, this trend did not hold true in Massachusetts, as table 13 indicates. Perhaps in Massachusetts, the difference is between lawyer-legislators whose first loyalty is to their law practices, as opposed to those who see politics as their first priority. Later chapters will discuss further differences among different types of lawyer-legislators.

Another difference between lawyer and nonlawyer members is in their role orientation toward representing their constituents in the legislature. Political scientists have long used three general terms ("delegate," "trustee," and "politico") to describe legislators' role orientations, or the ways that legislators approach representing their constituents (see Eulau and Sprague 1964, 89–93; Rosenthal 1981, 95–96; Davidson and Oleszek 1990, 127–29). As defined by two leading legislative scholars, "the trustee is a representative who acts as a free agent, making decisions according to principles, convictions, and conscience. The delegate consults with constituents and follows their instructions, even when these run contrary to his or her own judgment. The term politico is sometimes used to describe legislators who seem to combine both roles, who shift role orien-

Table 14

Ohio Legislators' Views of Their Role as Legislators

Legislators	Delegate	Politico	Trustee
All lawyers (N = 30)	0%	43%	57%
All nonlawyers (N = 96)	18%	39%	43%

Note: gamma = .37 / tau-b = .17

Table 15

Maryland Senators' Views of Their Role as Legislators

Senators	Delegate	Politico	Trustee
All lawyers (N = 12)	17%	25%	58%
All nonlawyers (N = 33)	15%	39%	46%

Note: gamma = .17 / tau-b = .08

Table 16

North Carolina Senators' Views of Their Role as Legislators

Senators	Delegate	Politico	Trustee
All lawyers (N = 14)	7%	50%	43%
All nonlawyers (N = 27)	22%	37%	41%

Note: gamma = .17 / tau-b = .09

tations because of issues or circumstances" (Jewell and Patterson 1986, 67–68). Davidson and Oleszek note that the differences between these terms turn in part on differences in legislators' styles of representation: whether they accept instructions (the Instructed Delegate), act upon their own initiatives (the Burkean Trustee), or some combination of the two (the Politico) (Davidson and Oleszek 1990, 128). As Eulau and Sprague note, "Of the three representational roles that express the legislator's style in his relationship with his clienteles, that of trustee is evidently more or less equivalent to the lawyer's traditional conception of his fiduciary role vis-à-vis his clients" (Eulau and Sprague 1964, 90–91).

Table 17

Ohio Legislators' Definition of Themselves

Legislators	Full-Time	Part-Time
All lawyers (N = 30)	33%	67%
All nonlawyers (N = 96)	74%	26%

Note: gamma = .70 / tau-b = .36

Table 18

Massachusetts Legislators' Definition of Themselves

Legislators	Full-Time	Part-Time
All lawyers (N = 18)	50%	50%
All nonlawyers (N = 46)	89%	11%

Note: gamma = -.78 / tau-b = -.43

Table 19

Ohio Legislators' Self-Reported Salaries, Including Their $30,000 Base Salary

Legislators	Salary (in Thousands of Dollars)					
	<40	40–60	60–80	80–100	100–200	>200
All lawyers (N=28)	18%	28%	14%	11%	18%	11%
All nonlawyers (N=95)	31%	40%	17%	8%	4%	0%

Note: gamma = .42 / tau-b = .23

Not surprisingly, almost none of the lawyer-legislators in Ohio, Maryland, and North Carolina accepted the instructed delegate role orientation. Almost all either preferred the role of trustee or the combination role of politico, which includes many of the components of the trustee role. As tables 14, 15, and 16 indicate, in Ohio and in North Carolina lawyer members were much less likely than their nonlawyer colleagues to accept the instructed delegate role. Lawyer-legislators apparently see themselves as free agents, elected to follow their own principles and convictions, but always with the best interests of their constituents in mind. Just as a lawyer is hired because he or she has more knowledge or expertise than the client, the lawyer-legislator does not feel constrained to accept instructions from his or her less-informed constituents. As Eulau and Sprague conclude, "The pattern of responses may be indicative of a different style and stance that lawyers and non-lawyers bring to politics. Lawyers may be more candid than non-lawyers, more realistic and less stereotypic" (Eulau and Sprague 1964, 71).

Another clear difference between lawyer-legislators and the nonlawyers in the two state legislatures in this study is that the lawyer members are much less likely to consider themselves to be full-time legislators, as indicated in tables 17 and 18. Both the Ohio and Massachusetts legislatures are generally considered to be highly professionalized, full-time legislatures (see Rosenthal 1981, 41), yet in both states nonlawyers are much more likely than lawyers to be full-time legislators. Many lawyer-legislators in these highly professionalized state legislatures continue to practice law while holding their legislative seats. In addition, in Ohio the lawyer-legislators report much higher total incomes (in addition to their base annual salary of thirty thousand dollars, 1989 rate) than nonlawyers, as is indicated in table 19. It is also interesting to note that in their study from the late 1950s of four state legislatures, including Ohio, Eulau and Sprague also found strong income differences between lawyers and nonlawyers (Eulau and Sprague 1964, 37).

The differences between lawyer and nonlawyer legislators in how they perceive each other and in their career paths, leadership positions, and desire to run for higher office are important, because lawyerly approaches greatly influence the decision-making process in legislatures in this country. The conventional wisdom, that the dominance of lawyers in American legislatures has no effect on those institutions, appears to be wrong.

CHAPTER SIX

How Lawyer-Legislators
and Nonlawyer-Legislators
View the Courts

In order to understand more fully how lawyers dominate the legislative process, it is important to understand how lawyers affect the ways in which Congress and the state legislatures interact with other governmental institutions, especially the courts. Congress does not exist in a vacuum; it must coexist with other political entities. In this chapter, the individual legislator will be the unit of analysis. One key area in which the legal training and professional socialization of lawyer-legislators affects their political attitudes and behavior is their attitudes toward the courts and court opinions. Based primarily on my interviews with legislators in the Massachusetts legislature, the Ohio legislature, and the U.S. House of Representatives, I conclude that there are clear and important differences between lawyer-politicians and their nonlawyer colleagues in their general approaches to the courts.

Although American courts and American legislatures have been studied extensively by both traditionalist and behavioralist scholars, much less research has been done on the routine interactions between these two institutions. Various political scientists and other scholars have reminded us that the eventual determination of public policy in this country is often a result of the continuous interactions and dialogues between Congress and the federal courts (see, e.g., Dahl 1958; Bickel 1962; Casper 1976; Agresto 1984; Barber 1984; Johnson and Canon 1984; Murphy 1986; Roberts 1989; Henschen and Sidlow 1989; Marshall 1989; Katzmann 1992; and, especially, Fisher 1985, 1988). As one prominent scholar has concluded, "How courts and Congress interact has ramifications beyond those branches. . . . The interplay of Congress and the courts has vital consequences for the administrative state itself" (Katzmann 1988, 12).

Continuing with a neo-institutionalist perspective, this chapter will examine the general attitudes and approaches of legislators toward the courts in their respective systems of government. March and Olsen, the leaders of the neo-institutionalist approach to politics, remind us that the general attitudes of members who comprise an institution help trigger the routine reactions of that institution toward the decisions of other groups (March and Olsen 1989, 21). And as Fiorina reminds us, attributes such as custom and practice are very important in understanding how institutional factors affect the decisions of individuals (Fiorina 1990, 444). Therefore, in order to understand more fully how lawyers shape the political culture of Congress and the state legislatures, it is important to examine how lawyers differ from their nonlawyer colleagues in their attitudes toward the courts.

Research on court-legislative interactions has centered almost exclusively on extraordinary events: when Congress has voted to overturn a Supreme Court decision.[1] The traditionalist literature on court-Congress interactions has stressed how and when Congress would vote to overturn or modify unpopular Supreme Court decisions (see, e.g., Nichols 1935, Schubert 1960, Pritchett 1961, Murphy and Pritchett 1961, Murphy 1962, Beaney and Beiser 1964, Stumpf 1965, Nagel 1969, Becker 1969, Breckenridge 1970, Johnson and Canon 1984, Mikva and Bleich 1991). For example, Morgan (1966) wrote an extensive and highly informative series of seven case studies dealing with congressional attempts to overturn court decisions between 1935 and 1965, based in large part on interview data. A 1958 Harvard Law Review Note examined congressional reversal of court decisions from 1945 to 1957. Other scholars have argued that the courts are protected from attacks by Congress because of their prestige and because of their special role in our system of government (see Murphy 1962, Pritchett 1961, Murphy and Pritchett 1961, Schubert 1960).

A few behavioralist works used roll-call analysis to examine how individual members of Congress voted on bills to overturn Supreme Court decisions (see, e.g., Schmidhauser, Berg, and Melone 1972; Schmidhauser and Berg 1972; Berg, Green, and Schmidhauser 1974). One study attempted to test empirically several hypotheses, including the role of prestige in protecting the courts from congressional attacks (see Stumpf 1965). Another study tested the hypothesis that historical periods of conflict between Congress and the courts are cyclical in nature (see Nagel 1969). Finally, Schmidhauser, Berg, and Melone's analysis of floor roll-call votes from 1945 to 1968 found that there were some weak regional, partisan, and ideological patterns that might help explain differences in how individual members of Congress approach court decisions.[2]

All of these works have examined extraordinary conflicts between the courts and Congress, but little if any research has focused on the everyday attitudes of legislators toward the courts. When exploring how legislatures interact with the courts, it is essential to understand the general approaches and attitudes of members toward the courts, because these attitudes help shape the routine, standardized, and informal patterns of interaction with other institutions. In order to understand these routine patterns of reaction to court decisions, we must understand how the legal training and background of so many legislators affects this standardized pattern of interaction.

One way to study the general attitudes of legislators toward the courts is to see if lawyer-legislators and nonlawyer-legislators have different attitudes and general feelings about the courts. As a keen political observer reminds us, "For all the talk of the insidious influence of special-interest contributors on the modern-day Congress, many members' voting behavior is most affected by their experiences in the working world before they were elected to the House" (Duncan 1991, 87). The conventional wisdom has been that there are no behavioral differences between lawyer-legislators and nonlawyer-legislators (see Eulau and Sprague 1964). This study presents strong evidence that the conventional wisdom is wrong. The attitudes and behavior of lawyers and nonlawyers can be quite different, especially when dealing with the courts.

Three Different Governmental Systems

This chapter and the following chapters will examine the ramifications of an abundance of lawyer-legislators in three different governmental systems: the federal system, the Ohio state government, and the Massachusetts state government. Because this chapter is concerned primarily with legislators' attitudes toward the courts, it is necessary to describe the legislatures and the court structures in these three systems. The structure of the federal government is quite familiar, and will not be described in great detail here. The structures of the Ohio and Massachusetts systems, however, may be less familiar.

The legislatures in these three governmental systems—the Congress, the Ohio General Assembly, and the Massachusetts General Court—are similar in many important aspects. Both the Ohio and Massachusetts state legislatures are highly professionalized legislative bodies that appear to be evolving toward the congressional model. Based on length of legislative sessions, frequency of turnover, legislator salaries, staffing, and so forth, both the Ohio and Massachusetts legislatures have been rated as two of the top seven most professionalized state legislatures in the country (Jewell 1982, 7–8). Both are heavily lobbied by various interest groups in their states (see Sheridan 1989; Dalton, Wirkkala, and Thomas 1984). In 1988, the Council of State Governments (CSG) listed both Ohio and Massachusetts as examples of the nine full-time professional state legislatures in the United States, based on length of session, salary levels, and occupational self-definition of members (Council of State Governments 1988, 78).

Although the Ohio and Massachusetts legislatures resemble their federal counterpart in many ways, the courts of the three governmental systems are quite different, especially in their procedures for selecting judges. Of course, federal judges are appointed by the president for life terms after being confirmed by the Senate, and they are often selected based on the president's perceptions of their policy preferences (see, e.g., Slotnick 1983; Abraham 1985; Goldman 1985, 1987, 1991; Baum 1990, 114–29).

The title of Jacob's (1990) essay on comparative state politics, "Courts: The Least Visible Branch," could easily have been referring to the Massachusetts Supreme Judicial Court (SJC). Unlike the activist and partisan policy-making role played by some state courts, the SJC is perceived by most members of the Massachusetts legislature as an extremely passive actor in state politics. As a Massachusetts representative who also practices law in the state said, "Comparatively speaking, the courts in Massachusetts are not very political. Of course the courts here are somewhat influenced by politics, but not nearly as much as in other states." Echoing these words, a Massachusetts representative concluded, "Generally, there is a much quieter bench in Massachusetts than in some other states."

The court system in Massachusetts follows the usual three-tiered trial and appellate court structure, although the organization of the lower courts is quite complex. In Massachusetts, the state supreme court is officially known as the Supreme Judicial Court (SJC). The state judges at all levels are appointed by the governor for life terms (see Hand, Hill, and Gould 1981, 158), with confirmation by the anachronistic and obscure Governor's Council (see Turner 1992, 19). Although not constitutionally required, since 1991 the governor by executive order has used so-called merit selection nominating commissions to help select candidates for the state bench (see Warrick 1993).

Created in colonial times as the people's envoy to the royal governor, today the Governor's Council has few formal duties except to confirm the governor's judicial and quasi-judicial appointees (e.g., coroners, notaries public, justices of the peace, and the solicitor general) and to approve of gubernatorial pardons. The council consists of eight members elected for two-year terms from special districts, plus the lieutenant governor (see Levitan and Mariner 1980, 32–33). Because the council confirms judicial appointments, lawyers are the most likely candidates for council seats. Only two states (Massachusetts and New Hampshire) still maintain the Governor's Council (see Levitan and Mariner 1980, 32); Maine abolished its Governor's Council in 1975. In fact, the Governor's Council is so obscure that its members are not even listed in the *Massachusetts Political Almanac*. Many people in Massachusetts are now calling for its abolition (see McHugh 1994; Turner 1992; Loth 1991, A19).

The legislature plays no formal role in the judicial-selection process in Massachusetts, and has little informal influence on the selection decisions. Generally, the selection process is almost invisible to the public and to the legislature, although rare newspaper articles discuss the process (see, e.g., Loth 1991). The perception among many Massachusetts legislators interviewed in this study is that judicial selection in the Bay State is often driven by pure patronage concerns and not by expertise or ideology. The entire selection process receives very little attention in the state legislature or in the media. As one Massachusetts representative put it, "It is hard to understand who judges are and what they do in a life-tenure state. We need better PR for the courts. Their decisions can't be made in a vacuum."

Various scholars (see, e.g., Porter and Tarr 1982, 54–59) and judges have suggested that state judgeships often serve as "consolation prizes for those who fail in big-time elected politics" (Neely 1983, 41). These feelings were certainly reflected in the Massachusetts interviews. A Massachusetts senator said, "Too many judges in this state receive their judicial appointments purely as a political favor. Some are appointed just to free up a legislative seat. It is shocking that it happens at all. These judges are not appointed on the basis of merit, but just to get them out of the way of the legislature."

In general, the Massachusetts legislators were surprised that academics would even be interested in their state courts. The decisions of the Supreme Judicial Court receive very little attention in the media and in the legislature. During the interviews for this project, only 37 percent of the legislators spontaneously mentioned any policy-making role for the SJC, and only 52 percent could even mention a specific SJC decision when asked to do so.[3] Most of the legislators who mentioned a specific decision discussed the SJC's rulings on applying the state sales tax to services or rulings on the beverage bottle deposit and recycling system in the state. These issues are not highly salient to the general public, although some legislators did mention the court's controversial ruling in the early 1980s declaring that the death penalty violates the state constitution.

Massachusetts legislators' perception that their state supreme court is passive is at odds with some other measures. For example, on Caldeira's 1975 reputational scores, the SJC ranked fifth among the states (Caldeira 1983, 89), and forty-seven state courts cited the SJC in their opinions (Caldeira 1988, 37). But the longstanding activist reputation of the Massachusetts SJC could be deceiving. According to Glick's work, Massachusetts ranked tenth in the absolute number of challenges to the constitutionality of state statutes in the 1981–85 period, but only twenty-fifth in the percentage of state laws declared unconstitutional by the state courts (see Glick 1991). And on Canon and Baum's overall tort doctrine innovation scores for the post–World War II period, Massachusetts ranked forty-eighth among the states (Canon and Baum 1981, 978). Thus the SJC is highly respected outside of Massachusetts, but on more objective measures it does not appear to hand down major policy pronouncements with any frequency. Nevertheless, the important point is that Massachusetts legislators perceive the SJC to be a passive actor in the state government.

Part of the reason the Massachusetts state courts are not perceived to play an active role in state policy making is that for several decades, and until the election of a Republican governor in 1990, the Democratic Party had controlled most of the apparatus of state government (see Dalton, Wirkkala, and Thomas 1984). In the late 1980s, Massachusetts was one of the most heavily one-party states in the nation, and until the 1990 elections, the Republican minority in the state senate was too small even to force roll-call votes in that chamber (Sedgwick 1992, 70–72). In the 1992 elections, the Republicans again lost seats in both houses of the legislature. In the new legislature, which first met in January of 1993, the Democrats controlled 124 seats in the 140-member House, and 31 of the 40 seats in the state senate (Aucoin 1992, 33, 39). As Tarr and Porter argue, "In one-party states, political elites (which would include the justices) characteristically share an ideological consensus, often times supporting institutions and practices that diverge from prevailing national norms. . . . Rather than seeking to develop an independent policy role, the state supreme court typically serves an important but subordinate role in defending state values" (Tarr and Porter 1988, 56). A Massachusetts representative supports this view, declaring, "The governors in this state have generally been in the mainstream of thinking in Massachusetts, and they have appointed mainstream judges. Thus the Massachusetts courts are very much in step with the legislature." Another Massachusetts representative agreed: "In the history of Massachusetts, the legislature has had little reaction to the courts. The legislature does not view itself in a contentious mode with the courts, maybe with the governor, but never with the courts."

In Ohio, on the other hand, state judges are elected from top to bottom in technically nonpartisan elections following nomination from partisan primaries. During the general election campaign season in Ohio, the two parties widely distribute party voting cards listing the judicial candidates of their party. The media in Ohio covers most judicial races, especially those for seats on the Ohio Supreme Court, as extremely partisan events. In reality, the Ohio courts, and especially the Ohio Supreme Court, are partisan bodies whose decisions tend to change depending on which party controls the bench (see Tarr and Porter 1988, 124–83; Baum 1988; Hojnacki and Baum 1992).

Ohio legislators' perception of the Ohio courts is much different from the reactions of their federal or Massachusetts colleagues. The Ohio courts, and especially the Ohio Supreme Court, are seen as active and partisan actors in the state's policy-making process. As one legislator complained about the partisan nature of the Ohio courts, "I am personally disappointed with the amount of party politics that go on in the court's decision making. I realize that people can't be separated from their 'political animal.' But I feel that the courts should interpret the law, not make law. Coming out of law school, I was quite naïve to the amount of partisan politics that goes on at the Ohio Supreme Court."

In Ohio, the relationship between the courts and the legislature is often confrontational because the courts are seen by the legislators as playing a highly partisan role in the state's policy-making process. This confrontational relationship is due in part to the tradition of split-party government in Ohio. Before 1978, the Ohio appellate courts had long been controlled by the Republicans. Between 1978 and 1986, the Democrats controlled the Ohio Supreme Court. In 1986, the GOP again took control of Ohio's high court (Tarr and Porter 1988, 124–32). During most of this period, the legislature was under split party control, with Republicans holding the state senate and Democrats having a solid majority in the state house. The parties alternated control of the governor's office during this time. The split-party tradition in Ohio politics adds to the highly partisan nature of the Ohio Supreme Court and adds to the costs of judicial elections in Ohio. Since the Democrats gained control of the Ohio Supreme Court in 1978, Ohio judicial elections have become very expensive partisan fights. In 1980, the candidates for chief justice of the Ohio Supreme Court spent $100,000 in the campaign; in 1986, the price skyrocketed to $2.7 million (Baum 1989, 126).

In the interviews, many Ohio legislators assumed that it was quite natural for the state courts to make policy. As one senior Ohio legislator described the situation, "Judges in Ohio are subject to the same influences as legislators. They get wined and dined by the utilities and other interests in the same restaurants we do. All business interests seek to control their future, to press their influence, to maintain control over the courts' decisions, basically to keep us out of their decisions." Commenting on the policy-making role of the Ohio Supreme Court, one Democratic senator stated, "The Ohio Supreme Court serves as a convenient whipping boy for the media and others who are upset with the political outcomes of their decisions. I didn't like the way [the former Democratic chief justice] handled himself, including his tactics and manipulation, but on policy questions he led the court in the right direction."

In addition, Ohio legislators are not shy about taking action to overturn or modify Ohio Supreme Court decisions that they perceive to be incorrect on policy grounds. Eighty-eight percent of the Ohio legislators said that they would take legislative action to overturn a decision of the Ohio Supreme Court that they perceived to be incorrect. But a more important lesson from the interviews is the fact that only 9 percent of the Ohio legislators volunteered that they could foresee circumstances in which they would do nothing in response to an unfavorable Ohio court decision.

In the interviews, Ohio legislators repeated said that state court decisions became important issues in their own reelection campaigns. Because they perceive the Ohio courts as important players in the state policy game, Ohio legislators are not at all hesitant to overturn state court decisions. The following statements are fairly typical of the passion Ohio legislators feel when discussing Ohio court decisions. When asked how he/she would react to an unfavorable decision by the Ohio Supreme Court, one Ohio legislator responded, "I would issue a press release to scare the court to their senses. I don't hesitate to overturn court decisions. The courts are just another political group, in my opinion." Another Ohio legislator stated that "if the courts issue a bad opinion, I'd go and talk to [first name of Ohio Supreme Court justice] first. They are really aloof and disconnected with the legislature. They have a great deal of power, but most judges are unknown and are not understood by the people. I'd make sure they understand how wrong they are."

The very real conflicts between the Ohio Supreme Court and the Ohio legislature do not necessarily center around the court's overturning of recent legislative enactments. Instead, the Ohio Supreme Court has begun to tackle issues that the legislature has failed to address in any fashion, such as workers' compensation decisions and other social issues that the Ohio legislature has refused to address for many years because of the split-party nature of the Ohio General Assembly (see Hojnacki and Baum 1992). Because the legislature could not come to an agreement on these sensitive partisan issues, the concerned interests turned to the Ohio courts for relief. In the 1980s the Democratically controlled Ohio Supreme Court became very activist on liberal social, consumer, and labor issues. According to Tarr and Porter, "A long line of precedent pertaining, inter alia, to restrictions on suits against state and local governments and limitations on medical malpractice claims and on the rights of tenants, consumers, and workers injured during the course of employment was reversed. Virtually overnight the court became pro-labor and highly urban in orientation" (Tarr and Porter 1988, 128–29). These generally liberal social decisions generated a great deal of criticism from many members of the more conservative Ohio legislature. This judicial activism is probably the major reason Ohio legislators perceive the Ohio courts to be highly partisan.

This conflict between the Ohio legislature and the Ohio courts is not unexpected, due to the key role played by the parties in the nomination and election of Ohio judges, even though the judges run on technically nonpartisan ballots in the general election (see K. Barber 1971, 1984). Ohio judges are certainly partisan animals. As Tarr and Porter note, "Where parties participate in selecting judicial candidates, those selected tend to be not merely candidates with party ties but partisans. Systems that provide for a limited tenure for judges and require them to run for reelection on partisan ballots may reinforce the partisan perspective that a judge has brought to the bench" (Tarr and Porter 1988, 57).

Thus the Ohio legislators perceive the Ohio Supreme Court to be an active and highly partisan player in the state's policy-making processes. But the Ohio courts became more activist and more visible in part because they needed to prove to the voters that the change in party control of the Ohio Supreme Court had produced important substantive changes in policy outcomes. Thus, the highly partisan judicial selection system used in Ohio helps produce highly partisan state judges who feel that they need to play an activist role in the state's policy-making process in order to get themselves reelected, and to help their fellow partisans in the other institutions of state government stay in power.

These three judicial-selection systems can also be compared using the number of participants in the initiation, screening, and affirmation stages of the recruitment process. Using Sheldon and Lovrich's (1991) terminology, the Ohio judicial-selection system is a highly articulated system because many actors (e.g., interest groups, the parties, and the voters) play key roles in the various judicial-recruitment stages. The federal selection system is a moderate articulation system because of the relatively modest number of actors involved in all stages of recruitment. Of course, the federal selection system can become much more articulated when nominations are for the U.S. Supreme Court (see, e.g., Baum 1992, Goldman 1991, O'Brien 1988). The Massachusetts selection is a very low articulation system because very few actors participate in any of the recruitment stages. These differences in judicial selection are important because organizationally all three court systems have a similar three-tiered structure with an intermediate court of appeals below the supreme court level that handles appeals from the trial-level courts. As discussed previously, however, the three court systems play very different roles in the policy-making process.

Lawyer-Legislator Attitudes toward the Courts

As an additional challenge to the conventional wisdom about the lack of differences between lawyer- and nonlawyer-legislators, this study reveals some clear differences in their attitudes toward the courts. As table 20 suggests, lawyer members of Congress tend to hold more positive attitudes toward the courts as an institution than do nonlawyer members. The lack of negative attitudes toward the courts among lawyers is especially telling. Because of their legal training and background, lawyers have a much better understanding of how the courts work and why they make the decisions they do. Lawyers are often referred to as officers of the court. Thus, despite the conventional wisdom, it should not be surprising that lawyer members see the courts somewhat differently than do nonlawyer members.

In order to explore further the differences between lawyers and nonlawyers, it would be useful to examine this distinction while controlling for other factors that could be causing these differences. The committee of membership is one factor that could affect a U.S. representative's general feelings about the courts. But there are only very small differences in general feelings toward the courts based on congressional committee of membership. Seventy percent of the Judiciary Committee members in this study expressed positive feelings toward the courts, 63 percent of the Interior members expressed positive feelings, and 56 percent of the Energy and Commerce Committee members expressed positive feelings toward

Table 20

Congress Members' Views on Federal Courts

	Lawyers (N = 35)	Nonlawyers (N = 26)
Generally positive	71%	50%
Generally negative	6%	27%
Felt decisions based mainly on politics	6%	32%
Distinguished between Constitutional and statutory interpretation decisions	80%	13%
Saw Congress's reaction to court decisions as routine	14%	40%
Would strip courts of jurisdiction	9%	39%
Saw Congress as reacting faster to agencies than to courts	63%	20%

the courts. These small differences indicate that the committee of membership has little effect on the legislators' attitudes toward the courts.

As another test of the effects of the committee of membership on attitudes toward the courts, it is useful to examine differences between lawyers and nonlawyers on the same committee. Because the House Judiciary Committee is comprised exclusively of attorney members, and very few attorneys serve on the Interior Committee, this analysis will now turn to the U.S. Energy and Commerce Committee, 60 percent of whose members are lawyers. Among that committee's members, there are considerable and noticeable differences between lawyers and nonlawyers in their attitudes toward the courts. Eighty percent of the lawyers on this committee expressed positive attitudes toward the courts, but only 13 percent of the nonlawyers did. To further this analysis, it is useful to compare the views of lawyer members on the Energy and Commerce Committee with the lawyer members on the Judiciary Committee. Here there are only slight differences. Eighty percent of the Judiciary Committee lawyer members and 70 percent of the Energy and Commerce Committee lawyer-legislators expressed positive attitudes toward the courts. Taken together, these analyses strongly suggest that the differences between how lawyers and nonlawyer members view the courts are not due to the committee of membership.

Partisanship and ideology are two additional factors that could influence feelings toward the courts. In this congressional sample, there is fairly extreme ideological polarization along partisan lines. In other words, the vast majority of the Democrats on these three congressional committees are liberals, and almost all of the Republicans are conservatives (see Miller 1992). These determinations were made by averaging the members' ADA scores for 1985–88. In this congressional sample, it is very difficult to separate partisan and ideological influences. An analysis of the interview data reveals some fairly clear partisan (and of course for this sample, ideological) differences in members' general views of the courts. Democrats in Congress have a much more positive view of the federal courts than do Republicans (78 percent to 33 percent, respectively, reported positive attitudes).

To further the analysis of lawyer/nonlawyer differences in their general attitudes, one should also look at the partisan differences in attitudes toward the courts among members of Congress, controlling for lawyer or nonlawyer background. Among Democrats in Congress, lawyers are generally more positive in their feelings toward the federal courts than are Democratic nonlawyers (88 percent to 50 percent, respectively). Among Republicans, however, the lawyer/nonlawyer differences are much more stark. Republican nonlawyers have a generally negative view of the federal courts (only 17 percent expressed positive views toward the courts), whereas Republican lawyers hold a generally positive view (60 percent). Although partisan differences certainly exist, the lawyer/nonlawyer distinction is important for understanding differences within the parties. Members' feelings about the courts are affected by their legal backgrounds. The differences between lawyers and nonlawyers remain in this sample of Congress when controlling for partisanship differences, ideological differences, or committee of membership differences.

Another way to look at lawyer/nonlawyer differences is to examine whether the members see the courts and court decisions as primarily politically motivated. Table 20 also indicated that almost none of the lawyers in this congressional sample see the courts as being primarily motivated by political considerations. Almost one-third of the nonlawyers, however, see federal court decisions as being politically motivated. Again, these differences are probably due to the legal training of lawyers and their familiarity with the decision-making processes of courts. Almost all law schools teach that the courts are driven by legal considerations, not by politics. As one key committee staffer said in the interviews, "Lawyers understand court decisions better than nonlawyer members of Congress. The nonlawyers tend to read the decisions for all they're worth. But lawyers take a more balanced and realistic view of court decisions."

Again, it is useful to explore other factors that could cause this difference. The analysis indicates that committee of membership has almost no effect on whether U.S. representatives see the courts as primarily motivated by politics, although there are some partisan differences on this question. Almost no Democrats see the courts as political in nature, but about a third of Republicans believe the courts are politically motivated. When controlling for legal background, however, clear differences within the parties again appear. Democratic nonlawyers are somewhat more likely than their lawyer colleagues in the party to view the courts politically (4 percent to 21 percent, respectively). But among Republicans, the lawyer/nonlawyer differences are quite clear. Republican nonlawyers are about evenly split on the question, whereas only about 10 percent of the Republican lawyers see the court decisions as primarily motivated by political concerns. The lawyer/nonlawyer distinction remains important for understanding congressional feelings about the federal courts.

These clear differences between lawyers and nonlawyers appear in the House of Representatives, but do they also appear in the interviews with the members of the Ohio General Assembly and the Massachusetts legislature? The following section will explore attitudinal differences toward the courts in both the Massachusetts and Ohio state legislatures.

In the Massachusetts legislature, there appear to be both attitudinal and behavioral differences between the lawyer and nonlawyer members. Especially on the issue of court reform, there is a perception among the pro-reform members that the practicing lawyer-legislators in Massachusetts band together to block any court-reform legislation. Court-reform proposals got a fair amount of attention in the Massachusetts legislature in the early 1990s, due to tight state budgets and an extraordinary September 1990 *Boston Globe* investigative series entitled *Half-Day Justice* on state trial judges who often did not show up for work and on politically well-connected lawyers (such as members of the state legislature) who had unusually high success rates in the Boston Municipal Court and other state criminal trial courts.[4] For several years, however, court-reform proposals were bottled up in the state legislature by the practicing lawyer members.

During these interviews, the Massachusetts legislators were asked their opinions on what changes were needed in their state court system and on various specific court-reform proposals then circulating. On many points, there was much agreement between the lawyer members and their nonlawyer colleagues, as indicated in table 21. For example, neither many lawyers nor nonlawyers supported changing the Massachusetts gubernatorial appointment system for state judges, and both groups seemed generally satisfied with the quality of judges produced by that process, although nonlawyer members were somewhat less satisfied. Both lawyer and nonlawyer members were equally divided on whether life tenure was a good idea for Massachusetts state judges, and majorities of both groups generally supported abolishing the seemingly anachronistic Governor's Council. Of those who took a position, majorities of both lawyer and nonlawyer members supported giving the Massachusetts state courts more authority over their budgets and over their personnel decisions. Currently, the legislature has control over all the details of the judiciary's budget in the state.

More generally, about half of both the lawyer members and the nonlawyers in Massachusetts cited concern over the caseloads and backlogs in the state trial courts. Large proportions of both groups felt that

Table 21

Massachusetts Legislators' Concerns about State Courts

	Lawyers (N = 18)	Non-Lawyers (N = 46)
Decisions are political	67%	76%
Efficiency and caseload	50%	41%
Administration and personnel are political	50%	39%
Accountability of judges	44%	30%
Abolish Governor's Council	39%	43%
Abolish life tenure for judges	33%	24%
Give courts more budget control	28%	39%
Discipline of bad judges	28%	30%
Change selection system	28%	24%
End two-trial criminal system	28%	20%
Tough on crime / victims' rights	28%	13%
Liberal reforms	28%	33%
Physical facilities / technology	22%	13%
Cost / consolidation of courts	17%	30%
Poor quality judges	11%	24%

the decisions of the state courts are often politically motivated. About half of the lawyer members expressed the view that court personnel and administrative decisions should be made without regard to political considerations; 39 percent of the nonlawyer members supported this assertion. Thirty percent of the nonlawyers and 28 percent of the lawyer-legislators mentioned that the courts needed to be stronger in disciplining judges who were not performing their duties properly. This was certainly in response to the *Half-Day Justice* series.

Although on many points regarding court reforms the opinions of the lawyers and nonlawyers were similar, on other questions there was some disagreement, as indicated in table 21. For example, 30 percent of the nonlawyer members felt that the cost of the state court system needed to be trimmed, and that consolidation of many state courts was necessary. Only 17 percent of the lawyer members mentioned this point. But 44 percent of the lawyers were concerned that the state courts be more accountable to the citizens and to the legislature, whereas only 30 percent of the nonlawyers mentioned this. Another difference arose when 28 percent of the lawyers expressed concern over victims' rights and the need for the courts to be tougher on crime; only 13 percent of the non-lawyer members expressed these traditionally conservative views. On the other hand, traditionally liberal reforms, such as more efforts by the courts toward rehabilitation of convicted criminals, were called for by 33 percent of the nonlawyer members and by 28 percent of the lawyer members.

Twenty-two percent of the lawyers and 13 percent of the nonlawyers expressed concern that the physical and technological resources of the state courts needed to be improved. Due to a budget crisis in the state, during the early 1990s the budget for the courts was cut, as were the budgets for most other state agencies. Several legislators described the Massachusetts state courts as the forgotten orphans of state government. One lawyer senator said, "The courts don't have enough resources like they do in other states. Massachusetts has fewer judges per capita than any other state. There are no good physical facilities in the state. There is an antilawyer establishment in the leadership of the legislature."

Because Massachusetts judges are appointed for life terms without any real input from the voters or from the legislature, these judicial appointments are not perceived by the legislators to have important policy consequences. In part because the Massachusetts courts have been traditionally perceived as passive in the policy-making process in this one-party state, the relatively invisible and apolitical selection system seems to perpetuate this passivity. Legislators were asked if they felt that the legislature should play a role in the selection of Massachusetts state judges by confirming the governor's choice. Giving the legislature a role could make the judicial-selection system more policy oriented. As table 22 indicates, of those who took a position on the question, lawyer mem-

Table 22

Massachusetts Legislators' Views on State Legislature Confirming State Judges

Legislators	Should Confirm	Should Not Confirm
All lawyers (N = 18)	56%	44%
All nonlawyers (N = 44)	39%	61%

Table 23

Massachusetts Legislators' Evaluation of Massachusetts Supreme Judicial Court

Legislators	Excellent	Good	Fair	Poor
All lawyers (N = 15)	33%	53%	13%	0%
All nonlawyers (N = 32)	16%	50%	28%	6%

Note: gamma = .47 / tau-b = .25

bers were somewhat more likely to support legislative confirmation of judicial candidates. Currently, the legislature plays no formal role in the process and has little informal influence over the process.

In Massachusetts, there were also some clear differences between lawyer and nonlawyer members in their general ratings of the state supreme court, as table 23 indicates. The lawyer-legislators generally had a more favorable perception than nonlawyers of the state supreme court. But the amazing factor about the Massachusetts interviews is the very large number of legislators who could not or would not give the Supreme Judicial Court a rating at all. Of the 64 members interviewed, 17 (27 percent) said that they were unable to rate the job performance of the SJC. In Ohio, only 7 members of the 127 interviewed (6 percent) refused to rate the state supreme court. Obviously, the Ohio Supreme Court has a much higher profile in Ohio politics than the SJC has in Massachusetts.

In the Ohio legislature, one might also expect to find such stark differences between lawyers and nonlawyers in their general attitudes toward the state courts. However, largely because in reality Ohio state judges are elected in what are highly partisan elections, the lawyer/nonlawyer differences do not appear as starkly in the Ohio legislators' general evaluations of the job performance of the Ohio Supreme Court. As table 24 indicates, the lawyer/nonlawyer differences in legislators' evaluations of the Ohio Supreme Court are really quite small. The only difference is that lawyer members tend to be somewhat less extreme than nonlawyers in their views of the courts. As one Ohio lawyer-legislator commented, "I'm intrigued by court decisions, but I don't get overly excited by bad decisions. We need the give and take between the legislature and the courts. I rarely find that the court has misinterpreted a statute. Usually, the legislative language is inadequate."

Table 24

Ohio Legislators' Evaluation of Ohio Supreme Court

Legislators	Excellent	Good	Fair	Poor
All lawyers (N = 28)	4%	68%	28%	0%
All nonlawyers (N = 89)	10%	61%	27%	2%

Note: gamma = .07 / tau-b = .03

Table 25

Ohio Legislators' Evaluation of Ohio Supreme Court, by Party

Legislators	Excellent (%)	Good (%)	Fair (%)	Poor (%)
All Democrats (N = 67)	3	51	43	3
All Republicans (N = 51)	17	77	6	0
Democrat lawyers (N = 16)	0	56	44	0
Democrat nonlawyers (N = 51)	4	49	43	4
Republican lawyers (N = 12)	8	83	8	0
Republican nonlawyers (N = 38)	18	76	5	0

Note: All Democrats and Republicans: gamma = .81 / tau-b = .45; Democrat lawyers and nonlawyers: gamma = -.05 / tau-b = -.02; Republican lawyers and nonlawyers: gamma = .35 / tau-b = .12

The most stark differences in general attitudes toward the courts in the Ohio legislature are partisan in nature, as table 25 indicates. The partisan nature of the Ohio courts tends to blur the lawyer/nonlawyer differences that can be seen in Congress. There are also some clear ideological differences in legislators' general evaluation of the Ohio Supreme Court (see Felice and Kilwein 1993). As one Republican legislator commented, "I think the Ohio Supreme Court is doing a pretty good job today because my party is controlling the court. It's a change like night and day from when the Democrats had control. The previous court [con-

Table 26

Massachusetts Legislators' Evaluation of Massachusetts Supreme Judicial Court, by Party

Legislators	Excellent (%)	Good (%)	Fair (%)	Poor (%)
All Democrats (N = 29)	28	59	14	0
All Republicans (N = 18)	11	39	39	11
Democrat lawyers (N = 9)	44	44	11	0
Democrat nonlawyers (N = 20)	20	65	15	0
Republican lawyers (N = 6)	17	67	17	0
Republican nonlawyers (N = 12)	8	25	50	17

Note: All Democrats and Republicans: gamma = .61 / tau-b = .36; Democrat lawyers and nonlawyers: gamma = .39 / tau-b = .21; Republican lawyers and nonlawyers: gamma = .70 / tau-b = .42

trolled by Democrats] made laws. Today's court [controlled by the GOP] just interprets them."

Breaking these partisan differences down by lawyer/nonlawyer background, one finds in table 25 that within the Republican Party there are some differences between the attitudes of Republican lawyer members and the Republican nonlawyer members, with Republican lawyers being somewhat less positive in their views of the Ohio Supreme Court. There are almost no differences in the general evaluations of the Ohio Supreme Court between lawyers and nonlawyers on the Democratic side of the aisle.

As table 26 indicates, in Massachusetts there were also some partisan differences in the ratings of the SJC, but separating the parties into lawyer and nonlawyer groupings reveals that within the parties, lawyer-legislators in Massachusetts generally had a more positive overall feeling about the court. Thus, although the lawyer/nonlawyer background of members of the Massachusetts legislature and members of the U.S. House seems to greatly affect their general attitudes toward the appointed federal courts, the lawyer/nonlawyer distinction is not as important in shaping the general attitudes of Ohio legislators toward the elected judges in their state.

Differences in Attention toward and
Understanding of the Courts

Moving from general attitudes toward the courts, this study also reveals that lawyer-legislators pay more attention to the courts and are much more familiar with legislative options in reacting to court decisions than are their nonlawyer colleagues. Another clear difference between lawyer and nonlawyer members of Congress concerns their understanding of differences in congressional reactions to court decisions based on whether a particular court case was decided on Constitutional grounds or on statutory interpretation grounds. Because congressional options are so different in the two situations, this distinction is extremely important (see Wasby 1988, 299–313; Baum 1989, 223–25). As table 20 indicated, almost all of the lawyers in the congressional sample spontaneously differentiated between congressional reactions to statutory-interpretation court decisions and court cases decided on Constitutional grounds. Very few of the nonlawyers mentioned this distinction without prompting. Because of the critical nature of this distinction, it is surprising that so few nonlawyers mentioned it. Again, legal training and background appear to have subtle but important effects on the legislative process and on the members' attitudes toward the courts.

Although the formal interview structure did not allow for Ohio legislators to focus on the Constitutional/statutory-interpretation distinction, the legislators were asked about how much attention they paid to the decisions of the Ohio Supreme Court. The amount of attention legislators pay to the decisions of the Ohio courts differs according to their occupational background. As one Ohio senator who is a lawyer stated, "I pay a great deal of attention to Ohio court decisions. I pay more attention than the normal legislator because I am a lawyer." As table 27

Table 27

Ohio Legislators' Attention to Ohio Supreme Court Decisions

Legislators	Great Deal	Some	Not Much	None
All lawyers (N=30)	63%	30%	7%	0%
All nonlawyers (N=96)	26%	50%	22%	2%

Note: gamma = -.62 / tau-b = -.31

indicates, lawyer members of the Ohio General Assembly pay much more attention to the decisions of the Ohio courts than do the nonlawyer members of that body.

Part of the difference between how lawyers and nonlawyers get information about court cases in Ohio may be due to the fact that many lawyer-legislators in Ohio continue to practice law while holding their legislative seats. In fact, lawyer-legislators in Ohio are much less likely than their nonlawyer colleagues to refer to themselves as full-time legislators, and lawyer-legislators are more likely than nonlawyers to earn higher incomes. It is also interesting to note that in their study from the late 1950s of four state legislatures, including Ohio, Eulau and Sprague found strong income differences between lawyer-legislators and nonlawyer-legislators (Eulau and Sprague 1964, 37). Lawyers in the Ohio legislature, because of their law practices, must know more about court decisions in the state.

Table 28

Massachusetts Legislators' Attention to Massachusetts Supreme Judicial Court Decisions

Legislators	Great Deal	Some	Not Much	None
All lawyers (N=18)	39%	50%	11%	0%
All nonlawyers (N=46)	15%	39%	41%	4%

Note: gamma = .60 / tau-b = .33

Table 29

Ohio Legislators' Sources of Information about Ohio Supreme Court Decisions

Legislators	Media	Read Cases	Lobby/ Constituent	Member/ Staff	Judges	Other
All lawyers (N=30)	53%	97%	7%	7%	7%	0%
All nonlawyers (N=96)	77%	13%	16%	13%	7%	5%

Note: Individual legislators may have given up to three responses, so percentages will not add to 100.

In Massachusetts, lawyer members also pay more attention than nonlawyers to the state supreme court, as table 28 reveals. Many non-lawyer members in Massachusetts seemed surprised that I would even ask them about state court decisions. A typical response from the non-lawyer members was, "I don't pay much attention to the courts. They are not part of my day to day concerns. I'm not on the Judiciary Committee, and the courts have never been an issue in my campaigns." In Massachusetts many lawyer-legislators continue to practice law while they serve in the state legislature, and nonlawyer members of the Massachusetts legislature are much more likely to consider themselves full-time legislators.

Another aspect of this issue is whether lawyer-legislators and their nonlawyer colleagues use different sources of information to find out about court decisions. As table 29 indicates, lawyers in the Ohio legislature find out about the decisions of the state courts using quite different means than their nonlawyer colleagues. In Ohio, lawyers-legislators use the traditional legal sources for finding out about court decisions, that is, they either read the cases themselves from the Official Reports, or they read about them in the *Ohio Bar* magazine. Nonlawyers are much more likely to rely on the media for their information about the decisions of the Ohio courts. One nonlawyer Ohio legislator expressed his frustration with court decisions: "There is a real need for a layman publication about the courts. The information the public—and those of us who are nonlawyers in the legislature—get is blurred. There's an isolation here between those who understand most cases [the lawyer-legislators] and those of us who are only informed about isolated cases, and then without all the facts. The lawyer members have an unfair advantage."

Table 30

Massachusetts Legislators' Sources of Information about Massachusetts Supreme Judicial Court Decisions

Legislators	Media	Read Cases	Lobby/ Constituent	Memb/ Staff	Judges	Other
All lawyers (N=18)	73%	67%	28%	11%	17%	6%
All nonlawyers (N=46)	85%	4%	39%	33%	22%	7%

Note: Individual legislators may have given up to three responses, so percentages will not add to 100.

Another interesting note on this topic is that seven nonlawyer members of the Ohio legislature and two lawyer members received information about the decisions of the Ohio courts through personal contact with the justices of the Ohio Supreme Court. In other words, they called the justices personally or, more likely, the justices alerted them about any politically sensitive decisions. The members of my congressional sample went out of their way to declare that they had very little personal professional contact with federal judges. But the political culture of the Ohio legislature seems to indicate that Ohio legislators know their state judges well, and they are not afraid to make personal contact with them regarding their judicial decisions (see also Felice and Kilwein 1993 for further discussion of this practice).

In Massachusetts, lawyer-legislators also were more likely to use the traditional sources of information about court decisions, as table 30 indicates. Although Ohio courts seem to be more active in policy making in that state, the sources of information about the courts are more limited in Ohio than they are in Massachusetts. Massachusetts legislators use a wide variety of sources to find out about court decisions, including interest groups, constituent groups, and other members of the legislature. But in Massachusetts a large number of members find out about court decisions directly from the judges themselves.

Differences in Reactions to Court Decisions

In addition to differences in their attention and attitudes toward the courts, are there differences between lawyers and nonlawyers in how they react to court decisions they perceive as incorrect or unfavorable? This study finds some clear differences in this area.

Another indicator of general attitudes toward the courts is the willingness of legislators to prevent the courts from hearing certain types of highly controversial cases. In the jargon, this action is usually referred to as "stripping the court of jurisdiction over certain cases," or, more simply, as "court stripping." For example, in the 1970s and early 1980s many people in the pro-life movement wanted to strip the courts of jurisdiction over abortion cases. There is some current sentiment to strip the courts of jurisdiction over some environmental questions. Although the vast majority of the members of Congress in this sample opposed such extreme congressional measures, table 20 indicated that lawyers are much

less likely than nonlawyers to support court stripping. Again, legal training may affect legislative attitudes and actions. Law schools proclaim the
necessity of having a legal forum to settle disputes and to decide the constitutionality of various legislative actions. As Abel and Lewis note, "There
is some evidence that professional identity strengthens the independence
of the judiciary and its willingness to defy or at least obstruct grossly
illegal acts by the more political branches" (Abel and Lewis 1989, 482).
Stripping the courts of jurisdiction over certain controversial issues could
prevent the courts from serving the needs of justice in society, according
to most law school courses.

Seeing court-stripping proposals as direct attacks on the institutional
integrity of the courts, it is not surprising that the vast majority of lawyer members would not support such actions. As one House Judiciary
Committee member noted, "Lawyers are different from other members.
They have an unusual respect for laws. Lawyers like clean and neat solutions; they don't like ambiguity." Stripping the courts of jurisdiction is
anything but a clean, neat, and unambiguous solution to any perceived
policy problem.

As table 20 indicated, lawyer members of Congress are more likely
to see congressional reactions to court decisions as unusual, rather than
a part of their day-to-day routine. When asked how he approached re-
quests to overturn federal court decisions, one lawyer member of Congress said, without prompting, "You should draw a distinction in your
research between lawyer and nonlawyer members of Congress. Lawyers
are more willing to accept court decisions as fait accompli than are non-

Table 31

How Massachusetts Legislators Would React to an Unfavorable Massachusetts Supreme Judicial Court Decision

Legislators	File Bill/ Constitutional Amendment	Attack Court	Tell Judges	Tell Others	Do Nothing
All lawyers (N=18)	78%	6%	11%	67%	61%
All nonlawyers (N=46)	43%	4%	11%	50%	74%

Note: Individual legislators may have given up to three responses, so percentages will not
add to 100.

lawyer members." And as table 20 indicated, lawyer members are also more likely to see congressional reactions to court decisions as happening much more slowly than congressional reactions to agency decisions. Nonlawyer members of Congress did not distinguish between the speed of congressional reactions to court decisions versus the speed of reactions to agency decisions. The lawyer members of Congress see legislative reaction to the courts as outside the norm, whereas nonlawyers members see congressional reactions to court decisions as part of the normal, day-to-day political activities of a legislator.

In the Massachusetts legislature, there were some clear differences between the lawyer and nonlawyer members in how they would react to an unfavorable court decision. Table 31 reveals that lawyers in Massachusetts are much more likely than nonlawyers to file legislation or Constitutional amendments to overturn court decisions. Although both groups indicated that they would often do nothing in response to a court decision they perceived as unfavorable, nonlawyers were more likely to give this response. Note very few members of either group would attack the courts or the judges for "wrong" decisions.

In the Ohio interviews regarding reactions to court decisions, lawyer/nonlawyer differences were less pronounced. In general, Ohio legislators would be more active in their reactions to the courts; a very small percentage would do nothing. As table 32 indicates, Ohio legislators were fairly uniform in their reactions to court decisions they perceived as being incorrect or unfavorable. One difference worth noting is that none of the lawyer members would contact the justices directly to voice their op-

Table 32

How Ohio Legislators Would React to an Unfavorable Ohio Supreme Court Decision

Legislators	File Bill/ Constitutional Amendment	Attack Court	Tell Judges	Tell Others	Do Nothing
All lawyers (N=30)	93%	3%	0%	3%	10%
All nonlawyers (N=96)	86%	4%	6%	4%	8%

Note: Individual legislators may have given up to three responses, so percentages will not add to 100.

Table 33

How Members of Congress Would React to an Unfavorable Federal Court Decision

Legislators	File Bill/ Constitutional Amendment	Attack Court	Tell Judges	Tell Others	Do Nothing
All lawyers (N=37)	100%	3%	0%	5%	76%
All nonlawyers (N=26)	100%	8%	0%	12%	62%

Note: Individual legislators may have given up to three responses, so percentages will not add to 100.

position to a particular decision, but six nonlawyer members of the Ohio General Assembly said they would contact the justices directly to convey their displeasure with a decision. The nonlawyer members are somewhat more likely to see the Ohio courts as just one more political actor. Table 33 indicates few differences between lawyer and nonlawyer members of Congress in their reactions to unfavorable court decisions.

Although the tabular differences between lawyers and nonlawyers in the Ohio legislature are small, there were some more pronounced qualitative differences in the types of remarks lawyers and nonlawyers made during the Ohio interviews. As one lawyer-legislator stated, "If the courts issued a wrong opinion in an area of the law where I have some expertise, I would initiate a law suit to use the courts themselves as a correcting procedure to fix the problem." Another Ohio lawyer-legislator, when asked how he would react if the Ohio courts issued a wrong opinion, said, "I would support legislation to overturn a court decision. But I feel very strongly about the need for a separate, independent judiciary to keep bozos like me in line." Whereas nonlawyer members tended to be much more harsh in their criticism of the Ohio courts, lawyer members tended to use more muted language in discussing how they would react to court decisions they perceived as incorrect or unfavorable.

The conventional wisdom has been that there are no differences between lawyer-legislators and nonlawyer-legislators. Using the individual legislator as the unit of analysis, this project presents strong evidence that the conventional wisdom is wrong, especially in terms of how lawyers and nonlawyers deal with the courts. After controlling for committee of membership, party, and ideology, differences between lawyers and nonlawyers remain.

The question again arises: Does the preponderance of lawyers in American legislative bodies make any difference? Certainly when exploring how Congress interacts with the courts, the fact that so many members of Congress are lawyers seems to protect the courts from congressional attacks. Lawyer-legislators are especially unwilling to strip the courts of jurisdiction over controversial issues. Lawyers may disagree with specific court decisions, but they are unwilling to prevent the courts from carrying out their functions.

In order to understand court-legislative interactions, we must understand on a macroinstitutional level how the legal training of so many members of Congress affects how Congress as an institution reacts to the courts. When Congress does act to modify or to overturn a federal court decision, the lawyers in Congress will assure that Congress does not act with undue haste and that the proper procedures are always followed. Henschen (1983, 1985) has found that congressional reactions to federal court decisions are infrequent and unusual. Lawyers' beliefs that the courts must be treated as a special institution, combined with lawyers' procedural preferences, produces a Congress that rarely attacks the courts as an institution and overturns federal court decisions only after careful deliberation.

CHAPTER SEVEN

Are All Lawyer-Legislators the Same?
A Typology

After examining various differences between lawyers and nonlawyers, the question arises, are all lawyer-legislators alike? Much of this study has revealed that lawyers and nonlawyers differ substantially, especially in their views of the courts. But further study of the lawyer-legislator is needed. This chapter will develop a typology of lawyer-legislators, and then examine what insights this typology provides by looking at differences among different types of lawyer-legislators who serve in the U.S. House and in the Massachusetts legislature.

During the congressional and Massachusetts interviews for this project, many respondents strongly hinted that not all lawyer-politicians approach their roles from the same perspective. Professional socialization seems to have a great deal of effect on how lawyer-politicians approach their political activities, but are all lawyer-legislators socialized the same way? Could there be differences between those who see their primary career as the law and those who see their primary career as politics? Could there also be differences between those who practiced law for a substantial period of time before getting involved in politics and those who went almost directly from law school into a political career?

In my three-category typology of lawyer-legislators (the categories based on their professional socialization and career paths), "nominal legislators" are those who continue to practice law full time but also serve as part-time legislators. Law is their first and primary career; they dabble in politics. This type of lawyer-legislator is often found in state legislatures, especially in those that are less professionalized. Nominal legislators are not generally found in Congress, due to the time demands of this most professionalized legislature and to its conflict of interest requirements.

The second category, "nominal lawyers," are those legislators who are full-time lawyer-legislators but practiced law for less than five years before being elected to a legislative seat. Many of these lawyer-legislators see politics as their primary profession, and they often obtained a law degree merely to help them become more electable. They are trained in the law, but their real passion is politics. In many ways, they are the exact opposites of the political amateurs studied by Canon (1989 and 1990).

Finally, "real lawyers" are those full-time lawyer-legislators who practiced law for more than five years before being elected to a legislative position at either the state or federal level. These lawyer-legislators have been fully socialized into both the legal profession and the profession of politics. Although they certainly see the world through political eyes, they also retain their lawyerly outlook and perspectives. Real lawyers, for example, dominate the membership of the House Judiciary Committee, which has jurisdiction over many issues of importance to the legal community.

Much of the perceived differences among lawyer-legislators in Congress are due to the differences between real lawyers, who have actually made careers practicing law before coming to Congress or to the state legislatures, and nominal lawyers, who obtained a law degree merely for political expediency but have never spent a great deal of time practicing law. The nominal lawyers see their primary profession as politics and they used law school as a stepping stone to help them in their political careers. As Canon (1990, 26) implies, they are often very ambitious professional politicians who do not want to waste time serving in local political office or establishing law practices. Nominal lawyers desire a career in politics and gravitate toward law school merely to enhance their political fortunes. Because the opportunities for political advancement in the United States are many and varied, and almost all of them depend on self-starting ambitious individuals, it is not surprising that many lawyers in Congress fit into the category of nominal lawyer.

Other scholars have also suggested that there are very real differences between various types of lawyer-legislators. Without using these category labels, Eulau and Sprague hinted at differences between lawyer-legislators whose primary interest is politics and who got a law degree for utilitarian purposes and those whose primary interest is the law (Eulau and Sprague 1964, 64). The nominal lawyer is very common among American lawyer-legislators. Several of the state legislators interviewed by Eulau and Sprague volunteered that they became lawyers merely to facilitate their entry into politics. As one state legislator said, "I picked law as my major in college with an eye on politics" (Eulau and Sprague 1964, 55). In response to a question about why he got involved in politics, another state legislator said, "I thought a legal background qualified a fellow for anything in public life. . . . In high school I thought of the study of law and the legislature for a career" (Eulau and Sprague 1964, 61). As Eulau and Sprague conclude, "Law may be a convenient occupation for budding young politicians" (Eulau and Sprague 1964, 55).

Of course, many politically ambitious individuals use law school as a stepping stone for a political career. Stevens reported in a study of six major law schools (Boston College, University of Connecticut, Iowa, University of Pennsylvania, University of Southern California, and Yale) that a desire to enter politics is for many students one of the motivational factors in their decision to attend law school. This factor greatly increased from the class of 1960 to the early 1970s classes. In the early 1970s, a clear majority of the students at all six of these law schools reported a desire to enter politics as of some importance in their decision to enter law school (Stevens 1973, 578–79).

Several scholars have implied that the distinction between real lawyers and nominal lawyers is very much a part of the reality on Capitol Hill, with nominal lawyers perceived as being much more powerful (see, e.g., Schlesinger 1966, Ehrenhalt 1991). As Roger Davidson notes, "Some members of Congress have had extensive legal careers (especially as prosecutors), but many others with law degrees have practiced little or not at all" (Davidson 1988, 92). Alan Ehrenhalt draws an even greater generalization:

> It is an often repeated fact that more members of Congress identify themselves as lawyers than as practitioners of any other profession. But the large number of lawyer-legislators obscures the truth about who these people are. They are not, by and large, successful lawyers who left thriving partnerships to run for public office. Rather, they are political activists with law degrees. This does not mean that they are failures; it simply means that they are lawyers by training rather than by profession. (Ehrenhalt 1991, 16)

Many real lawyers feel that their legal experience has served them well in the legislature. Former U.S. Senator James Abourezk has said, "Indeed, I believe that lawyers, trial lawyers especially, may have the potential to be the best politicians. Certainly their backgrounds should help them in avoiding many of the pitfalls of a political career" (Abourezk 1977, 24). Former U.S. Representative Mo Udall has been quoted as saying, "I had a passion to become a lawyer since my boyhood days. World War II slowed me down some. I practiced law privately after my graduation in 1949 until my election to the U.S. House of Representatives in 1961. But I do not regret my decision to get into what my dad used to call 'public service.' . . . The training I got in trial preparation and courtroom persuasion during my years of private and public practice have served me well in the Congress" (Hegland 1983, 402–4).

According to one comparative scholar, the real lawyer–nominal lawyer distinction is also true in Britain:

> Many people [in Britain] qualify as lawyers without practicing, and perhaps without any intention of practicing. They get themselves called to the bar, as other people take a university degree, in order to secure a hall-mark that will be useful to them in their subsequent careers, and not necessarily as a technical qualification for a particular profession. So the number of members of parliament who are entitled to call themselves barristers-at-law considerably exceeds the number who are, or have been, practicing in that capacity. (Ross 1955, 441)

The distinction between real lawyers and nominal lawyers is important, but how does one determine the difference? One rough measure would be to examine how long lawyer-legislators practiced law before entering legislative service. Because the state legislatures are important stepping stones for those who desire to serve in Congress,[1] the nominal lawyer category includes those with five or fewer years of practicing law before they entered either the state legislature or the U.S. House. Conversely, real lawyers are defined for these purposes as those with more than five years of experience in the practice of law (or who served as a judge for at least five years) before they were elected to a legislative seat at either the state or federal level. Of the 195 lawyers who served in the House in 1989, 45 percent fell into the nominal lawyer category and 55 percent were real lawyers with considerable experience in the practice of law before getting into politics.

The next logical question to answer is, How do different types of lawyer-legislators differ in their legislative behavior? The following sections of this chapter will first explore differences between real lawyers and nominal lawyers who serve on three committees in the House of Representatives (Judiciary, Energy and Commerce, and Interior). In order to explore further the differences among the three types of lawyer-legislators, the final section of this chapter will examine how the behavior of lawyer-legislators differs in the Massachusetts legislature. More specifically, this chapter will examine how the three types of lawyers in the Massachusetts legislature differ in their approaches to the issue of court reform in that state.

The Congressional Committees

This chapter and the next focus primarily on the three U.S. House committees: the House Judiciary Committee, the House Interior and Insular Affairs Committee (recently renamed the Resources Committee), and the House Energy and Commerce Committee (recently renamed the Commerce Committee). These committees were chosen for a variety of reasons. First, they roughly represent the three types found in Fenno's (1973) typology of congressional committees: Interior is a classic reelection committee (see Smith and Deering 1984, 107–8), House Judiciary is almost always classified as a policy committee (see Smith and Deering 1984, 102–3), and the Energy and Commerce Committee is fast becoming typical of the power within the chamber committees (see Dodd and Oppenheimer 1989, Miller 1992). Second, these committees have overlapping jurisdictions that produce many multiple referrals among them (see Davidson, Oleszek, and Kephart 1988), and overlapping memberships that made comparisons among the three committees easier, especially for members and staff who had had contact with several of these committees. Finally, the committees have varying proportions of members who are lawyers. Traditionally, House Judiciary members are exclusively attorneys, about 60 percent of Energy and Commerce members were attorneys in 1989, and Interior has traditionally been dominated by nonlawyer members. Table 34 breaks down the committees' memberships into three groups: real lawyers, nominal lawyers, and nonlawyers. At the beginning of the 101st Congress, when the interviews for this study were conducted, 42 percent of the total membership of the House were lawyers (Ornstein, Mann, and Malbin 1990, 20–22). These three committees were also chosen in part because they have different proportions of the three categories of lawyer-legislators.

Table 34

Real, Nominal, and Nonlawyer Membership of Congressional Committees

Committee	Real Lawyers	Nominal Lawyers	Nonlawyers
Judiciary (N=35)	57%	40%	3%
Energy and Commerce (N=43)	23%	37%	40%
Interior (N=38)	21%	11%	68%

SOURCES: 1989–1990 Official Congressional Directory; Brownson 1989; Duncan 1989.
Note: gamma = .61 / tau-b = .44. Figures based on spring 1989 committee memberships. Real lawyers are defined as those with more than five years of practicing law before election to a state legislature or to the U.S. House.

The House Interior and Insular Affairs Committee (renamed the Natural Resources Committee in 1993 and renamed the Resources Committee in 1995) attracts relatively few lawyer members, as indicated in table 34. House Interior has traditionally been a reelection or constituency committee, which helps especially western members to provide money, projects, and other assistance to their districts (Smith and Deering 1984, 107–8). The committee recently has attracted more policy-oriented members, especially eastern liberals who are concerned about environmental issues (see Smith and Deering 1990, 87, 97). However, Interior has not lost its heavy constituency orientation. As one Interior staffer said in the interviews for this project, "While the westerners have an obvious constituency link which makes Interior attractive, most of the eastern liberals come to the committee for a cheap green vote for all those environmentalists back home. Few come to Interior to make grand policy initiatives."

The second committee, House Judiciary, has traditionally been classified as a policy committee that draws members who are interested in handling the legalistic policy issues under the committee's jurisdiction (see Smith and Deering 1984, 102). Members on this committee traditionally are exclusively attorneys, and the committee is known for its courtlike deliberative style and culture. Most of the members of this committee have had considerable experience in the practice of law, and thus the committee is dominated by "real lawyers." Today, House Judiciary draws policy-oriented lawyer-legislators of both the far right and the far left (Davidson 1988, 105) who feel comfortable with the highly legalistic subject matter of the committee (Perkins 1981, 358–59). Conservative Republicans are drawn to the committee to attempt to highlight a conservative social agenda, and liberals attempt to block just such issues (see Cohodas 1986, 1307). As one member declared, "Judiciary is special because there are so many lawyers there."

During the interviews for this project, members of Congress and their staff frequently implied that the House Judiciary Committee is different from other committees in the chamber mainly because its members are exclusively attorneys with considerable private law practice experience. Recall the member of congress who said, "It's great to work with all those lawyers on Judiciary. The members have more experience and are higher quality than most. They are also brighter than most." When asked directly if lawyers and nonlawyers in Congress behaved differently, many lawyer members said no, but then they quickly added that the lawyers who are attracted to the Judiciary Committee may indeed be different from other lawyer members. Thus many of those interviewed for this project implied that the Judiciary Committee is unique precisely because it is the "Committee of Lawyers," or perhaps because it is the committee of a special type of lawyer. What came across clearly in the interviews is that the real lawyers on Judiciary are not the same as many of the lawyer-legislators on other congressional committees. The difference lies in the socialization into the legal profession that most Judiciary Committee members have experienced because of their extensive prior work in the private practice of law.

This sense that the lawyers on the Judiciary Committee are somehow unique has also appeared in the scholarly literature. One roll-call study from the early 1970s implied that lawyers who serve on the Judiciary Committee may indeed be different from lawyer members who serve on other committees (Green, Schmidhauser, Berg, and Brady 1973, 450). Many of the members of the Judiciary Committee interviewed by Perkins mentioned that they were attracted to the Judiciary Committee because of their prior substantial experience in the practice of law. When asked why they sought seats on the Judiciary Committee, members were quoted as saying, "My first choice was Judiciary because I'm a lawyer and had been a judge." Another Judiciary Committee member explained, "I thought I'd like the Judiciary Committee. I'm a lawyer; it's my life work." A third committee member said, "Being on the committee helped me retain my lawyer skills" (Perkins 1981, 358). Thus the Judiciary Committee attracts those lawyers with considerable experience in the practice of law who are interested in maintaining their ties to the legal profession and to legal issues.

The third committee in this study, the Energy and Commerce Committee (in 1995 it returned to its former name, the Commerce Committee), draws members for a variety of reasons (see Smith and Deering 1990, 96), but in the 1990s it is fast becoming typical of Fenno's third committee type, the power committee (see Dodd and Oppenheimer 1989). One measure of Energy and Commerce's new status is the fact that it is now an exclusive committee for Republicans (Smith and Deering 1990, 116–17), and the Democratic Caucus gave serious consideration to making it an exclusive committee for their party as well (see House Democrats 1990, 4068). The committee draws a sizable proportion of lawyer members, as was indicated in table 34. Although roughly 60 percent of its members are lawyers, most are nominal lawyers who got into politics very quickly after finishing law school.

One of the clear differences among these three committees is the proportion of real lawyers compared to the proportion of nominal lawyers. As table 35 indicates, the three congressional committees in this study have very different proportions of real-lawyer members among their lawyer-legislators. The House Judiciary Committee is not only made up exclusively of lawyer members, but these policy-oriented lawyers are overwhelmingly real lawyers. Although Ehrenhalt is not totally correct when he says that few members of Congress have much experience practicing law (Ehrenhalt 1991, 16), he does articulate the perception among many Congress watchers that those lawyer-legislators with considerable practical legal experience stand out on the Hill. It should not be surprising, then, that the House Judiciary Committee, with its extremely high proportion of real lawyers, is perceived to be a very special congressional committee.

On the other hand, the lawyers who serve on the House Energy and Commerce Committee are overwhelmingly nominal lawyers. Recall that in 1989, 45 percent of the lawyer members of the U.S. House fell into the nominal lawyer category, and 55 percent were real lawyers with considerable experience in the practice of law before getting into politics. However, almost two-thirds of the Energy and Commerce lawyers fell into the nominal lawyer category. Recall that those with early political ambitions naturally gravitate toward the legal profession because individuals with law degrees are much more likely than nonlawyer politicians to achieve their political goals. The power-oriented Energy and Commerce members seem to fit this description well.

Table 35

Real and Nominal Lawyer Membership of Congressional Committees

Committee	Real Lawyers	Nominal Lawyers
Judiciary (N=34)	59%	41%
Energy and Commerce (N=26)	38%	62%
Interior (N=12)	67%	33%

SOURCES: 1989–1990 Official Congressional Directory; Brownson 1989; Duncan 1989. Note: gamma = .07 / tau-b = .04. Figures based on spring 1989 committee memberships. Real lawyers are defined as those with more than five years of practicing law before election to a state legislature or to the U.S. House. Figures are percentages of all lawyer-legislators serving on that committee.

Although their numbers are not large, the relatively high proportion of real lawyers on the Interior Committee is somewhat surprising. Only 33 percent of the members of the Interior Committee are lawyers, a much lower percentage than for many other committees in the House, but fully two-thirds of these lawyers are real lawyers, as indicated in table 35. Of course, the fact that this committee is numerically dominated by nonlawyer members blunts the effects of the presence of these real lawyers. The perception is that Interior has few real lawyers. As one Interior Committee staffer noted, "There are few differences between the lawyers and nonlawyers on our committee, but we don't have many real lawyers on our committee. Some of our members have law degrees, but most have never really practiced. Unlike the lawyers on the Judiciary Committee, most of our members with law degrees have been away from lawyering for too long. They no longer act like real lawyers." Another Interior Committee staffer agreed: "We have fewer lawyers on our committee than on most. But the lawyers we have aren't real lawyers like they have on Judiciary. The ones that act like real lawyers are obvious on the committee."

Types of Lawyers in the State Legislatures

Although almost non-existent in Congress, the third type of lawyer-legislator, the nominal legislator, is common in the state legislatures. At the state level, there are three categories of lawyer-legislators. There are those who get law degrees merely as a means to achieving their political goals (nominal lawyers), those who have extensive experience in the legal profession but then choose to change priorities and pursue a political career instead (real lawyers), and those who enter the legislature merely to enhance their legal careers (nominal legislators). At the state level, one measure of these differences would be those lawyer-legislators who consider themselves to be full-time legislators (the real lawyers and the nominal lawyers) and those who consider themselves to be part-time legislators, almost certainly because they actively continue to practice law while holding their legislative seats.

In his landmark work on state legislatures, Barber (1965) has suggested that lawyer-legislators may be divided into "real legislators" or "nominal legislators," although Barber uses the terms "Advertiser" and "Lawmaker." For Barber, lawyers come to the legislature with two very different goals in mind. Barber's Lawmakers are lawyer-legislators who put their political ambitions above their legal careers. This type is very similar to Fenno's (1973) members whose goal is to make good public policy. Barber found that about a third of the legislators in this category were lawyers (Barber 1965, 168). On the other hand, Advertisers were those lawyer-legislators who entered the legislature merely to enhance their legal careers. Barber's Advertiser is often a young, upwardly mobile lawyer experiencing professional difficulties (Barber 1965, 215). Lawmakers are "young and mobile, but with deeper and more varied political roots and much more interest in full-time elective office" (Barber 1965, 216). The "real legislators" often have ambitions of running for Congress, where they become either the nominal lawyers or the real lawyers.

The third category of lawyer-legislators, the "nominal legislators," rarely end up in Congress, because their priorities rest with their legal careers and they can earn much more money in their law practices (see Fowler and McClure 1989, 127–28). As a leading student of state legislatures notes, "[Most lawyer-legislators] at some point must choose between leaving the legislature and leaving their firms" (Rosenthal 1981, 43). And another commentator observes, "Full-time jobs in Congress and in legislatures attract people who want to devote most of their waking hours to politics. There is no reason to suppose that this is the same set of people who would want to do politics in their spare time. . . . Politics in the 1990s is for people who are willing to give it vast amounts of their time. It is also for people who are not particularly concerned about making money" (Ehrenhalt 1991, 14–15). Thus at the state level, there is a clear difference between the nominal legislator and legislators in the other two categories.

In the highly professionalized state legislatures in Ohio and Massachusetts, a sizable number of lawyer-legislators continue to practice law while serving in the legislature (recall tables 17 and 18 in chap. 5). Most of the nonlawyer members of these state legislatures considered themselves to be full-time public servants. On the other hand, in Ohio only a third of the lawyers in the legislatures considered themselves to be full-time legislators, and in Massachusetts only half of the lawyer members labeled themselves as full-time legislators. Table 19 (chap. 5) indicates that the lawyer members of the Ohio legislature have much higher salaries than the nonlawyer members, in large part because so many of the lawyer-legislators in Ohio continue to practice law full-time while they are in the legislature.

In Massachusetts, the differences among these three types of lawyer-legislators became very clear when discussing the issue of court reform in that state. In the Massachusetts legislature, the Joint Committee on the Judiciary has jurisdiction over most court-related matters. And traditionally, the Judiciary Committee in Massachusetts has been dominated by practicing lawyer-legislators, or nominal legislators in our terminology. As a member of the Massachusetts joint Judiciary Committee stated, "I'm one of the very few nonlawyers currently on the Judiciary Committee. That's a plus, because I look at the world much differently than all the other lawyer members." Another nonlawyer member of the Judiciary Committee in Massachusetts commented, "It is unusual to have nonlawyers serving on the Judiciary Committee. I think it is good for the committee to hear a different point of view. All the lawyer members have a uniform view of the world." Members of the state legislature in Massachusetts see clear differences between the lawyer and the nonlawyer members of that body.

It was somewhat amazing that during my Massachusetts interviews many members repeatedly used the term "lawyer-legislator" to describe their colleagues who were practicing lawyers. Many of the lawyer-legislators in Massachusetts continue to practice law in the state, even though most of their nonlawyer colleagues in the legislature consider themselves to be full-time legislators. During my Massachusetts interviews, several members mentioned clear distinctions between different types of lawyer-legislators. The full-time legislators saw politics as their primary career, whereas the part-time lawyer-legislators clearly saw the practice of law as their primary concern. These differences then translated into stark differences on the issue of court reform in the state. As one lawyer member put it, "I am much more reform-minded than most of the other lawyers here. Unfortunately, they act only on their own self-interests."

This distinction between nominal legislators and the other types of lawyer-legislators arose in many of the legislative interviews in Massachusetts. An astute nonlawyer representative said that in the Massachusetts legislature, there is a clear difference between the "old-boy lawyers" and the "new-boy lawyers." The old-boy lawyers continue to practice law in Boston, whereas the new-boy lawyers spend most of their time on their legislative work (see chap. 5). "The new-boy lawyers may or may not practice law," he noted, "but they have a clear understanding of the role of a legislator. They put their job in the legislature first, and their law practices second."

Practicing Lawyer-Legislators and
Court-Reform Efforts in Massachusetts

As mentioned briefly in the previous chapter, court reform was a major issue before the Massachusetts legislature in the early 1990s. This issue illustrates nicely the clear differences between nominal legislators and the other two types of lawyer-legislators in our typology.

In response to the *Boston Globe* series on politically well-connected lawyers and state trial judges who often did not show up for work, the Massachusetts Supreme Judicial Court requested a special report on various court-reform issues from Paul R. Sugarman, dean of the Suffolk University Law School in Boston.[2] The Sugarman report endorsed the following court-reform proposals: more power for the courts independently to handle personnel, administrative, resource allocation, and court consolidation issues (currently the state legislature must approve all such changes); the merger and consolidation of the Boston Municipal Court into the rest of the state trial court system;[3] and a prohibition on lawyer-legislators practicing before the state courts while they are members of the legislature (Sugarman 1991, 258).

Prompted mainly by the public outcry that resulted from these *Boston Globe* series and the Sugarman report, the legislature in the early 1990s considered various court-reform proposals. None of the proposals would have affected the way the state supreme court functions in the state; they were focused primarily on the state trial courts. Court-reform proposals were drafted by the state's Republican governor, the Massachusetts attorney general (a Democrat), a joint effort by the Speaker of the House and the president of the senate (both Democrats), the Boston Bar Association, the Massachusetts Bar Association, the League of Women Voters, and Massachusetts SJC members (Wong 1992b, 41, 45). Although these proposals differed somewhat in detail, all were strikingly uniform in their stated goals (see Wong 1992a, 21, 23): to simplify the organization of the state trial courts; to consolidate the Boston Municipal Court into the rest of the state court system; to create a statewide juvenile court system; to end unique state practices such as the criminal trial de novo (in which if a criminal defendant is convicted in a bench trial, that defendant is automatically granted a second completely new jury trial and the bench trial conviction is ignored) (see Sugarman 1991, 24–30); to allow the SJC and other courts to have more control over court consolidation actions and other personnel and administrative matters; and to reduce legislative control over the details of the annual appropriations for the state courts (see Wong 1992c, 17, 24). None of the legislative proposals would have barred lawyer-legislators from practicing before the state courts.

After much stalling, on the last day of the 1992 legislative session, Massachusetts passed a watered-down version of court reform. This legislation eliminated the two-trial system in criminal cases, created a statewide juvenile court, and established evaluation procedures for judges and court personnel. However, the court-reform law did not give the courts more control over most budget matters, thus preserving the power of the legislature over many personnel and budgetary questions (see Williamson 1993, B1). Most judges in the state were not happy with the bill (see Williamson 1993, B1). The legislature in effect enacted cosmetic court reform but did not give the courts the needed flexibility to solve administrative, personnel, and other resource issues.

Are Lawyer-Legislators Blocking Real Court Reform?

During the course of the interviews for this study, it became clear that practicing lawyers who serve in the Massachusetts legislature have very different views on the state courts in general and on the issue of court reform than their colleagues whose main concern is their legislative work.

The Joint Committee on the Judiciary, which is dominated by lawyer members, has primary jurisdiction over the state courts and court reform proposals (see Center for Leadership Studies 1991, 8–9). One nonlawyer senator declared:

> The administration of the courts needs to be corrected. But the problem is the Judiciary Committee. It's all lawyers on that committee. The Judiciary Committee is controlled by lawyers who all practice law in Boston. It is the worst run committee in the legislature. There are just too many Boston lawyers in the legislature. We'll probably never get court reform. It's been a decade of frustration for me trying to get any improvements in the court system. There is a real lawyer/nonlawyer split in this legislature.

Getting court reform enacted in Massachusetts was very difficult because the general feeling in the legislature was that the lawyer-legislators benefit personally and financially from the current system, and that they were loath to make any changes in the manner that the Massachusetts courts operate. A leader in the court-reform movement observed, "Court reform stabs at the old habits of the legislature. The Supreme Judicial Court is not infallible. But the experiences of the lawyers with the courts should not be persuasive. The experiences of the lawyer-legislators drive the entire legislature on this issue. On court reform, the legislature just has not done a good job because of the dominance of the lawyers."

Continuing on the issue of court reform in Massachusetts, a nonlawyer representative said, "Unfortunately, court reform failed in the House last year. All those lawyers on the Judiciary Committee all do business in the Boston courts, and they all stuck together on that vote. There is a clear lawyer/nonlawyer gulf in the legislature on this issue." One nonlawyer representative concluded that the lawyer members have a herd mentality and thus vote as a block on many issues. As this nonlawyer explained, "The practicing lawyer-legislator is always aware of his lawyer peers. They feel that they must watch out because the whole bar is watching them very closely. They must act like a lawyer; they can't afford to act independently." Along these lines, a pro-reform lawyer member noted, "There is a difference in the perspective of lawyer and nonlawyer members here. I am much more of a reform-minded lawyer than most here because the law is not my first profession. Unfortunately, most of the lawyer members look out only for their own self-interests." One senator who is a lawyer took the opposite side of the argument: "There is an antilawyer establishment in the leadership of the legislature. Thus the legislature has ignored the needs of the courts."

There is a perception among the pro-reform members of the Massachusetts legislature that the practicing lawyer-legislators in Massachusetts (the so-called nominal legislators) band together to block any court-reform legislation. There also is a perception among court-reform advocates that the Joint Committee on the Judiciary, the legislative committee with jurisdiction over court-reform issues, is captured by the lawyer-legislators who continue to practice law in the state.

During these interviews, the Massachusetts legislators were asked about their opinions on what changes were needed in the Massachusetts state court system and on various specific court-reform proposals then circulating. The legislators' responses, broken down between lawyer and nonlawyer members, were reported in the previous chapter. Although on many points regarding court reforms the opinions of the lawyer and nonlawyer legislators were similar, on other questions there was some sharp disagreement between the two groups. For example, 30 percent of the nonlawyer members felt that the cost of the state court system needed to be trimmed and that consolidation of many state courts was necessary. Only 17 percent of the lawyer members mentioned this point, and none of them practiced law full time. This difference could be due to the fact that lawyer-legislators who practice in the state courts are quite comfortable with the current arrangements, and the *Boston Globe* series discussed above indicated that lawyer-legislators are often big winners in the state trial courts. Any changes in judicial personnel or arrangements could be seen as an attack on their lucrative law practices.

Thus, in the Massachusetts legislature there seems to be a great deal of conflict between the various types of lawyer members, especially on the issue of court reform. As one senator complained, "The lawyer members resent the time they spend on legislative business. They make a lot more money in their law practices." As previous chapters indicated, the legislators themselves were quick to point out behavioral and attitudinal differences between the lawyer and nonlawyers members in Massachusetts.

The 1991 Sugarman report to the SJC called for lawyer-legislators to discontinue practicing law in the state courts because of potential conflict of interest concerns. Carpinello (1989, 1991), among others, has raised ethical questions about the ability of lawyer-legislators to avoid potential conflicts of interests: "Legislators who are also practicing at-

Table 36

Massachusetts Legislators' Views on Lawyer-Legislators Practicing in Massachusetts State Courts

Legislators	Should Practice	Should Not Practice
All lawyers (N=12)	75%	25%
All nonlawyers (N=12)	0%	100%

Note: gamma = 1.00 / tau-b = .78

torneys face a special problem not shared by other legislators. Attorneys in the legislature bring with them their private interests, as well as the interests of each and every client. Thus the attorney, unlike the farmer or the doctor, inevitably has a wider range of potential conflicts" (Carpinello 1991, 12).

When asked, the vast majority of the lawyer-legislators in my study felt that they should be able to continue practicing law while serving in the legislature, as indicated in table 36. None of the nonlawyer legislators who commented on this issue shared that view. Note that a sizable percentage of the legislators refused to answer this question.

One lawyer explained his ambivalence on the subject: "I agree there is a certain unfairness when lawyer-legislators practice before the state courts. If we are to require that this be a full-time legislature in Massachusetts, then don't allow the lawyers to practice. But I don't believe a full-time legislature is a good legislature. We need lawyers in the legislature. All professions should be represented in the legislature. This should be a citizen-legislature; don't exclude the lawyers." Another lawyer-legislator stated, "They can't prohibit practicing by lawyer-legislators; we'd need much higher legislative salaries to do it. But one ought not to serve on the Judiciary Committee if practicing, because that creates a perceived conflict of interest. Lawyer-legislators should not have a primary role in setting policies that directly affect their sources of income, i.e., the courts." A nonlawyer member stated, "It is unfair to allow lawyer-legislators to continue practicing. But I won't deal with that issue. I won't attack the lawyer-legislators because they are too powerful in this state."

The clear perception among advocates of court reform in Massachusetts is that the practicing lawyer-legislators block any court-reform efforts because these lawyers benefit personally and financially from the status quo. Although publicly supportive of court reform, the practicing lawyer-legislators (nominal legislators) privately block efforts aimed at reform because they are comfortable and familiar with the current byzantine court system. Fearful of reducing their own influence and power over the state court system, the lawyer-legislators have been able to torpedo court-reform efforts in the state.

Clearly, the state courts in Massachusetts are not an important part of the day-to-day work of many Massachusetts legislators. The courts are rarely, if ever, an issue in their campaigns, and most members of the Massachusetts legislature perceive the state courts as outside the normal political give-and-take in the state. In a similar vein, court reform does not appear to be an important issue to most members of the legislature. According to one 1992 newspaper report, "Court reform is an issue that has garnered little interest among rank-and-file lawmakers, who are facing reelection campaigns" (Wong 1992a, 21, 23).

The exception to this general indifference comes from the members of the legislature who are also practicing lawyers. The lawyer-legislators who practice law in the Massachusetts state courts appear to pay a great deal of attention to the courts and to issues of court reform. These lawyer-legislators tend to see court reform as an attack on their personal financial and political interests. They prefer that the Massachusetts courts remain a passive and nonsalient part of the state government. From their perspective, the less that is known about the courts in the state, the happier they are.

✦✦✦

CHAPTER EIGHT

Lawyers on Congressional Committees

In order to understand more fully how lawyer-politicians affect the functioning of American political institutions, this chapter will examine how the proportion of different types of lawyers on various congressional committees affects the committees' decision-making styles and processes. As Woodrow Wilson first observed in 1885, "Congress in session is Congress on public exhibition, whilst Congress in its committee-rooms is Congress at work" (Wilson 1973, 69). Therefore, in this chapter I will shift the level of analysis from the individual legislators examined in previous chapters to the congressional committees. The first section of this chapter will explore how congressional committees differ in their decision-making processes and deliberative styles according to how many lawyers serve on the committee. In order to provide some concrete examples of how different types of lawyer-legislators approach their legislative work, this chapter will also examine how congressional committees dominated by "real lawyers" approach constitutional questions differently than committees dominated by "nominal lawyers."

Differences in Committee Decision-Making Styles

Previous chapters have found clear behavioral and attitudinal differences between individual lawyers and nonlawyers in Congress. These differences become even more evident when one examines how the decision-making styles of the three congressional committees in this study differ according to the proportion of lawyer members on each committee, and according to the most common type of lawyer on the committee. The political cultures, decision-making styles, and jurisdictions of different congressional committees can vary greatly.[1] These differences are in part due to the varying proportions of lawyers who serve on these committees.

According to David Price, a political scientist who served in Congress from 1986 to 1994, "Committees are collections of individuals who bring different goals, values, identifications, and skills to their committee roles; the performance of a committee may be seen in part as a function of these characteristics of its membership" (Price 1985, 175). As March and Olsen, two key proponents of the neo-institutionalist approach to politics, argue, "The bureaucratic agency, the legislative committee, and the appellate court are arenas for contending social forces, but they are also collections of standard operating procedures and structures that define and defend interests. They are political actors in their own right" (March and Olsen 1984, 738).

In order to explore how various types and proportions of lawyer members affects the decision-making processes of congressional committees, this section will return to an examination of how the House Judiciary Committee, the House Energy and Commerce Committee (now known as the Commerce Committee), and the House Interior Committee (in 1995 renamed the Resources Committee) differ in their decision-making styles. Recall from the previous chapter that the Judiciary Committee is dominated by real lawyers, the Energy and Commerce Committee is dominated by nominal lawyers, and the Interior Committee is dominated by nonlawyers.

During the congressional interviews, there seemed to be a clear understanding among those interviewed in Congress that the lawyers on the House Judiciary Committee were somehow different than the lawyers on the House Energy and Commerce Committee. The policy-oriented real lawyers on the Judiciary Committee often take on the role of judges, whereas the power-oriented nominal lawyers on Energy and Commerce seem to prefer the prosecutor as a role model. I wish to explore in greater detail how the real-lawyer-dominated Judiciary Committee behaves differently from either of the other two committees examined.[2]

House Judiciary's formal jurisdiction includes all matters dealing with federal courts and judges; federal crimes and prisons; civil rights and liberties; the Federal Bureau of Investigation (FBI); immigration and naturalization of citizens; bankruptcy; patents, copyrights, and trademarks; antitrust law and monopolies; and administrative law. It is also the only House committee that has jurisdiction over proposed Constitutional amendments (see Davidson 1988; *Congressional Quarterly Almanac* 1989,

49-E). Congress has entrusted the committee with some of its most important constitutional and judicial issues (see Ralph Nader Congress Project 1975, Davidson 1988, Eskridge 1991).

House Judiciary has usually been classified as a policy-oriented committee that draws members who want to make good public policy (see Smith and Deering 1984, 102; see also Ralph Nader Project 1975). By tradition, members on this committee are almost exclusively attorneys, and the committee is known for its courtlike deliberative style and culture. Committee members tend to be ideologically polarized on Judiciary, meaning that the Democrats tend to be much more liberal than their colleagues in the full House, and Republicans tend to be much more conservative than their party colleagues (see Davidson 1988).

In the 1960s and 1970s, House Judiciary handled extremely important and significant legislation dealing with the burning civil rights and civil liberties issues of the day. At that time, it was a much desired and visible committee for policy-oriented members, especially liberals. After the election of Ronald Reagan to the White House in 1980, however, the committee's Democratic leadership changed the focus of the committee in order to attempt to kill the president's conservative social agenda. In the 1980s, the committee became a graveyard for many conservative initiatives, including proposed Constitutional amendments (see Cohodas 1980, 1982; Biskupic 1990, 4079–81). Many members of the full House, both liberals and conservatives alike, were often privately pleased that the committee did not act on the many emotionally charged issues before it, thus protecting them from difficult votes.

The House Interior Committee (now the Resources Committee) has jurisdiction over public lands and national parks, natural resources in general, mining and mineral issues, interstate water compacts and other water rights issues, nuclear power and nuclear waste issues, Native American issues, and issues concerning U.S. territorial possessions.

The third committee in this study, Energy and Commerce (now the Commerce Committee) in the late 1980s and early 1990s had an ever-growing jurisdiction that covered topics such as any issues dealing with interstate and foreign commerce; national energy policy; various aspects of energy resources, including nuclear power and other nontraditional energy sources; inland waterways; railroads and their employees; securities; telecommunications and communications issues; consumer affairs; public health and health care; and biomedical research and development (see *Congressional Quarterly Almanac* 1989, 44-E; see also Ralph Nader

Project 1975b). According to one commentator, "The [Energy and Commerce] Committee is on the cutting edge of fundamental issues that are central to the U.S. economy. . . . As a result, the committee has attracted what many observers believe are the best, brightest, and most independent representatives, most of whom had to fight just to get on the panel" (Plattner 1983, 501–8).

Energy and Commerce, fast becoming typical of Fenno's (1973) power committees, also now has enormous fund-raising potential, adding to the evidence that it is evolving into a power-oriented committee (see Alston 1990, 1991). One member of Congress defined the differences between policy committees and power committees by noting, "You have to decide whether you want to be on a powerhouse committee where you can raise funds or go to a committee that handles the issues that motivated you to take an interest in public office in the first place" (Smith and Deering 1990, 61). Many members now see Energy and Commerce as a clear example of the former.

Energy and Commerce has been described as "an octopus of a committee" that aggressively attempts to steal as much jurisdiction as possible from other committees (Duncan 1989, 769–71). As one commentator has said, "The [Energy and Commerce] Committee has the largest jurisdiction in Congress, and its members are not bashful about seeking more" (Plattner 1983, 501). In part because of the fierce determination of the committee's former longtime chair, Representative John Dingell (Democrat-Michigan), the committee actively attempts to enlarge its jurisdiction and thus its visibility and power in the House. As one Republican member of the committee is quoted as saying, "John Dingell feels about his committee much as Lyndon Johnson felt about his ranch. Johnson didn't want to own the whole world, he just wanted to own all the land surrounding his ranch. Dingell doesn't want his committee to have the whole world, just all the areas surrounding its jurisdiction" (Smith and Deering 1984, 179).

Sometimes other committees blow up at Energy and Commerce's insatiable appetite for an ever larger jurisdiction. In the summer of 1994, for example, a serious jurisdictional squabble over an insurance redlining bill broke out on the floor of the House between Energy and Commerce and the House Banking Committee. Both committees claimed jurisdiction over the bill, but the House parliamentarian ruled that Energy and Commerce could take ultimate control over the measure. The original sponsor of the bill and a member of the Banking, Finance and Urban

Affairs Committee, Congressman Joseph Kennedy (Democrat-Massachusetts), offered an amendment on the floor to reclaim control over the issue for the Banking Committee. The rebuke to the Energy and Commerce
Committee failed on the floor by a vote of 88 to 343 (see Hager 1994,
2010), which is further evidence of the new power position of the Energy and Commerce Committee. During the floor debate, Congressman
Kennedy bitterly attacked the Energy and Commerce Committee's claim
of jurisdiction in this case. After complaining that many key issues were
now improperly under the control of Energy and Commerce (including
the mutual fund industry, the securities industry, health care, transportation, energy, railroads, and interstate commerce), Kennedy exploded:

> Enough is enough. At some point the fact is that this is nothing more
> than a further power grab by [Energy and Commerce] on the Commit-
> tee on Banking, Finance and Urban Affairs' jurisdiction, and it is time
> to stop getting bullied around by the Committee on Energy and Com-
> merce. Time and time again, whether it is legislation pertaining to how
> we are going to come together as a land and have financial institutions
> that can go out and compete with the Germans and Japanese and other
> foreigners, as long as it treads on the Committee on Energy and Com-
> merce jurisdiction, it cannot pass the Congress of the United States. (Rep.
> Kennedy, *Congressional Record*, 20 July 1994, H-5907).

Dodd and Oppenheimer have classified Energy and Commerce as one of
the five elite committees in the House that form "The New Oligarchy":
Appropriations, Ways and Means, Budget, Rules, and Energy and Commerce (Dodd and Oppenheimer 1989, 39, 49). This list is very similar to
Fenno's power committees, except for the addition of Energy and Commerce. Although Smith and Deering continue to categorize Energy and
Commerce as a policy committee (Smith and Deering 1990, 87), their
most recent interviews concerning member goals and committee preferences were conducted only with freshmen members. What Smith and
Deering miss is the fact that the goals of many of the members who already serve on Energy and Commerce have changed a great deal over the
last decade. Members may have originally come to Energy and Commerce
for policy or constituency reasons, but once there they view the committee
as one that can also help them increase their power in the House.

My interviews confirm that Energy and Commerce members see their
committee as one of the most powerful in Congress. As one Republican

member stated, "Energy and Commerce is the most powerful committee in the House because it combines strong legislative jurisdiction with extremely effective oversight." An Energy and Commerce staffer stated, "We have members who are highly motivated on Energy and Commerce. It is now the most sought after committee in the House. It's very tough placement to get on Commerce. Thus we get a better quality of members; we get the most ambitious members in the House." Alluding to the power from campaign contributions that now surrounds Energy and Commerce, another staffer said, "We take care of our constituents through the Interior Committee; we do our fundraising on Energy and Commerce."

The Courtlike Style of the Judiciary Committee

The House Judiciary Committee, the "Committee of Lawyers," is dominated by real lawyers who have had a great deal of experience in the practice of law before getting into politics. Judiciary prides itself on its extremely formal, lawyerlike deliberative style (see also Perkins 1980, 383). In many ways, the Judiciary Committee functions like a court. It is hard to imagine a committee not dominated by real lawyers adopting the courtlike style of the Judiciary Committee. Formality of procedures is always observed in Judiciary Committee proceedings. As Tocqueville noted, "Some of the tastes and habits of the aristocracy may consequently be discovered in the characters of lawyers. They participate in the same instinctive love of order and formalities" (Tocqueville, 1841, 266).

Judiciary is the only House committee with a formally designated parliamentarian, and its hearings and mark-up sessions often look and sound more like courtroom proceedings than political events. Judiciary uses formal mark-up sessions where the exact proposed language is debated by the members. The members rarely delegate the drafting of final legislative language to the staff, a practice common on many other committees. Unlike most House committees, Judiciary has formal rules against interfering in any way with ongoing litigation, and the committee has a norm that no bills should be take effect retroactively. Many of the interviews for this project indicated that this formal style was a direct result of the fact that only attorney members serve on House Judiciary. As one staffer observed, "Judiciary Committee members are sensitive to the proprieties of rules. All committee members revere the rules qua rules."

Members of the Judiciary Committee also spend a great deal of time debating the constitutionality of the legislation they approve. Judiciary members and staff pride themselves on their ability to anticipate how the federal courts will read the legislative language produced by the committee. With lawyerlike precision, Judiciary members will spend a great deal of time and energy worrying about the constitutionality of the bills that pass through the committee. Other committees seem much less concerned about writing legislation that the courts will uphold as constitutional. The Judiciary Committee expends sometimes enormous efforts to anticipate how the courts will react to specific legislative provisions. As one staffer said, "Judiciary Committee members see federal judges as their colleagues. That's not always true on other committees."

Judiciary staffers function much as law clerks do for judges, or as junior associates in a law firm do for senior partners. Hired for their legal skills and political savvy, they are prohibited from talking to the press and are very cautious in talking with academics. They have the reputation for being top-notch attorneys as well as top-notch political operatives.

Hearings on House Judiciary are designed to bring out both sides of any controversy, and they serve to build a record in support of any legislative action. Comparing Judiciary hearings to those on Energy and Commerce, one staffer observed, "On Energy and Commerce, they will move legislation without hearings, and what hearings they have support only the chair's point of view. Judiciary is very careful to build a proper hearing record." The Judiciary Committee is very procedurally oriented. Another observer noted that "Judiciary hearings are so thorough and so workmanlike. The intellectual level of questioning is much higher than on other committees. There is less rhetoric and less bombast. There is also a substantive difference in the treatment of court cases in Judiciary hearings than on other committees." Thus the real lawyers on the Judiciary Committee will not sacrifice adherence to proper procedures to mere political expediency.

Agency oversight activities on Judiciary tend to occur in a slow and methodical manner. As is its habit, the committee wants to hear all sides of an issue before it acts. Oversight hearings are a method for the committee to build a record against an agency, in preparation for a legislative remedy if necessary. In their oversight role, Judiciary members seem to act more like judges than prosecutors.

The legal training and world view of the members of the Judiciary Committee have probably fundamentally altered their view of the proper role and decision-making style of the committee. One also suspects that the professional socialization of its members has greatly altered the substantive decisions the committee is willing to make. In many ways, the Judiciary Committee functions in a manner analogous to that of a court or a large law firm. The judges or the senior partners (the members of the committee) react to the important issues before them (for example, the pronouncements of the courts) and leave the lesser issues (for example, reactions to agency decisions) to their law clerks or to their junior associates (the committee staff). Lawyers on other committees, such as the Energy and Commerce, show glimpses of how their legal training affects their work, but these members are more likely to be token lawyers who merely want a law degree on their résumé for purposes of political expediency. The lawyers on Judiciary are different; they are real lawyers who bring a unique mix of politics and law to their work.

The Nonlawyer Informality of Interior

In contrast to the courtlike style of the Judiciary Committee, the Interior Committee, dominated by nonlawyers, tends toward an informal deliberative style. Interior members are more likely to delegate drafting details to staff, and the committee is more likely to have a "conceptual mark-up": it agrees about the general gist of legislation and the staff is left to work out the details of the final legislative language. This preference for informality exists despite the fact that the committee is often polarized along ideological, party, and regional lines (see Parker and Parker 1985, 92–97, 252–58). Interior does sometimes hold more formal mark-up sessions, with roll-call votes on particular amendments; however, whenever possible, the Interior members seem to prefer informality, leaving the details of their work to the staff.

Hearings on Interior are often highly political affairs, with witnesses often being determined by the political agenda of the presiding chair. Unlike the Judiciary Committee, there is little feeling that hearings should reflect the evidence on both sides of an issue. The staff, many of them lawyers, play a large role in recruiting witnesses, preparing questions for the members to ask, and generally setting the tone to the nonlawyer dominated committee. However, the lawyers on the Interior Committee staff do not direct the actions of the committee. They merely serve as legal advisors to their clients, the committee members.

A Middle Style: House Energy and Commerce

In many ways, Energy and Commerce's deliberative style is closer to Judiciary's formal style than it is to the more informal style of the Interior Committee. This is not surprising, because a little more than half of Energy and Commerce's members are lawyers. But recall that lawyers on Energy and Commerce tend to be nominal lawyers. Also, the proportion of lawyer members is higher for the Democrats than it is for the Republicans (see Miller 1992). Yet in many ways Energy and Commerce is less formal than the courtlike Judiciary Committee.

Mark-up sessions are usually quite formal on Energy and Commerce, although the committee does not have a formal parliamentarian. The scholarly and legally oriented arguments that carry the day on the Judiciary Committee, however, do not play well on the power-oriented Energy and Commerce Committee. As a staffer who had worked for both House Judiciary and Energy and Commerce noted, "A good legal argument wins on Judiciary; power wins on Energy and Commerce. Power, not legal training, is the most important thing on Commerce. Commerce doesn't listen to legal arguments, just ideology." Another staffer concurred: "As a nonlawyer myself, I have trouble understanding hearings and mark-ups on Judiciary. Judiciary members argue for hours over the exact wording of the most unimportant section of the bill. They spend a lot of time on legalistic, esoteric concepts that I frankly don't see the point of." The staffer continued, "Energy and Commerce is more responsive than Judiciary to public needs, and thus E&C moves more quickly. Judiciary is a bunch of lawyers asking stupid lawyerlike questions. Judiciary reflects how courts make decisions, more methodical, more careful, more easily bogged down over details. E&C is full of hands on members who get the job done any way they can."

The congressional interviews elicited many responses comparing the Judiciary Committee's decision-making processes with those of the Energy and Commerce Committee, especially when dealing with the courts. It seems that members and staff see these two committees as operating in almost totally different worlds. An Energy and Commerce staffer said, "On Judiciary, they worry about the fundamental functioning of the courts. They can afford to take a broader picture. We just don't have the time for that." One representative who serves both Energy and Commerce and Judiciary commented, "Both committees have a great deal of respect for the courts. But Energy and Commerce bounces around the courts more. You just don't go trampling on the courts on the Judiciary Committee." A staffer who has worked for both committees observed, "The Judiciary Committee won't interfere with court cases in progress. Energy and Commerce is less cautious in going after court decisions. Commerce is more reactive or proactive than Judiciary. The Judiciary Committee tends to wait until the final decision from the Supreme Court before moving a bill; they are very sensitive to the appeals process. Commerce reacts more quickly. Commerce is very economically driven. It must consider economic issues with great impact. Commerce has more program oriented members who want to fix problems immediately. Judiciary is more legally oriented, less power- and policy-oriented." The real lawyers on the Judiciary Committee would no doubt feel quite out of place with Energy and Commerce's deliberative style, which reflects the needs of its nominal lawyer majority.

Although the preponderance of lawyer members on Energy and Commerce has not produced the courtlike deliberative style of Judiciary, it has affected Energy and Commerce's approach to agency oversight. During oversight activities, Energy and Commerce's members seem to behave like a collection of prosecutors grilling the same defendant. One staffer noted that former Chairman Dingell actively recruited attorney members to the Democratic side of the committee, because "the lawyer side of John Dingell comes out in his approach to agency oversight. It's Dingell and his young band of attorneys on the committee versus those cowering bureaucrats."

The Judiciary Committee is dominated by real lawyers, the Energy and Commerce Committee is roughly equally divided among the three groups, and the Interior Committee is dominated by nonlawyer members. But the nominal lawyers have been able to maintain their preferred deliberative style on the Energy and Commerce Committee. When the lawyer members are divided into real lawyers and nominal lawyers, it is easier to understand why the Judiciary Committee has such a courtlike deliberative style, whereas the number of lawyer members on the Energy and Commerce Committee seems to have less effect on that committee's processes. The Judiciary Committee appears to attract policy-oriented real lawyers who enjoy the legalistic subject matter of the committee and its deliberative style. On the other hand, the power-oriented nominal lawyers of the Energy and Commerce Committee probably prefer the rough-and-tumble world of hardball politics.

Congress and the Constitution:
A Tale of Two Committees

This section will examine how the House Judiciary Committee and the House Energy and Commerce Committee differ in their approaches to constitutional matters (see also Miller 1993d). Specific examples of how each committee has reacted to a federal court decision will help illustrate the difference between the real lawyers on the Judiciary Committee and the nominal lawyers who dominate Energy and Commerce.

Henschen has been one of the few scholars to examine court-Congress interactions at the committee level (see Henschen 1983, 1985; see also Eskridge 1991). As she has rightly pointed out, "Previous examinations of congressional reaction to the interpretations of the Court have limited their focus to proposals which have reached the floor-consideration or roll-call stage of the legislative process. In doing so, they ignore the significant decisions that are made at the committee level, and muffle much of the 'noise' in the legislative system" (Henschen 1983, 443–44). Echoing this theme, Solimine and Walker note that "both the House and Senate are decentralized institutions, and the actions of individual committees in both institutions may well have an impact on the interaction between the Court and Congress" (Solimine and Walker 1992, 438). This section provides a more in-depth understanding of how two congressional committees treat constitutional issues in their day-to-day deliberations, as well as providing more insights about the political environments in which these committees function.

A recent debate in the *North Carolina Law Review* between Abner Mikva and Louis Fisher about the ability and willingness of members of Congress to interpret the Constitution also indicates the need to examine how different congressional committees approach constitutional questions (see Mikva 1983, Fisher 1985). Former congressman, judge, and presidential counsel Abner Mikva assumes that both political and institutional pressures create an atmosphere in which Congress has neither the willingness nor the capacity to give careful consideration to constitutional issues. According to Mikva, "Most Supreme Court decisions never come to the attention of Congress" (Mikva 1983, 609). But even when Congress does consider constitutional issues, its "hallmark has been superficial and, for the most part, self-serving constitutional debate" (Mikva 1983, 610). On the other hand, Louis Fisher, a noted scholar from the Congressional Research Service, argues that Congress is quite careful and competent in its consideration of constitutional issues. In his defense of Congress's ability to understand and resolve constitutional disputes, Fisher argues, "That a congressional interpretation or understanding of the Constitution may differ from the Court's is hardly reason to conclude that Congress *ignores* the Constitution—a charge that imputes legislative bad faith" (Fisher 1985, 744). Fisher concludes: "Despite institutional and political limitations shared with the President and the courts, . . . Congress can perform an essential, broad, and ongoing role in shaping the meaning of the Constitution" (Fisher 1985, 708).

The differences between the perceptions of these two prominent observers of Congress may be due to the fact that congressional committees differ in their handling of constitutional questions. Being sensitive to the fact that Congress is a highly complex political institution that should not be treated as a monolith, both Mikva and Fisher agree that "the ability of Congress to participate effectively in constitutional interpretation depends in part on the strength of its committee system" (Fisher 1985, 746; see also Mikva 1983, 610). I argue that Mikva's position reflects the insensitivity to constitutional issues often found in the House Energy and Commerce Committee's deliberations, and Fisher's position mirrors the care that the House Judiciary Committee almost always uses in its deliberations on constitutional issues.

The House Judiciary Committee gives very careful consideration to the constitutional implications of all of its legislative actions. Judiciary has a great deal of respect for the courts as an institution and for the constitutionally based decisions handed down by the federal courts. Although not shy about overturning Supreme Court decisions with which it disagrees on policy grounds,[3] the committee only overturns federal court decisions after very judicious consideration and reflection of all the ramifications of its actions. Judiciary treats the Constitution and the courts with a respect bordering on reverence.

On the other hand, the House Energy and Commerce Committee, a committee whose main currency is power, treats constitutional questions no differently that it treats any other political issues. Because raw political power is the driving force behind the committee, it treats the federal courts as just one more political actor playing the game of hardball politics and rarely pays much attention to the constitutional ramifications of its decisions. Thus, if politics demand it, the Energy and Commerce Committee will not hesitate to overturn or to circumvent a constitutionally based federal court decision, and constitutional questions play very little role in the committee's day-to-day deliberations. Thus while the best legal or constitutional argument often wins in the Judiciary Committee, the interests with the most political muscle almost always win in the Energy and Commerce Committee, irrespective of constitutional considerations.

Another difference between the Commerce Committee and the Judiciary Committee is that Commerce members spend much less time worrying about the constitutionality of the legislation they approve. As one staffer explained, "On Energy and Commerce, the members take the Constitution seriously, but are nevertheless willing to delve into controversial First Amendment issues because they are important political issues. Energy and Commerce members move quickly to fix the problems before them without getting bogged down in fruitless debates over the possible constitutionality of the bills before them. The Energy and Commerce Committee is quite willing to take chances on passing possibly unconstitutional legislation."

Echoing these statements, another Energy and Commerce staffer noted that "our members take their constitutional responsibilities seriously, but they don't see that including a duty to take the most conservative constitutional interpretation. Thus the members often support approaches that are borderline constitutionally. Just because constitutionality is uncertain is not a bar to action on this committee." Another staffer explained, "Energy and Commerce treats constitutionality aspects and previous court decisions as one of many aspects to consider. We don't give constitutional questions overwhelming concern, just one more thing to consider. Energy and Commerce has a pressing agenda; we must act quickly." The deliberate, judgelike decision-making style of the Judiciary Committee is quite out of place on the more free-wheeling Energy and Commerce Committee.

Thus the House Judiciary Committee and the Energy and Commerce Committee have very different approaches to constitutional issues. While Judiciary agonizes over the constitutionality of all legislation it approves, Energy and Commerce spends very little time or energy considering how the courts will react to its legislative enactments. The Judiciary Committee is certainly a committee of lawyers, trained in both the law and politics. The real lawyers on the Judiciary Committee cause the committee to have a more elevated and intellectual approach to constitutional issues than does the more power-oriented Energy and Commerce Committee.

Energy and Commerce Committee members see lengthy discussions over the esoterica of constitutional issues as efforts to delay committee action, instead of a useful contribution to the public debate over the great issues of the day. The primary question on Judiciary seems to be, How will the committee's actions affect constitutional considerations? On the other hand, the primary question on Energy and Commerce is whether its actions are politically advantageous. Energy and Commerce is happy to leave questions of constitutionality to others, including the federal courts. But, of course, if the Energy and Commerce Committee disagrees with a court's ruling, it will not hesitate to take whatever actions are necessary to circumvent or overturn the court's decision. Some specific examples of how the Energy and Commerce Committee has reacted to constitutionally based federal court decisions will help illustrate the difference between the real lawyers on the Judiciary Committee and the nominal lawyers on the Energy and Commerce Committee.

Dial-a-Porn

Throughout much of the 1980s, various members of the Energy and Commerce Committee attempted to outlaw so-called dial-a-porn telephone services, that is, sexually explicit adult live or recorded messages accessible through 900, 976, and sometimes 800 telephone numbers.[4] The issue bounced back and forth between the courts, the Congress, and the Federal Communications Commission (FCC) for most of the decade.[5] At the insistence of several Energy and Commerce members, in 1988 Congress outlawed all obscene or indecent telephone communications (*School Improvement Act of 1987*, Public Law 100–297, H. Rept. 5). Although in June of 1989 the Supreme Court struck down most of the legislation on First Amendment grounds,[6] at the earliest possible opportunity in early July of 1989, the Energy and Commerce Committee attempted to circumvent the court's decision by attaching a provision to the annual budget reconciliation bill that effectively regulated the dial-a-porn industry out of business.[7] The legislation was eventually attached to an annual appropriations bill and enacted into law.[8] This story is illustrative of how the committee generally approaches constitutional issues.

On 30 September 1987, Energy and Commerce's Subcommittee on Telecommunications and Finance held hearings on a bill to outlaw all dial-a-porn telephone services. The bill would have totally banned all obscene or indecent telephone communications. The witness list for the hearings was fairly short. The chair of the subcommittee, Congressman

Edward Markey (Democrat-Massachusetts), attempted to set the tone for the hearings when he stated that among other political and technological issues, "the hearings will focus on the constitutional implications of regulating obscene or indecent telephone speech" (Dial-a-Porn Hearings, 1). Despite this introduction, statements such as the following were typical from committee members: "The concern I have in this piece of legislation is whether we are going too far; whether, constitutionally, this passes muster. I have some doubts, just having briefly read the [bill]. But I do think it is an appropriate vehicle that we should use, in terms of remedying this very serious problem" (statement of Congressman Bill Richardson [Democrat-New Mexico], Dial-a-Porn Hearings, 19). A liberal on the committee stated, "I don't cosponsor this legislation lightly, because . . . I have great concerns about attempts to impose restrictions on free speech. . . . At the same time, I have to recognize that this is an instance in which this speech is being put out for all to consume. There is not protection for minors. . . . It is my hope that this legislation, being carefully drafted, can meet the constitutional test" (statement of Congressman Thomas Tauke [Republican-Iowa], Dial-a-Porn Hearings, 19–20). Another member concluded, "I am proud to be a sponsor of [this bill]. I think we need a remedy. I hope this is constitutional. I am not a constitutional lawyer. I don't know" (statement of Congressman Dan Coats [Republican-Indiana], Dial-a-Porn Hearings, 18).

Although there was no disagreement during the hearings that Congress could constitutionally ban obscene telephone messages, various witnesses testified that it would be unconstitutional for Congress to ban merely indecent messages designed for consenting adult callers, as the bill proposed to do. Thus among the witnesses who testified that the proposed legislation would be unconstitutional were lawyers representing the American Civil Liberties Union, the FCC, the Justice Department, and a prominent Washington law firm.[9] Privately, committee counsel also warned the members that the legislation would probably be declared unconstitutional by the courts. Despite these warnings, Congressman Bliley, the author of the bill, urged the committee to ignore the probable unconstitutionality of the bill and enact it anyway. As Congressman Bliley concluded, "I firmly believe that [this legislation] is constitutional. Good men differ on this. It is unquestionably a sensitive area of constitutional law. Freedom of speech is a value that Americans hold dear, especially those who have seen the repression of speech in other countries. But there comes a time when, in a strained effort to reach a perfect balance of interests, we mistakenly emphasize one group's rights over that of another. I believe that has happened here" (statement of Congressman Bliley [Republican-Virginia], Dial-a-Porn Hearings, 4).

Although the committee did not act on H.R. 1786, members of the committee allowed its provisions to be attached to an education bill that was eventually enacted (Public Law 100-297). However, the conference report on the education bill did not mention the dial-a-porn provisions.[10] Several key members of the Energy and Commerce Committee (including the committee chair, the Telecommunications Subcommittee chair, and the ranking Republican on the Telecommunications Subcommittee) served as conferees for the education bill, and under pressure from various members of the House they allowed the dial-a-porn provisions to remain in the final version of the legislation despite the grave concerns about its constitutionality (see *Congressional Quarterly Almanac* 1988, 330–37). In response to the questionable constitutionality of the measure, one Energy and Commerce Committee member said on the floor of the House, "I think we should make every assault upon pornography that we can make, direct or indirect. I think that this is the first line of defense, outright banning of it. I think we ought to send it to the courts. Logically they get the last guess at whether the law is constitutional but let us let them vote on it" (statement of Congressman Ralph Hall [Democrat-Texas], 134 Cong. Rec. H1698, 19 Apr. 1988). Another member of the committee stated on the floor, "Now some say that they are worried about constitutional problems [with the legislation]. We are not elected in this body to stand here and make a constitutional decision, that is done across the street at the Supreme Court" (statement of Congressman Dan Coats [Republican-Indiana], 134 Cong. Rec. H1699, 19 Apr. 1988). Finally, the chairman of the Energy and Commerce Committee stated on the floor of the House, just before he voted in favor of the bill, that "if the House adopts this measure, then there will be a prohibition on dial-a-porn. I would point out to my colleagues that this proposal is of extraordinarily shaky and doubtful constitutionality" (statement of Congressman John Dingell [Democrat-Michigan], 134 Cong. Rec. H1699, 19 Apr. 1988). Chairman Dingell's words proved correct when the Supreme Court upheld the ban on obscene telephone messages, but also ruled that the portion of the legislation that attempted to ban merely indecent speech was an unconstitutional infringement of the First Amendment rights of consenting adults (*Sable Communications of California v. FCC*, 109 Sup. Ct. 2829 [1989]).

Although the Court struck down most of the dial-a-porn legislation in June 1989, only several weeks later the Energy and Commerce Committee attempted to circumvent this First Amendment decision by attaching a provision to the annual budget reconciliation bill that effectively regulated the dial-a-porn industry out of business.[11] The 1989 provision was passed by the committee without hearings and with very little discussion of its constitutionality. It was coupled with attempts to enact the so-called Fairness Doctrine into law (see *Report on the Budget Reconciliation Act of 1989,* 101st Cong., 1st sess., H. Rept. 101–247).

The new attack on dial-a-porn required that potential customers sign up in advance with federal regulators if they wanted to use the dial-a-porn services. Customer lists of those requesting dial-a-porn services would be made available to the public. The committee report on these provisions simply stated that "these provisions are intended to clamp down further on dial-a-porn providers, leaving unaffected other information service providers, and pass constitutional muster under the test articulated in the *Sable Communications* decision."[12] Only one member of the committee objected to the odd procedure of attaching this proposal to the annual budget bill. According to this member, "As a member who has cosponsored both Fairness Doctrine legislation and Dial-a-Porn legislation, I must object to the fact that the Committee has addressed these issues in the Energy and Commerce budget reconciliation bill. . . . It is clear that these issues should be addressed in separate individual bills and should not have been attached to budget reconciliation. Appropriate procedure requires that budget and money bills be considered separately from policy bills."[13]

Although dropped from the final version of the budget reconciliation bill, the proposal was eventually attached to an annual appropriations bill and enacted into law.[14] Several federal courts declared the new dial-a-porn provisions to be unconstitutional,[15] but eventually the constitutionality of the new regulations was upheld by the U.S. Circuit Courts of Appeals.[16] Clearly, this case study indicates that the Energy and Commerce Committee does not hesitate to overturn or to circumvent a federal court decision with which it disagrees, even when the decision is based on the First Amendment.

In another committee action regarding a constitutionally based Supreme Court decision, in 1986 the Energy and Commerce Committee effectively overturned the Court's Eleventh Amendment decisions in *Atascadero State Hospital v. Scanlon* (473 U.S. 234 [1985]) and *Hans v. Louisiana* (134 U.S. 1, 10 Sup. Ct. 504, 33 L.Ed 842 [1980]), regarding state claims of sovereign immunity, without ever mentioning these court decisions in the committee report on the legislation.[17] As part of its massive 1986 Superfund reauthorization bill, the Energy and Commerce Committee effectively overturned these two Supreme Court decisions by specifically abrogating state sovereign immunity for claims regarding the state's handling of hazardous waste disposal. In other words, the Superfund legislation exposed states to private citizen suits to recover the costs of hazardous-waste cleanup in spite of the Court's rulings that this was prohibited under the Eleventh Amendment.[18] This action was very similar to action taken by the House Education and Labor Committee in the Rehabilitation Act Amendments of 1986 regarding making states liable for discrimination in certain federally assisted enterprises.[19] In *Pennsylvania v. Union Gas Company* (109 S. Ct. 2273 [1989]), the Supreme Court ruled that Congress, and by implication the Energy and Commerce Committee, had indeed intended to overrule both *Atascadero* and *Hans* in the Superfund legislation by specifically allowing suits against the states for environmental damage, and that Congress had the power to do so. Although it is not that unusual for Congress to overturn Supreme Court decisions (see Eskridge 1991), it is somewhat shocking that the Energy and Committee took this action without ever mentioning either Supreme Court decision in its report on the legislation.

Flag Burning

Contrast Energy and Commerce's actions with the Judiciary Committee's reactions to the Supreme Court's July 1989 ruling in *Texas v. Johnson* (109 Sup. Ct. 2533 [1989]), which stated that flag burning is protected political speech under the First Amendment. Under intense political pressure from an outraged public, from President Bush, and from many of their colleagues in the House, the Judiciary Committee eventually approved legislation designed to circumvent the Court's decision upholding flag burning as protected speech.[20] Before taking any action, however, the Judiciary Committee held extensive hearings that built a considerable record reflecting the views of diverse legal and constitutional scholars, interest groups, and politicians on all sides of the complex issue (see Biskupic 1989b, 2255–58). Although politically impossible, many members of the Judiciary Committee privately preferred to take no action at all regarding the Court's decision, but the committee felt compelled to pass a statute restricting flag burning, even if that statute might also be declared unconstitutional. The fear was that without such a statute, Congress might approve a Constitutional amendment that would rewrite the First Amendment.

Before acting on legislation dealing with flag burning, the Judiciary Committee's Subcommittee on Civil and Constitutional Rights held four days of exhaustive hearings on the question.[21] The subcommittee heard testimony from twenty-six witnesses, including at least five prominent constitutional law scholars, such as Professors Robert Bork, Walter E. Dellinger, Charles J. Cooper, Charles Fried, and Laurence Tribe. The committee also received statements and letters from another twenty-seven individuals and groups including at least seven additional legal scholars. Of course, the committee also heard from lawyers representing the Bush administration and various interest groups. The hearings were very balanced among those who advocated a Constitutional amendment, those who favored a statutory response to the Court's decision, and those who urged the committee to take no action regarding the Court's ruling. The hearings examined at least three statutory proposals, and thirty-eight proposed Constitutional amendments on the subject, including one submitted by President Bush. Congressman Don Edwards (Democrat-California), the subcommittee chair, set the tone for the careful consideration of the constitutionality of these proposals when he stated in his opening remarks, "All of these proposals will be regarded and treated with careful respect by the subcommittee. . . . In accepting this large responsibility, I'm confident that the members of this subcommittee, all experienced lawyers, will remember that the flag is sturdy, flying proudly throughout every fierce battle of every war and through times of social upheaval. The Constitution, however, is fragile and can be amended by the votes of legislators caught up in the emotional whirlwinds of the moment" (statement of Congressman Don Edwards [Democrat-California], Flag Burning Hearings, 2). Another committee member stated, "I would think even as we respect the flag, we ought to respect the Constitution and the Bill of Rights that is encompassed thereby" (statement of Congressman Robert Kastenmeier [Democrat-Wisconsin], Flag Burning Hearings, 4). Note how the subcommittee chair stressed the fact that lawyers served on the committee and that they would consider questions of constitutionality very carefully.

Although criticized for its lack of haste on the issue (see Biskupic

1989a, 1790), the Judiciary Committee followed its usual pattern of carefully considering all sides of an issue and judiciously weighing all the alternatives before attempting to overturn or modify a federal court decision. One of the Republican members of the committee commented at the hearings, "I would like to commend [the subcommittee chairman] for having hearings on the flag desecration issue with such lightning speed. Never have I been more pleased to see such a quick response by this subcommittee to overturn a Supreme Court decision. After all, this subcommittee is commonly known as the graveyard for legislation which the Democrats don't want to get to the House floor" (statement of Congressman James Sensenbrenner [Republican-Wisconsin], Flag Burning Hearings, 3).

The Judiciary Committee eventually decided to approve a statute to prohibit flag burning.[22] The committee report on the bill included a rather lengthy analysis of the constitutional questions surrounding the proposed legislation. It discussed many relevant decisions from the Supreme Court, and it cited the views of many prominent legal scholars on the question. In many ways, the committee's report reads like a text on constitutional law, and specifically a text on the question of symbolic political speech. It is much different in tone and in substance from the Energy and Commerce Committee's statements on the dial-a-porn issue. It directly addresses the constitutionality issue, arguing in carefully chosen legalistic language that the proposed legislation would meet constitutional muster. The statements of the committee members on the floor of the House during the debates on the legislation also showed a keen sensitivity for the constitutionality of the committee's actions. On this issue, the Judiciary Committee acted like real lawyers, carefully considering all sides of an issue and judiciously weighing all the ramifications before attempting to circumvent or modify the Court's decision. However, the Supreme Court later ruled that this statute was also unconstitutional. (*United States v. Eichman,* 110 Sup. Ct. 2404 [1990]).

In the area of civil rights and antidiscrimination measures, the House Judiciary Committee has taken several critical actions to overrule various Supreme Court decisions. Although Supreme Court rulings on civil rights are usually technically based on statutory interpretation principles, these decisions are certainly "rooted in constitutional soil" (Mikva and Bleich 1991, 745). Between 1982 and 1988, the Judiciary Committee was able to overturn seven Supreme Court decisions in the area of antidiscrimination measures (see Mikva and Bleich 1991, 740). Two of the most famous decisions overruled by Judiciary Committee action include *City of Mobile v. Bolden*, which required proof of intentional discrimination in order to violate the 1965 Voting Rights Act,[23] and *Grove City v. Bell*, which held that the federal prohibition on sex discrimination in federally funded schools applied only to the specific funded program rather than to the entire school.[24] The tone of the committee's report on the *Grove City* legislation is quite telling: "The Supreme Court exercised its proper constitutional role in interpreting one of those [critical] statutes, but the result was an incorrect reading of what Congress intended the law to be. Now, mindful of the implications for other statutes, Congress must enact new legislation to preserve the old."[25] Notice that one would never expect such calm and even-handed language to come from an Energy and Commerce Committee report. Probably the most famous recent instance of the Judiciary Committee taking action to overturn the Supreme Court's civil rights decisions occurred with the enactment of the Civil Rights Act of 1991 (Public Law 102–166). Finally enacted after several years of struggle in Congress and despite President Bush's veto of an earlier version of the bill, this landmark legislation overrules at least nine Supreme Court decisions (see Biskupic 1991a, 3200; Biskupic 1991b, 3463).

However, it is important to note that the Judiciary Committee held exhaustive hearings on all of these bills before it took any action to overturn these civil rights decisions. At these hearings, the committee heard testimony from constitutional scholars, from the legal community, and from the affected interest groups. The committee carefully weighed the constitutional ramifications of all of its actions, and certainly did not act in haste or without due deliberation. Although the Judiciary Committee, and eventually the full Congress, strongly disagreed with the Court's decisions in these cases, the committee did not attack the courts as an institution, nor did it attempt to limit the power of the courts to make further decisions in this area. Although disagreeing with the Court for policy reasons, the Judiciary Committee approached all of these efforts to overrule court decisions with great care and respect for the judicial decision-making process.

A Judiciary staffer attempted to explain how members of both parties on the committee approach constitutional questions in particular and the courts in general: "Just like one can disagree with different schools of thought among legal scholars or other academics, Judiciary members disagree with the courts without attacking the courts as an institution. When Judiciary members disagree with a court's decision, they don't call

for the impeachment of the judge; they file amicus briefs for the appeal."
Another staffer noted, "Even in the flag burning case, the Judiciary Committee took great pains not to attack the courts as an institution. Judiciary members have an elevated and formal concept of separation of
powers. They will correct wrong judicial interpretations of the intent of
Congress without attacking the courts. Judiciary members have a more
elevated intellectual view of court decisions than do other committees."
Or recall how one staffer described the committee: "Judiciary functions
like a body of individuals schooled in both politics and the law."

Generally, the Judiciary Committee reacts to constitutional questions
in a very judicial, courtlike fashion. Although political considerations are
always important, the best constitutional or legal argument almost always wins. Constitutional issues are at the forefront of every action the
committee takes. On the other hand, the Energy and Commerce Committee spends little time worrying about the constitutionality of the legislation it passes, nor does it give legal or constitutional arguments much
weight in its deliberations. Energy and Commerce reacts to its perceptions of raw power politics. In the debate over whether Congress has the
will or the ability to give proper consideration to constitutional matters,
those watching the Energy and Commerce Committee would say no,
whereas those using the Judiciary Committee as a model would say yes.

In one of the most comprehensive works on congressional attempts
to overturn federal court decisions, Eskridge conceptualizes the interactions between Congress and the courts as a dynamic game (Eskridge
1991, 334). With great insight, Eskridge identifies the players in this game
as the Supreme Court, *the relevant congressional committees,* Congress as
a whole, and the President (Eskridge 1991, 334; emphasis added). In the
game, "ultimate statutory policy is set through a sequential process by
which each player—including the Court—tries to impose it policy preferences. The game is a dynamic one because each player is responsive to
the preferences of other players *and* because the preferences of the players change as information is generated and distributed in the game"
(Eskridge 1991, 334). Eskridge's work is very important because he em-
phasizes the role of congressional committees in this continuing dialogue
between Congress and the courts. This chapter's examination of two congressional committees provides additional information for Eskridge's
game theory, because it has shown that congressional committees differ
greatly in their approaches to constitutional questions. If we are to under-

stand fully how Congress interprets the Constitution, we must understand how congressional committees differ in their approaches to this task.

Clearly, the nominal lawyers on the Energy and Commerce Committee do not hesitate to act expediently to circumvent a court decision with which they disagree, even when the decision is based on the First Amendment. In contrast, members of the Judiciary Committee act like real lawyers, carefully considering all sides of an issue, and judiciously weighing all the ramifications before attempting to circumvent or modify the Court's decision.

CHAPTER NINE

Lawyers' Views and Lawyers' Ways: The Institutional Effects of Lawyer-Politicians

Because lawyers numerically dominate American political institutions and the American public-policy-making process, it is essential to explore what general effects this lawyer domination produces for our broader political system. Because our law schools are for the most part uniform in their teaching approaches and techniques, American lawyers are socialized into a common professional legal ideology. This legal ideology then pervades our political institutions, shaping their behavior, and the behavior of these institutions greatly limits our society's political alternatives and choices. According to Scheingold, in the United States "legal values condition perceptions, establish role expectations, provide standards of legitimacy, and account for the institutional patterns of American politics" (Scheingold 1974, xi).

In keeping with the neo-institutional perspective that has guided this book, this chapter will again shift the unit of analysis from the congressional committee to a macroinstitutional level, exploring the broader macroinstitutional effects of an abundance of lawyer-legislators in Congress. In many ways, the behavior of our political institutions is shaped by the background characteristics of their dominant members. As explained by Kim, "Similar social background characteristics [of legislators] provide similar contexts of formative experiences and consequently lead to similar attitudes and behavior" (Kim 1973, 401). Therefore, it becomes apparent that thinking like a lawyer is the link among all politicians in this country with legal training.

The real effect of having so many lawyer-legislators serving in Congress is the fact that the Congress and many state legislatures have adopted lawyers' ways, lawyers' language, as well as lawyers' approaches to problem solving. In many ways, the behavior of American political institutions is shaped by the large group of the institution's members who think like lawyers. As Davidson reminds us, "The demographic composition of Congress doubtless affects its functioning as a social group. Members of the U.S. Congress, like those of other legislative assemblies, are more alike than different. This makes it hard to isolate the effects of differing backgrounds on their behavior. But it should not blind us to the subtle power of background characteristics" (Davidson 1990, 52).

Previous chapters highlighted the fact that lawyers tend to dominate any groups they join (see, e.g., Goldstein 1968; Murrin 1971, 442–43; Scheingold 1974; Seligman 1978; Thielens 1980, 427–29; Olson 1984, 8–11, 21–39; Provine 1986, 90). And institutions dominated by lawyers generally take on lawyerly approaches to decision making and a lawyerly internal political culture. As McCann notes, many of the leaders of the public interest reform movement in the 1960s and 1970s were lawyers, and "this striking number of lawyers in the movement further encouraged mutual intercourse built upon shared vernacular and specialized understanding of the world" (McCann 1986, 34). In other words, these groups adopted lawyers' language and lawyers' ways of problem solving. Like the contemporary reform movements, Congress and many state legislatures have also adopted lawyers' practices, lawyers' habits, and the lawyers' love for proper procedures and processes. As a former dean of the Harvard Law School said, "Lawyers are specialists in the normative ordering of human relations" (Legal Profession 1992, 3).

Because lawyers so dominate the decision-making processes in Congress, even the nonlawyers who serve in that body must learn to adapt to the lawyerlike political environment. As Robert Dahl once said, "To suppose that one can run a complex political system without first learning the trade is, as Plato pointed out, as silly as to suppose that one can be a doctor or a carpenter without prior training" (Schlesinger 1958, 3). Or as Randall Ripley states, "Once in Congress, socializing pressures may impose more uniformity on what was at the outset a reasonably diverse lot of people" (Ripley 1975, 86). In many ways, learning to legislate in Congress involves learning to think like a lawyer, even for the nonlawyer members.

Earlier chapters outlined the essential aspects of thinking like a lawyer. Recall that thinking like a lawyer involves developing keen analytical skills that promote a rationalistic approach to problem solving, with the ability to manipulate facts and rules accurately and quickly. Because of this rule orientation, lawyer-politicians are often preoccupied with proper procedures and processes over more substantive concerns. Another aspect of thinking like a lawyer involves believing in the "myth of rights." Thinking like a lawyer encompasses a narrow, rights-focused view of solutions to broad social problems, which tends to ignore other, less-incrementalist alternatives. Thinking like a lawyer also involves an appreciation of the current social order because both the American legal profession and American political preferences reflect strongly middle-class biases. Lawyer-politicians therefore tend to avoid calls for massive or radical social change. They tend to favor stability and predictability in the society at large. Finally, because lawyers dominate the internal political culture in the U.S. Congress, that institution tends to seek procedure-oriented, rights-oriented, incrementalist solutions to all of society's problems.

From a macroinstitutional point of view, I will in this chapter explore two very different aspects of how Congress as an institution is affected by the social background characteristics of its dominant lawyer members. First, I will examine how the lawyerly approach to decision making affects the substantive policy choices of Congress. Then, I will explore how the internal political culture of Congress is shaped by its controlling lawyer members. This duality is important, because according to Scheingold, it is necessary to explore "the two lives of the law in the United States. The concrete institutional existence of the law is the more familiar; it is readily researched and therefore better understood. Law, however, also has a symbolic life; it resides in the minds of Americans. The symbolic life of the law is often acknowledged but seldom analyzed, and the impact of legal symbols on political life accordingly remains obscure" (Scheingold 1974, xi).

How Lawyers Affect the Substantive
Decisions of Congress

Congress's domination by lawyer-legislators greatly shapes and subsequently limits its substantive legislative decisions. As previously indicated, lawyers tend to be very uncomfortable with calls for massive or radical social change. The legal ideology that guides lawyer-legislators also stresses a procedural, legalistic, rights-oriented approach to social problems. Thus Congress generally embraces a narrow, rights-focused view of solutions to social problems, which tends to ignore other broader approaches (see McCann 1986).

The lawyer-dominated Congress rarely enacts radical legislation. Take, for example, two landmark pieces of legislation enacted in the middle of Ronald Reagan's second term. Although billed as major reform efforts, both the Immigration Control and Reform Act (ICRA) of 1986 and the Tax Reform Act of 1986 were in reality just incrementalist adjustments to existing policies. The Immigration Control and Reform Act (ICRA) sought to restrict illegal immigration by, for the first time, imposing sanctions on employers who hired illegal aliens. Previously, illegal aliens would be deported when discovered, but the law placed no restrictions on the ability of employers to hire these illegal aliens. Under the new law, employers would have to be able to document that all their employees were legally present in this country. ICRA also granted amnesty to illegal immigrants already in the United States for a specified length of time (see Angle 1993, 710).

ICRA is a fine example of Congress's preoccupation with proper procedures and processes. The lawyer-dominated Congress wanted an incrementalist, rights-oriented approach to immigration reform, embracing neither the idea of totally blocking immigration nor of making illegal immigration too easy on either the employers or the illegals themselves. On the issue of immigration, Martha Angle notes that "Congress, at least, cannot make up its mind whether to reach for the drawbridge or spread out a welcome mat" (Angle 1993, 710). Although this legislation was hailed at the time as a major change in our immigration policies, in reality it was merely incrementalist tinkering with the immigration laws. More radical alternatives were never given serious consideration. In fact, in 1990 Congress was forced to enact a new Immigration Control and Reform Act to deal with many of the problems left unsolved by the so-called landmark 1986 legislation (see Biskupic 1990c). ICRA is a clear example of the incrementalist, procedure-oriented approach to problem solving favored by the lawyer members of Congress.

In addition to avoiding any radical changes in society, Congress is often very cautious in enacting even incremental reforms. The Immigration Control and Reform Act took more than five years to pass Congress in its final form, although Congress had considered immigration reform legislation for more than a dozen years before that (Biskupic 1990b, 1006). Congress had also considered various tax-reform proposals for decades before enacting the Tax Reform Act of 1986. As one legal scholar has noted, "The legal approach to problem solving is usually methodical and often slow" (Katsh 1993, xvii).

The Tax Reform Act of 1986 was another piece of legislation that was considered a major reform at the time, but in reality was just more incrementalist tinkering. The act sought to simplify the number of individual tax brackets and to reduce many individual marginal tax rates. It also sought to close many tax loopholes regarding tax deductions, credits, and so on, and it attempted to require all profitable corporations and wealthy individuals to pay a minimum income tax. Finally, it removed many low income individuals from the tax rolls. According to one case study of the legislation:

> Tax reform was, without doubt, a landmark piece of social legislation. It took more than four million impoverished working people off the income tax rolls. It also launched a no-holds-barred attack on tax shelters, a growing blight on the American economic landscape. In addition, it ended the ability of large and profitable corporations to escape paying taxes, which, whatever its economic merits or demerits, had become a galling spectacle to the American people. Most important, reform narrowed the enormous inequities that permeated the existing tax system. (Birnbaum and Murray 1987, 288–89)

Some even claimed that the bill was a historic rewrite of the tax laws. According to Albert Hunt, "The Tax Reform Act of 1986 was the best political story of its time, full of suspense, and with a vivid cast of characters. It marked the most significant achievement of the second Reagan Administration. Indeed, in the history of the Republic, very few pieces of legislation have more profoundly affected so many Americans" (Birnbaum and Murray 1987, xi).

Upon closer examination, however, the act is just another example of the incrementalist approach favored by the lawyer-dominated Congress. This major reform did not close all tax loopholes, nor did it end preferential treatment in the tax code for certain industries. As Birnbaum and Murray explain, "Although they failed to halt the bill, anti-reform lobbyists won significant battles: A coalition of labor groups and insurance companies staved off the effort to tax fringe benefits; life insurers succeeded in preserving the tax-favored status of their most lucrative product, cash-value insurance; oil and gas interests kept their pain to a minimum; and hundreds of individual companies won special transition rules" (Birnbaum and Murray 1987, 287–88). These special transition rules provided special tax treatment to certain industries and even to specific companies. Thus, the final version of the legislation produced much less real reform than its supporters had promised.

Another aspect of the incrementalist nature of the 1986 Tax Reform Act was the fact that it did not in any way redistribute wealth in this country. Even proponents of the legislation were forced to admit that the final product did little to alter the relative financial status of most Americans (Birnbaum and Murray 1987, 289). Its ultimate effect may have been to make the tax code appear to be more fair, but it did little to change the overall amount of taxes collected from middle-class taxpayers.

The Tax Reform Act's tinkering with the tax code did not produce a radical change in U.S. tax policy, but reflected Congress's lawyerly approach to problem solving. The final legislation was certainly incrementalist in nature, because "in terms of its substance, the tax bill was an awkward, hodgepodge attempt at reform, not at all like the pure proposals that so frequently came out of academia or Washington think tanks. It attacked tax breaks with an uneven hand . . . ; it had elements of deceit . . . ; and it certainly was not simple" (Birnbaum and Murray 1987, 289). The lawyerly approach to tax reform produced a bill that made some important changes in the tax code, but it certainly did not radically transform the distribution of wealth in this country or the basic ways the government collects the federal income tax.

It thus becomes clear that the predominance of lawyers in Congress forces a certain preoccupation with procedures and processes upon the institution, as well as a certain narrowness in the way that viable political alternatives are defined in this country. Take for example the Americans with Disabilities Act of 1990 and the Family and Medical Leave Act of 1993. The Americans with Disabilities Act (ADA) extends the 1964 Civil Rights Act's protections against discrimination in employment, public services, and in public accommodations to handicapped individuals. It also requires new buses and trains to be accessible to the disabled, and it requires telecommunications companies to provide various services for disabled persons (see Rovner 1990). Although certainly providing important benefits to disabled persons, the ADA is another good example of the rights-oriented, incrementalist approach favored by the lawyer-dominated Congress.

The ADA will force some changes in how our society treats disabled individuals, perhaps even some major changes, but it did not create massive new rights for the disabled. Instead, it used the incrementalist approach of adding the disabled to those already receiving protection under the Civil Rights Act of 1964. The disabled now have the same procedural rights granted to victims of discrimination based on race, sex, religion, and national origin. The specifics of many of these procedural rights will be left to the courts to define further. The ADA does not radically transform our society, but it does offer an incrementalist, procedure-oriented solution to the enormous problem of protecting the rights of the disabled. The ADA gives disabled persons new procedural avenues for asserting their new rights, but it does not give them new social programs or other less incrementalist alternatives.

The Family and Medical Leave Act of 1993 is another example of Congress's preference for incrementalist, procedurally oriented solutions to society's problems. In an attempt to solve the problem of workers needing to care for new babies and ill family members, the Family and Medical Leave Act of 1993 requires employers with more than fifty employees to grant workers up to twelve weeks of unpaid leave after the birth or adoption of a child or to care for a close family member who is ill (see Zuckman 1993a, 1993b). The problem in part arouse because in the last several decades more and more women have been entering the work force, either as single mothers or as a family's second wage earner. In the Ozzie and Harriett world where women did not pursue careers and one wage earner could support the traditional American family, finding time to care for new children and the ill was not a serious social problem. But as more and more middle-class women found child care to be a serious impediment to keeping their jobs, Congress responded in a lawyerly fashion with a rights-oriented, incrementalist approach.

Although the Family and Medical Leave Act of 1993 was attacked by its opponents as radical government interference with the ability of employers to negotiate such issues with their employees, it is an example of an incrementalist solution to the problem. This law does not go nearly as far as laws in most of Western Europe, whose citizens can enjoy as much as nine or twelve months of *paid* maternity and paternity leave after the birth of a child (see, e.g., Drozdiak 1994, A1). Also, those governments often provide free medical care to their citizens (see Coll 1994, A1). Congress's modest solution to balancing the family's child care needs with the needs of employers pales in comparison, and it took more than eight years for Congress to enact such incrementalist legislation. Obviously, the lawyer-dominated Congress never considered more radical solutions to our nation's child care problems. The incrementalist approach of the American legal ideology took many options off the table in the lawyer-dominated Congress. As Ragsdale reminds us, "American politics is well known for its practicality, give-and-take, compromise, and consensus-seeking. Policymaking in the United States rests not so much on determining the right or wrong approach but rather on adopting an approach on which a majority can agree" (Ragsdale 1993, 131).

The lawyerly approach to social problems in large part forms the foundation for how our political institutions operate and function. As one political commentator has written, "People in other lands look at our politics as essentially devoid of big issues. Our ideologies run from A to B. With few exceptions, we are all democrats and capitalists in both theory and practice" (Harwood 1992, A25). Non-Americans are often struck by how American campaigns and party platforms ignore the major substantive issues of the day. And one should quickly add, in this country our politicians have almost all adopted the liberal legal ideology's approach to problem solving. American politics uses the language of rights and procedures, of processes and rules, producing a government that is preoccupied with a rights-oriented, procedural approach to incrementalist change.

Lawyers Shape the Internal Political Culture of Congress

This next section now turns to an examination of how lawyers dominate the internal political culture in Congress. In order to understand the internal political culture of Congress, one must eventually learn to think like a lawyer, because the institution is so dominated by lawyers' ways and the lawyers' world view. This study then joins a larger body of work that has examined the internal political cultures or environments of Congress and the state legislatures.[1]

Although at times the impact of having so many lawyer-politicians in Congress is readily apparent, more often the effects of having our legislative bodies dominated by lawyer members are more subtle. From their behavioralist perspective, Eulau and Sprague argued that the professions of law and politics converged because the two require similar skills and because these scholars found few differences in the political behavior of lawyers and nonlawyers. According to these scholars, "It may be said that lawyers tend to become politicians more than members of other occupations do, or that politicians tend to choose law rather than another career, *because* law and politics are convergent professions. . . . The more law and politics converge as professions, the less distinct will be the particular kind of contribution that the lawyer-politician is likely to make to politics as a lawyer" (Eulau and Sprague 1964, 144–45).

What Eulau and Sprague and other behavioralist studies of this issue have missed, however, are the very real effects that lawyer-politicians have on the internal political culture of the institution, and on the practices of the institution. Analysis of voting patterns on the floor of either house in Congress will not reveal the true impact that lawyers have on the public-policy process. Instead, one must consider how lawyers' ways and lawyers' views come to dominate the entire internal political culture of the institution. This lawyerly approach greatly shapes the political behavior of the institution and limits the political choices available to its members.

At times the differences between individual lawyer-politicians and their nonlawyer colleagues are rather obvious. For example, during the Senate Judiciary Committee's 1991 hearings on the nomination of Clarence Thomas to the Supreme Court, it became quite apparent to almost all observers that the committee was dominated by lawyer members. The prosecutorial questioning of Anita Hill and Clarence Thomas clearly indicated that the questioners were well trained in the law. The confirmation hearings thus took on the aura of a court, with the senators serving as both prosecutors and as defense attorneys for their respective points of view. The Senate Judiciary Committee members often even objected to the statements and questions of their fellow committee members, as if the committee room had magically been transformed into a courtroom. Recall that one Massachusetts state representative said in an interview with this author, "The difference between lawyer and nonlawyer legislators is very real, but very abstract and very complex." Using both the individual senator and the committee as the units of analysis, the influence of lawyers in Congress in this example becomes readily apparent. But lawyers' ways and lawyers' practices tend to dominate the larger institution as well.

The internal political culture in Congress clearly is shaped by the fact that historically so many lawyers have served and continue to serve in the institution. As Roger Davidson concludes, "One suspects that social scientists may have missed the more subtle effects of legal training upon the legislative process. Oral debates and written reports display lawmakers' intense fascination with legal procedures, concepts, and terminology. And members often reveal a knack for turning substantive issues into matters of legal or procedural detail—perhaps a belated manifestation of legal training" (Davidson 1988, 92). Or as Nelson Polsby has argued about the effects of lawyers in Congress: "Not only do a great many lawyers serve in Congress; the occupational culture of Congress is dominated by lawyers' ways and lawyers' jargon. Committees are organized to elicit information by 'holding hearings' in which 'witnesses' 'testify' and are examined 'on the record' by questions from members and staff. At least one high-ranking staff member, and usually more than one, is a lawyer and is known as 'counsel' to the committee. Hearings make the legislative record that surrounds legislation" (Polsby 1990, 114). Recall the statement by the Supreme Court that "Congress is, after all, not a body of laymen unfamiliar with the commonplaces of our law. . . . Congress is predominately a lawyers' body" (*Callanan v. U.S.*, 364 U.S. 587, 594 [1961]).

Many legal commentators have stressed the lawyer's preoccupation with facts, rules, precedents, processes, and procedures as the key to thinking like a lawyer (see Blaustein and Porter 1954, 98–100; Davidson 1988 and 1990; and Polsby 1990; see also Shklar 1964; Vanderbilt 1979, 9; Provine 1986, 89; Epp 1992b, 704). In addition, recall that thinking like a lawyer involves developing keen analytical skills that promote a rationalistic and analytical approach to problem solving (see Van Loon 1970, 337). Thus in law school, "teachers and texts present the law as *a coherent, comprehensive system of rules* produced by an invisible process of democratic consensus that strips them of all political content" (Abel 1989b, 212; emphasis added). A critic of legal education writes about his own law school experiences: "Craft was rewarded over choice and *process over purpose*" (Auerbach 1976, 276; emphasis added). As a legal historian explains, "The lasting influence of the case method [used in law schools] was to transfer the basis of American legal education *from substance to procedure* and to make the focus of American legal scholarship—or at least legal theory—increasingly one of *process rather than doctrine*" (Stevens 1983, 56; emphasis added).

During the interviews for this project, many respondents alluded to the process and procedural orientation of the lawyer-legislators. Recall that a lawyer member of the House said nonlawyers "have a harder time understanding the process. Lawyers have an easier time understanding what goes on around here." Note the process-oriented language. According to this lawyer-legislator, "Lawyers in Congress have more awareness of the impact of legislative history and the dangers of ex parte communications. Lawyers are more familiar with administrative procedures. Nonlawyers tend to see unnecessary red tape in administrative and judicial procedures. Lawyers understand the necessity of proper procedures."

Other commentators have also argued that the presence of so many lawyers in government produces a concern for procedures and processes over substance. Kemp argues that the dominance of lawyers in federal regulatory agencies produces an "incremental, case-by-case approach to policymaking" (Kemp 1986, 267–68). Davis and Kohlmeier complained that the dominance of lawyers in federal agencies produces a case-by-case approach to problem solving and to policy making (see Davis 1971, Kohlmeier 1969). The institutional effects of the legal ideology are deeply rooted yet subtle. According to Scheingold, "What may make legalism a bit more deluding than some other world views is its covert character. Law professors and lawyers do not believe that they are either encumbered or enlightened by a special view of the world. They simply feel that their legal training has taught them to think logically" (Scheingold 1974, 161).

Congress and other American political institutions seem clearly to reflect the legalistic preoccupation and preferences of their lawyer-legislators. As Nelson and Trubek argue, "A hallmark of American lawyers has been their protean entrepreneurial spirit. They have promoted a distinct, instrumentalist conception of law as a mechanism for meeting changing social conditions" (Nelson and Trubek 1992, 6). And Congress as an institution has therefore adopted this same lawerly approach to problem solving. Thus the lawyer's preference for procedure- and rights-oriented decision-making processes produces a system of government that favors incrementalism and process-oriented debates on the major issues of the day. This procedure-oriented system of government in turn encourages more lawyers to enter the political arena, because lawyers' skills provide great advantages in our decentralized, non–party disciplined, and incrementalist legislative bodies.

Our political institutions have adopted the habits, practices, and language that lawyers learn in law school. Thinking like a lawyer involves accepting a narrow legal ideology, and this legal ideology pervades our American political institutions because these institutions are dominated, and have long been dominated, by lawyer members. This legal ideology is internalized by law students during law school, and stays with the lawyers throughout their professional careers. It then is passed on to our political institutions, where lawyer members dominate. The effects of having so many lawyer-politicians are widespread; the American legal ideology is pervasive in the American public policy process.

Using a neo-institutional approach, this study has helped map the internal political culture of American legislative bodies. Simple roll-call analysis, or even lengthy case studies, will not reveal the true effects of having so many lawyers in Congress. As Brigham argues, we must separate the study of an institution's actions from the study of its practices: "Understanding an institution requires us to be aware that there is a dynamic between what is believed to be possible [i.e., practices] and action in accord with the possibilities" (Brigham 1987, 21). Legislative roll-call analysis and extensive case studies of any legislative issue look only at the actions of individuals in institutions. These behavioralist techniques miss how the practices of an institution limit individual behavior. Again, as Brigham explains it, "When we say that institutions are bodies of practices existing in a society, we mean that there are communities who understand the practices and operate according to them" (Brigham 1987, 25).

On the other hand, from a macroinstitutional perspective, this chapter has attempted to explore how lawyers' ways and lawyers' views pervade the fundamental internal practices of the institution. Those in Congress almost automatically come to understand the practices that the American legal ideology dictates. Also those who deal with Congress understand that the body is dominated by lawyers' ways and lawyers' views, and they react accordingly: the effects of the American legal ideology on our political institutions are self-perpetuating.

In order to understand how our political institutions behave we must understand the pervasive effects of the American legal ideology. According to Scheingold, "The law is real, but it is also a figment of our imaginations. Like all fundamental social institutions it casts a shadow of popular belief that may ultimately be more significant, albeit more difficult to comprehend, than the authorities, rules and penalties that we ordinarily associate with law" (Scheingold 1974, 3). In this country, the law and our political institutions are perpetually intertwined.

By combining the behavioralist's concern with individual-level political action with the traditionalist's concern with the structure of political institutions, this neo-institutional study has shown some of the effects of having so many lawyer-politicians in this country. When discussing the effects of professional backgrounds on the attitudes and behavior of legislators, Roger Davidson and Nelson Polsby were both right when they said that social scientists have probably missed some of the very important effects that legislators' legal training have on the legislative process (see Davidson 1988, 92; Polsby 1990, 114). Philip Duncan is also right when he reminds us that the behavior of many legislators is most affected by their prior experiences in the working world before they were elected (Duncan 1991, 87). And Larson is probably right when stating that one can never really disbar a lawyer, even after they have achieved political office (Larson 1977). It seems almost impossible to separate the legally trained professional lawyer from the rest of the individual, even after that individual has been elected to Congress. It also seems impossible to separate the legally trained individual from the legalistically oriented political institutions in which they dominate.

The numerical dominance of lawyer-politicians in U.S. political institutions produces a government that is preoccupied with the procedurally oriented, incrementalist myth of rights, instead of with broader substantive questions of public policy. Because of their legal training and professional socialization, lawyer-politicians seem much more concerned about following proper procedures and processes, be it in the state legislatures, in committee, or on the floor of the U.S. House of Representatives. American political institutions are, therefore, dominated by the lawyerly approach to problem solving. Because American political institutions are dominated by lawyers and lawyers' ways of thinking, these institutions function in a very legalistic manner. Lawyers are truly the High Priests of American Politics, not only because they numerically dominate our political offices but also because lawyers' ways and lawyers' views determine how our political institutions behave in the broader system of government.

Notes

Chapter 1. The Study of Politics and of Lawyers

1. Students of the professions have long commented on the attempts of professions to colonize new areas of practice. See, for example, Hall 1948; Vollmer and Mills 1966; Moore and Rosenblum 1970; Larson 1977; Nelson, Trubek, and Solomon 1992; Harrington 1994.

2. See, for example, Agger 1956, Schlesinger 1957, Schubert 1960, Morgan 1966, Wasby 1970, and Halper 1970. Morgan's interviews with members of Congress in 1959, for instance, found several differences between lawyer and nonlawyer members, including the fact that nonlawyer members were much more willing to pass Constitutional questions on to the courts than were the lawyer members (Morgan 1966, 156–57, 336, 343–44).

3. For examples of the neo-institutional approach to judicial politics, see R. Smith 1988, 1989; Epstein, Walker, and Dixon 1989; Hall and Brace 1989, 1992; Nardulli 1991; Gates 1991; and Strine 1994. Other recent examples of the neo-institutional approach include McCubbins and Sullivan 1987; Atkinson and Nigol 1989; Cameron, Cover, and Segal 1990; Searing 1991; and Rockman 1994.

4. Fiorina 1990, 444. Several other recent works have used the neo-institutional approach. See McCubbins and Sullivan 1987; Smith 1988, 1989; Hall and Brace 1989, 1992; Atkinson and Nigol 1989; Cameron, Cover, and Segal 1990; Searing 1991; and Gates 1991.

5. Some of the leading discussions of the need for a behavioralist revolution in political science include Easton 1953, 1965, 1967; Dahl 1961; Eulau 1963; and Somit and Tennenhaus 1967.

6. I conducted all the congressional and Massachusetts interviews personally. The Ohio interviews were carried out by a team of interviewers, of which I was part, under the auspices of Professor Samuel (Pat) Patterson of the Ohio State University and the Ohio Legislative Research Project.

The congressional and Massachusetts interviews reported in the following chapters involved an open-ended question format that was designed to elicit the most information in the shortest amount of time. Notes were taken during the interviews, and details were added to the notes immediately following the interviews, which is the technique preferred by Peabody et al. (1990) and is very similar to the system that Kingdon (1989) used to interview members of Congress in his landmark work on congressional voting decisions.

7. The Maryland and North Carolina interviews were conducted by Professor Thomas Little, formerly with the American University and currently with the University of Texas at Arlington. I want to thank Professor Little for generously sharing his data with me.

8. See chapter 7 for more information on why these three committees were included in this study.

    All of the tables in this article reporting congressional data are based on combined responses from members of Congress and from key staff who stated that they could speak for their employers on these issues. This author was able to interview personally forty-two members of Congress who serve on at least one of the three committees, and thirty-five key staff (twenty-three committee staff and twelve key personal staff). When attempting to gain insights into the behavior of congressional committees, it is essential to interview both members and staff. As Aberbach stresses, "Staffers are undoubtedly better informants [than committee members] about many aspects of committee life because their work time is devoted almost entirely to the committee's tasks, and they play a crucial role in most of the decisions made" (Aberbach 1990, 227). All of the congressional staffers interviewed in this study were carefully chosen and were asked background questions concerning their title and responsibilities in the office, the length of time they had worked for their employer, and how regularly they spoke on behalf of their bosses. The staffers were also asked to clearly distinguish their own personal opinions from the opinions of their employers.

    Other scholars have also used staff responses as surrogates for the responses of the members of Congress themselves (see, e.g., Bullock 1976; Hall 1987; Smith and Deering 1984, 1990; Aberbach 1990). For further discussions of the importance and role of congressional staff, see Kofmehl 1962; Dexter 1969a; Fox and Hammond 1977; Malbin 1979; Salisbury and Shepsle 1981a, 1981b; Jewell and Patterson 1986, 157; and Bisnow 1990.

9.   None of the tables in this study report indicators of statistical significance, such as chi-squared, because such indicators require properly drawn probability samples. Not all the interviewees for this study were chosen by probability sampling. Also, statistical significance is largely a function of sample size and expected frequencies in the tables' cells. Because of the relatively small samples used in this project and the relatively large number of cells per table, almost every table has cells with expected frequencies below five. When tables have cells with expected frequencies below five, the chi-squared test reports distorted significance values (see Blalock 1979). Thus, to preserve the clarity of the reporting of this particular data, no statistical significance values are listed for any of the tables in this project.

Chapter 2. Socialization into the Legal Profession

1.   See the *Law & Society Review*'s special issue on law and ideology (vol. 22, no. 4, 1988), edited by members of the Amherst Seminar (John Brigham, Patricia Ewick, Christine Harrington, Sally Merry, Brinkley Messick, Austin Sarat, Susan Silbey, Adalaide Villmoare, and Barbara Yngvesson). According to the editors, "Ideology is a difficult term to discipline" (629).

2.   Not only do lawyers come to share a common legal ideology, but law professors are amazingly uniform in their backgrounds and approach to the law. As one law professor notes, "Law teachers [in the United States] come from similar educational backgrounds, teach similar courses, and employ the same range of teaching styles" (Bryden 1984, 500).

3.   For example, Turow quotes one psychiatrist as saying, "I have never seen more manifest anxieties in a group of persons under 'normal' circumstances than is visible in first-year law students" (Turow 1977, 154). Other studies have also found substantial increases in psychological distress among law students, even greater than those found in medical students (see, e.g., Benjamin et al. 1986). According to a legal sociologist, "Numerous empirical studies have found heightened symptoms of obsessive-compulsion, anxiety, depression, and hostility, beginning in the first six months of law school and persisting throughout the entire three years, even influencing the first two years of practice" (Abel 1989b, 213).

4.   Wice identifies three aspects of the legal personality: "The first is a strong ego, often manifested by an extroverted demeanor; second is an aggressive or contentious disposition; and third is a skeptical or cynical nature" (Wice 1991, 51). Wice also argues that lawyers as a whole are subject to

the occupational hazard of becoming arrogant, deceitful, and punitive (Wice 1991, 51). Along these lines, a Chicago Law School dean is quoted as saying to the wives of the then almost all-male first-year law class, "Your husbands are going to change; their personalities will become more aggressive, more hostile, more precise and more impatient" (Riley 1976, 90). Others have found that law school produces cynical individuals who are inclined to be skeptical and overly cautious (see Eron and Redmount 1957). One study even explores attitudinal changes and stress among working-class law students as they adjust their self-image to being a lawyer from an elite law school (Granfield 1991).

5. According to Scheingold, "Neither legal education nor professional experience are likely to alter the politics of lawyers in the more obvious ways. Party preferences will not change, nor will radicals be changed into conservatives. The influence is more subtle. It is the influence of ideology on behavior" (Scheingold 1974, 151).

6. Many advocates of the Critical Legal Studies movement believe that legal education should teach students how to transform society, but instead it only teaches students how to become cogs in the wheel of the status quo (see, e.g., Harvard Law Review, *Essays on Critical Legal Studies,* 1986; Kelman 1987; Hutchinson 1989; Kairys 1990). For example, Duncan argues that learning how to think like a lawyer often produces a strong probusiness and pro-establishment bias in law students. According to this law professor, "Law schools are intensely political places despite the fact that the modern law school seems intellectually unpretentious, barren of theoretical ambition or practical vision of what social life might be. The trade-school mentality, the endless attention to trees at the expense of forests, the alternating grimness and chumminess of focus on the limited task at hand, all these are only a part of what is going on. The other part is ideological training for willing service in the hierarchies of the corporate welfare state" (Duncan 1990, 38). Kahlenberg's (1992) recent memoirs of his experiences as a student at Harvard Law School bemoan the fact that so many Harvard students arrive at law school with public interest or public service careers in mind, but after graduation they overwhelmingly pursue individual financial rewards at large, corporate law firms.

Chapter 3. Lawyers, Lawyers Everywhere

1. For further debate on this issue, see the articles surrounding Epp (1992a), Sander (1992), and Magee (1992b) in the fall 1992 issue of *Law & Social Inquiry.* The debate was also continued in the letters to the editor section of the *Wall Street Journal* (see Epp 1992c, Magee 1992c).

2. In the Truman through Carter years, 40 percent of the cabinet-level posts were filled by persons with law degrees, 26 percent of the Reagan cabinet-level appointees were lawyers, and 40 percent of those in Bush cabinet-level posts had law degrees. In contrast, 67 percent of the original Clinton cabinet-level appointees had law degrees. See Dye 1993, 693–95.

3. Weaver notes, "The style of [a model lawyer in the Antitrust Division] and the attitudes his colleagues seem to find admirable are apparent. He is proud of having been trained to be an aggressive, bright but nonintellectual, technically competent, two-fisted prosecutor. He conceives of himself as an adversary, and he wants to win; but more than that, he wants to win by virtue of his character—his persuasiveness, hard work, canniness, and charm—as much as by force of his intellect. He conceives of his practice of law as an active and combative occupation rather than as a calling that at times resembles academic scholarship in the thoroughness of its research and its concern with clarity and distinctions" (Weaver 1977, 52).

4. See, for example, Dexter 1969b, Lowi 1979, Walker 1983, Schlozman and Tierney 1986, Birnbaum and Murray 1987, Berry 1989, H. Smith 1989, Salisbury 1990, Wolpe 1990, Petracca 1992, and Birnbaum 1992. According to one student of interest groups, American interest groups "lobby Congress and participate in election campaigns; litigate; raise a great deal of money and mobilize grassroots support for candidates and political issues; lobby the White House; form coalitions with other organizations; interact with other interest representatives and the bureaucracy; and mobilize mass publics" (Petracca 1992, 18).

5. See Provine 1986 for a discussion of the small number of nonlawyer judges in the United States. Provine argues that we need more nonlawyer judges in this country, in part because "America never made the judiciary into a true specialist's domain, requiring technical training geared to the responsibilities of office. Practitioners whose education is for law practice, not adjudication, are our 'professional' judges" (Provine 1986, 22–23).

Chapter 4. The Prevalence of Lawyer-Legislators in the United States

1. See, for example, Hurst 1950; Eulau and Sprague 1964, 15; Galanter 1974, 1983; Engle 1984; Olson 1984, xi–xv; Greenhouse 1989; and Polsby 1990, 114–16. In fact, in 1977 one journalist declared that the United States was in the midst of "one of the great unnoticed revolutions in U.S. history: the ever-increasing willingness, even eagerness, on the part of elected officials and private citizens to let the courts settle matters that

once were settled by legislatures, executives, parents, teachers—or chance" (Footlick 1977, 44).

2. See Murrin 1971, 430; and Haber 1991. Provine, however, argues that lawyers became important in colonial times "less because of their legal training than because of their wealth and social influence" (Provine 1986, 6).

3. Take, for example, neo-Nazi David Duke, who ran on the Republican ticket for both the U.S. Senate and the governorship of Louisiana over the strong objections of the national party organization. Or Lyndon Larouche, who has perennially run for president as a Democrat against the wishes of the party establishment. These candidates could never have appeared on party lists in countries where the party organization has control over candidate selection and nomination (see Epstein 1981, Ranney 1981).

Chapter 5. Are Lawyers Really Different from Nonlawyers?

1. See chapter 1 for more details on these interviews.

Chapter 6. How Lawyer-Legislators and Nonlawyer-Legislators View the Courts

1. One of the most comprehensive studies of this question can be found in Eskridge 1991. Other very good examinations of this question are Mikva and Bleich 1991, and Solimine and Walker 1992. See also Herrmann 1992.

    Other works have also focused on this question. For example, see Nichols 1935 (series of essays on a proposal for setting up routine procedures for Congress to overturn court decisions, much like the standard process used for overriding presidential vetoes), Morgan 1966 (an extensive and highly informative series of seven case studies dealing with congressional attempts to overturn court decisions between 1935 and 1965, based in large part on interview data), Murphy 1962, Pritchett 1961, Murphy and Pritchett 1961, and Schubert 1960 (all argue that the courts are protected from attacks by Congress because of their prestige and because of their special role in our system of government). Stumpf 1965 (attempted to test several hypotheses, including the role of prestige in protecting the courts from congressional attacks). Note: Harvard Law Review (1958) (examined congressional reversal of court decisions in the 1945–57 period), and Note: Georgia Law Review (1979). Lytle 1963, Breckenridge 1970, Fisher 1986, and Lee 1988 (all looked at specific issue areas where Congress and the Supreme Court have disagreed). Nagel 1969 (tested the hypothesis that historical periods of conflict between Congress and the courts are cyclical in nature). Culp 1929, Elliott 1958, Halper 1970, and Handberg and Hill 1980 (all have looked at general attempts by Congress to curb the jurisdiction of the Supreme Court). See also Schmidhauser et al. 1972 (analysis of floor roll-call votes from 1945 to 1968 found that there were some weak regional, partisan, and ideological patterns that might help explain differences in how individual members of Congress approach court decisions).

2. Other works of this type include Nichols 1935, Beaney and Beiser 1964, Becker 1969, Breckenridge 1970, Johnson and Canon 1984, and Mikva and Bleich 1991.

3. For comparison purposes, in a similar study only 19 percent of the members of the Ohio legislature said that they paid little or no attention to the decisions of the Ohio Supreme Court. See Felice and Kilwein 1993.

4. *Boston Globe.* Five-day Spotlight investigative series entitled *Half-Day Justice.* Daily front-page articles from Sunday, 23 Sept. to Thursday, 27 Sept. 1990.

Chapter 7. Are All Lawyer-Legislators the Same? A Typology

1. From 1978 until 1989, almost half of the newly elected members of the U.S. House of Representatives had previously served in state legislatures before coming to Congress (Canon 1990, xi; see also Eulau and Sprague 1964, 80; Davidson and Oleszek 1990, 63; Rosenthal 1981, 54–57).

2. Sugarman, Paul R. *In the Matter of the Boston Municipal Court, Department of the Trial Court.* Report of the Special Master and Commissioner to the Massachusetts Supreme Judicial Court, issued 4 February 1991.

3. According to the Sugarman report, "The Boston Municipal Court (BMC) is isolated from the rest of the trial court and has developed its own culture. Although the Court has district court jurisdiction, it does not operate as part of the district court system. There is no rotation of judges into or out of the BMC, and its systems and procedures have become inbred. There is an absence of coordinated management existing between the BMC and the district court system. Personnel, budget and other resource needs are not well coordinated with other parts of the judicial system. A management system that results in the court becoming a more integral part of the trial court system is required" (Sugarman 1991, 254).

Chapter 8. Lawyers on Congressional Committees

1. See, generally, Fenno 1973; and Smith and Deering 1984, 1990. The Smith and Deering 1984 edition is a better description of the political cultures of individual congressional committees; the 1990 edition is better for describing the workings of the committee system as a whole.

2. On the general differences among congressional committees on these points, see Fenno 1973; Smith and Deering 1984, 1990; Hinckley 1975, 1988; and Price 1979, 1985.

3. See Eskridge 1991, 341–43; Solimine and Walker 1992, 442–45, 449. For example, 58 percent of the Supreme Court decisions overridden by Congress during the 100th Congress (1987–88) were under the jurisdiction of the House Judiciary Committee (Eskridge 1991, 342). Of the twenty-three Supreme Court decisions that Mikva and Bleich (1991, 748 n. 103) identify as being overturned by Congress in the period between 1982 and 1986, eleven were overturned by Judiciary Committee action.

4. See, for example, the *Telephone Decency Act of 1987,* 100th Cong., 1st sess., 1987, H. Rept. 1786, introduced by Congressman Thomas J. Bliley (Republican-Virginia).

5. See, generally, *Telephone Decency Act of 1987: Hearings on H.R. 1786 Before the Subcomm. on Telecommunications and Finance of the House Comm. on Energy and Commerce,* 100th Cong., 1st sess., 30 Sept. 1987 (hereafter cited as Dial-a-Porn Hearings). See also *Carlin Communications, Inc. v. FCC,* 749 F.2d 113, 2d Cir. (1984), and *Carlin Communications, Inc. v. FCC,* 787 F2d. 846, 2d Cir. (1986).

6. *Sable Communications of California v. FCC,* 109 Sup. Ct. 2829 (1989).

7. Although eventually stripped from the 1989 budget reconciliation bill, Public Law 101-239, the committee's provision did finally get enacted into law as an amendment to the Fiscal Year 1990 Appropriations bill for the Departments of Labor, Health and Human Services, and Education, *Related Agencies Appropriations Act of 1990,* Public Law 101-166, 101st Cong., 1st Sess. See *Congressional Quarterly Almanac,* 1989, at 15–16.

8. The *Related Agencies Appropriations Act of 1990,* H. Rept. 3566.

9. See testimony of Barry W. Lynn, legislative counsel, American Civil Liberties Union, Dial-a-Porn Hearings, 29, supra note 5; testimony of Diane S. Killory, general counsel, Federal Communications Commission, Dial-a-Porn Hearings, 189, supra note 5; testimony of Brent Ward, U.S. attorney, District of Utah, Dial-a-Porn Hearings, 216–17, supra note 5; and letter from Timothy B. Dyk, attorney with the Washington, D.C., law

firm of Wilmer, Cutler and Pickering, Dial-a-Porn Hearings, 265, supra
note 5.

10. *Elementary and Secondary Education Conference Report to Accompany
H.R. 5,* 100th Cong., 2d sess., 13 Apr. 1988, H. Rept. 100-567.

11. Although eventually stripped from the 1989 budget reconciliation bill,
Public Law 101-239, the committee's provision did finally get enacted
into law as an amendment to the Fiscal Year 1990 Appropriations bill for
the Departments of Labor, Health and Human Services, and Education,
Public Law 101-166, 101st Cong., 1st Sess. See *Congressional Quarterly
Almanac,* 1989, 15–16.

12. Report on the *Budget Reconciliation Act of 1989,* 101st Cong., 1st sess.,
585, 1989, H. Rept. 101-247.

13. *Additional Views on Energy and Commerce Budget Reconciliation (Title
IV, Subtitle H) by the Honorable Howard C. Nielson (Republican-Utah),*
H. Rept. 101-247, 844.

14. The *Related Agencies Appropriations Act of 1990.*

15. See *American Information Enterprises, Inc. v. Thornburgh,* 742 F. Supp.
1255, S.D. N.Y. (1990).

16. See *Information Providers' Coalition for Defense of the First Amendment
v. FCC,* 928 F.2d. 866, 9th Cir. (1991); *Dial Information Services Corp.
of New York v. Thornburgh,* F.2d., 2d Cir. (1991).

17. *Superfund Amendments and Reauthorization Act of 1986,* H. Rept. 99-
253, pt. 1, 99th Cong., 1st Sess, 1985.

18. *Superfund Amendments and Reauthorization Act of 1986,* Public Law
99-499, sec. 101(b)(1), 100 Stat. 1613, 1615 (1986) (codified at 42
U.S.C. sec. 9601[20][d] [1988]).

19. *Rehabilitation Act Amendments of 1986,* Public Law 99-506, sec. 1003,
100 Stat. 1807, 1845 (1986) (codified at 42 U.S.C. sec. 2000d-7 [1988]).
For a discussion of the similarities of these two legislative enactments, see
Mikva and Bleich 1991, 743–44.

20. *Flag Protection Act of 1989,* Public Law 101-31, 103 Stat. 77 (codified at
18 U.S.C. sec. 700). This statute was eventually declared unconstitutional
by the Supreme Court in *United States v. Eichman,* 110 Sup. Ct. 2404
(1990).

21. *Statutory and Constitutional Responses to the Supreme Court Decision in
Texas v. Johnson: Hearings Before the Subcommittee on Civil and Constitutional Rights of the House Committee on the Judiciary,* 100th Cong.,
1st sess., 13, 18, 19, 20 July 1989.

22. See *Report on the Flag Protection Act of 1989,* 101st Cong., 1st sess., 1989, H. Rept. 101-231.
23. *City of Mobile v. Bolden,* 446 U.S. 55 (1980), overruled by *Voting Rights Act Amendments of 1982,* Public Law 97-205, 96 Stat. 131 (codified at 42 U.S.C. sec. 1973 [1988]).
24. *Grove City v. Bell,* 465 U.S. 555 (1984), overruled by *Civil Rights Restoration Act of 1987,* Public Law 100-259, 102 Stat. 28 (1987) (codified at 20 U.S.C. secs. 1681, 1687, 1688; 29 U.S.C. secs. 706, 794; 42 U.S.C. secs. 2000d-4a, 6107 [1988]).
25. *Civil Rights Restoration Act of 1987,* pt. 1.

Chapter 9. Lawyers' Views and Lawyers' Ways: The Institutional Effects of Lawyer-Politicians

1. For example, Fenno's (1966, 1973, 1978) classic studies looked at how the goals and motivations of congresspersons affect the broader institution. Caldeira and Patterson have written a series of articles on friendship and respect patterns in state legislatures (see Patterson 1959; Caldeira and Patterson 1987, 1988; Caldeira, Clark and Patterson 1993). Ross Baker's work, *House and Senate* (1989), examined differences in the internal political cultures of the two federal houses, often through interviews with those who had served in both bodies. The first edition of Smith and Deering's (1984) work on congressional committees also provided some very useful mapping of the internal political cultures of various committees. Unfortunately, their second edition (1990) is less useful for this purpose. Shepsle (1978) and Cooper (1970) looked at how Congress's rules and practices affected committee assignments within the institution. Asher's (1973, 1974, and 1975) studies explored how congressional norms change over time, as well as how these norms affect the internal political culture of the institution. These studies were largely based on earlier studies by White (1956), Huitt (1957 and 1961), and Matthews (1959 and 1960). Finally, Hedlund (1985) has prepared a review essay collecting other studies of organization attributes of American legislatures.

References

Abbott, Andrew. 1988. *The System of Professions: An Essay on the Division of Labor in Society.* Chicago: Univ. of Chicago Press.

Abel, Richard L. 1980. Redirecting Social Studies of Law. *Law & Society Review* 14:805–829.

———. 1988a. Lawyers in the Civil Law World. In *Lawyers in Society: The Civil Law World,* ed. Abel and Lewis.

———. 1988b. United States: The Contradictions of Professionalism. In *Lawyers in Society: The Common Law World,* ed. Abel and Lewis.

———. 1989a. Comparative Sociology of Legal Professions. In *Lawyers in Society: Comparative Theories,* ed. Abel and Lewis.

———. 1989b. *American Lawyers.* New York: Oxford Univ. Press.

Abel, Richard L., and Phililp S. C. Lewis, eds. 1988a. *Lawyers in Society: The Common Law World.* Berkeley and Los Angeles: Univ. of California Press.

———. 1988b. *Lawyers in Society: The Civil Law World.* Berkeley and Los Angeles: Univ. of California Press.

———. 1989. *Lawyers in Society: Comparative Theories.* Berkeley and Los Angeles: Univ. of California Press.

Aberbach, Joel D. 1990. *Keeping a Watchful Eye: The Politics of Congressional Oversight.* Washington, D.C.: Brookings Institution.

Abourezk, James. 1977. Lawyers as Politicians. *Trial,* Apr. 1977, 24–25.

Abraham, Henry J. 1985. *Justices and Presidents: A Political History of Appointments to the Supreme Court.* 2d ed. Oxford: Oxford Univ. Press.

Adamany, David. 1991. The Supreme Court. In *American Courts,* ed. Gates and Johnson.

Adler, Madeline, and Jewel Bellush. 1979. Lawyers and the Legislature: Something New in New York. *National Civil Review* 68:244–246, 278.

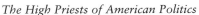

Agger, Robert E. 1956. Lawyers in Politics: The Starting Point for a New Research Program. *Temple Law Review* 29:434–452.

Agresto, John. 1984. *The Supreme Court and Constitutional Democracy.* Ithaca, N.Y.: Cornell Univ. Press.

Allen, Robert S. 1949. *Our Sovereign State.* New York: Vanguard.

Almond, Gabriel A. 1990. *A Discipline Divided: Schools and Sects in Political Science.* Newbury Park, Calif.: Sage Publications.

Alston, Chuck. 1990. As Clean-Air Bill Took Off, So Did PAC Donations. *Congressional Quarterly Weekly Report,* 17 Mar. 1990, 811–817.

———. 1991. Lobbyists Storm Capitol Hill, Clash Over Banking Bill. *Congressional Quarterly Weekly Report,* 24 Aug. 1991, 2313–2318.

Alter, Jonathan. 1991. And Now, Cuomo Agonistes. *Newsweek,* 9 Dec. 1991, 33.

———. 1992. The Language of Honesty. *Newsweek,* 20 Apr. 1992, 26.

An Address to Law Students. 1870. *Albany Law Journal* 1:165.

Angle, Martha. 1993. Immigration's Bridges Have Ups and Downs. *Congressional Quarterly Weekly Report,* 20 Mar. 1993, 710.

Aron, Nan. 1989. *Liberty and Justice for All: Public Interest Law in the 1980s and Beyond.* Boulder, Colo.: Westview Press.

Arron, Deborah L. 1991. *Running from the Law: Why Good Lawyers are Getting Out of the Legal Profession.* Berkeley, Calif.: Ten Speed Press.

Arthurs, Harry W., Richard Weisman, and Frederick H. Zemans. 1989. Canadian Lawyers: A Peculiar Professionalism. In *Lawyers in Society: The Common Law World,* ed. Abel and Lewis.

Asher, Herbert B. 1973. The Learning of Legislative Norms. *American Political Science Review* 67:499–513.

———. 1974. Committees and Norms of Specialization. *Annals of the American Academy of Political and Social Science* 411:63–74.

———. 1975. The Changing Status of the Freshman Representative. In *Congress in Change: Evolution and Reform,* edited by Norman J. Ornstein. New York: Praeger.

Atkins, Burton. 1987. A Cross-National Perspective on the Structuring of Trial Court Outputs: The Case of the English High Court. In *Comparative Judicial Systems: Challenging Frontiers in Conceptual and Empirical Analysis,* edited by John R. Schmidhauser. London: Butterworths.

Atkinson, Michael M., and Robert A. Nigol. 1989. Selecting Policy Instruments: Neo-Institutional and Rational Choice Interpretations of Automobile Insurance in Ontario. *Canadian Journal of Political Science* 22:107–135.

Aucoin, Don. 1992. Weld Tallies Vote's Bad News. *Boston Globe,* 5 Nov. 1992, pp. 33, 39.

Auerbach, Jerold S. 1976. *Unequal Justice: Lawyers and Social Change in Modern America.* New York: Oxford Univ. Press.

———. 1984. Legal Education and Some of Its Discontents. *Journal of Legal Education* 34:52.

Baker, John R. 1990. Exploring the "Missing Link": Political Culture as an Explanation of the Occupational Status and Diversity of State Legislators in Thirty States. *Western Political Quarterly* 43:597–611.

Baker, Nancy V. 1992. *Conflicting Loyalties: Law and Politics in the Attorney General's Office, 1789–1990.* Lawrence: Univ. of Kansas Press.

Baker, Ross K. 1989. *House and Senate.* New York: W. W. Norton.

Barber, James David. 1965. *The Lawmakers: Recruitment and Adaptation to Legislative Life.* New Haven, Conn.: Yale Univ. Press.

Barber, Kathleen L. 1971. Ohio Judicial Elections: Nonpartisan Premises with Partisan Results. *Ohio State Law Journal* 23:726–789.

———. 1984. Judicial Politics in Ohio. In *Government and Politics in Ohio,* edited by Carl Lieberman. Lanham, Md.: Univ. Press of America.

Barber, Sotirios. 1984. *On What the Constitution Means.* Baltimore, Md.: Johns Hopkins Univ. Press.

Bardach, Eugene, and Robert A. Kagan. 1982. *Going by the Book: The Problem of Regulatory Unreasonableness.* Philadelphia: Temple Univ. Press.

Barnhizer, David R. 1988. Prophets, Priests, and Power Brokers: Three Fundamental Roles of Judges and Legal Scholars in America. *University of Pittsburgh Law Review* 50:127–196.

Barone, Michael, and Grant Ujifusa, eds. 1985. *The Almanac of American Politics 1986.* Washington, D.C.: National Journal.

Bartee, Alice Fleetwood. 1984. *Cases Lost, Causes Won: The Supreme Court and the Judicial Process.* New York: St. Martin's Press.

Bartlett, Katharine T., and Rosanne Kennedy, eds. 1991. *Feminist Legal Theory: Readings in Law and Gender.* Boulder, Colo.: Westview Press.

Baum, Lawrence. 1988. Voters' Information in Judicial Elections: The 1986 Contest for the Ohio Supreme Court. *Kentucky Law Review* 77:645–670.

———. 1989a. *The Supreme Court.* 3d. ed. Washington, D.C.: Congressional Quarterly.

———. 1989b. State Supreme Courts: Activism and Accountability. In *The State of the States,* edited by Carl E. Van Horn. Washington, D.C.: Congressional Quarterly.

———. 1990. *American Courts: Process and Policy.* 2d. ed. Boston: Houghton Mifflin.

———. 1991. Courts and Policy Innovation. In *American Courts,* ed. Gates and Johnson.

Bay, Christian. 1992. Politics and Pseudopolitics: A Critical Evaluation of Some Behavioral Literature. In *Approaches to the Study of Politics*, edited by Bernard Susser. New York: Macmillan.

Bazar, Beth. 1987. *State Legislators' Occupations: A Decade of Change*. Denver: National Conference of State Legislatures.

Beaney, William M., and Edward N. Beiser. 1964. Prayer and Politics: The Impact of Engel and Schempp on the Political Process. *Journal of Public Law* 13:475–503.

Beard, Charles A. 1986. *An Economic Interpretation of the Constitution of the United States*. 1935. Reprint, New York: Free Press.

Becker, Howard S., Blanche Geer, Everett C. Hughes, and Anselm L. Strauss. 1961. *Boys in White: Student Culture in Medical School*. Chicago: Univ. of Chicago Press.

Becker, Theodore L., ed. 1969. *The Impact of Supreme Court Decisions*. London: Oxford Univ. Press.

Belenky, Mary Field. 1986. *Women's Ways of Knowing: The Development of Self, Voice, and the Mind*. New York: Basic Books.

Bell, Charles G. 1986. Legislatures, Interest Groups and Lobbyists: The Link Beyond the District. *Journal of State Government* (Spring): 12–18.

Bell, Derrick A., Jr. 1976. Serving Two Masters: Integration Ideals and Client Interests in School Desegregation Litigation. *Yale Law Journal* 85:470–516.

Bell, Susan J. 1989. *Full Disclosure: Do You Really Want to Be a Lawyer?* For the Young Lawyers Division of the American Bar Association. Princeton, N.J.: Peterson's Guides.

Benjamin, G. Andrew H., Alfred Kaszniak, Bruce Sales, and Stephen B. Shanfield. 1986. The Role of Legal Education in Producing Psychological Distress among Law Students and Lawyers. *American Bar Foundation Research Journal* (Spring): 225–52.

Bentley, Arthur. 1908. *The Process of Government*. Chicago: Univ. of Chicago Press.

Berg, Larry L., Justin J. Green, and John R. Schmidhauser. 1974. Judicial Regime Stability and the Voting Behavior of Lawyer Legislators. *Notre Dame Lawyer* 49:1012–1022.

Berry, Jeffrey M. 1977. *Lobbying for the People*. Princeton, N.J.: Princeton Univ. Press.

———. 1989. *The Interest Group Society*. 2d ed. Glenview, Ill.: Scott, Foresman; Little, Brown.

Bickel, Alexander M. 1962. *The Least Dangerous Branch: The Supreme Court at the Bar of Politics*. Indianapolis: Bobbs-Merrill.

Birnbaum, Jeffrey H. 1992. *The Lobbyists: How Influence Peddlers Get Their Way in Washington.* New York: Random House.

Birnbaum, Jeffrey H., and Alan S. Murray. 1987. *Showdown at Gucci Gulch: Lawmakers, Lobbyists, and the Unlikely Triumph of Tax Reform.* New York: Vintage Books.

Biskupic, Joan. 1989a. Critics of Flag-Burning Ruling Debate Next Step to Take. *Congressional Quarterly Weekly Report,* 15 July 1989, 1790.

———. 1989b. Scholars Split Over Response to Flag-Burning Ruling. *Congressional Quarterly Weekly Report,* 2 Sept. 1989, 2255–58.

———. 1990a. Politics, Debates of the '90s Fuel Scramble for Power. *Congressional Quarterly Weekly Report,* 8 Dec. 1990, 4079–81.

———. 1990b. Employer Sanctions Draw Fire after Report on Job Bias. *Congressional Quarterly Weekly Report,* 31 Mar. 1990, 1005–6.

———. 1990c. Sizable Boost in Immigration OK'd in Compromise Bill. *Congressional Quarterly Weekly Report,* 27 Oct. 1990, 3608–9.

———. 1991a. Senate Passes Sweeping Measure to Overturn Court Rulings. *Congressional Quarterly Weekly Report,* 2 Nov. 1991, 3200–3204.

———. 1991b. Bush Signs Anti-Job Bias Bill Amid Furor Over Preferences. *Congressional Quarterly Weekly Report,* 23 Nov. 1991, 3463.

Bisnow, Mark. 1990. *In the Shadow of the Dome: Chronicles of a Capitol Hill Aide.* New York: William Morrow.

Black, Jonathan, ed. 1971. *Radical Lawyers.* New York: Avon.

Blalock, Hubert M., Jr. 1979. *Social Statistics.* Rev. 2d ed. New York: McGraw-Hill.

Blaustein, Albert P., and Charles O. Porter. 1954. *The American Lawyer: A Summary of the Survey of the Legal Profession.* Chicago: Univ. of Chicago Press.

Blondel, Jean. 1973. *Comparative Legislatures.* Englewood Cliffs, N.J.: Prentice-Hall.

Bluhm, William. 1965. *Theories of the Political System.* Englewood Cliffs, N.J.: Prentice-Hall.

Bogue, Allan G., Jerome M. Clubb, Carroll R. McKibbin, and Santa A. Traugott. 1976. Members of the House of Representatives and the Process of Modernization, 1789–1960. *Journal of American History* 63:275–302.

Boigeol, Anne. 1988. The French Bar: The Difficulties of Unifying a Divided Profession. In *Lawyers in Society: The Civil Law World,* ed. Abel and Lewis.

Bonsignore, John J. 1979. Law School: Caught in the Paradigmatic Squeeze. In *Before the Law,* edited by John J. Bonsignore. 2d ed. Boston: Houghton Mifflin.

Boston Globe. 1990. *Half-Day Justice* (series), 23–27 Sept. 1990.

Bourdieu, Pierre. 1987. The Force of Law: Toward a Sociology of the Juridical Field. *Hastings Law Journal* 38:805–853.

Boyle, Elizabeth Heger, and Marc Ventresca. 1994. Professional Practices and the New Institutionalism: Legal Matters and Matters of Course. Paper presented at the annual meeting of the Law and Society Association, 1994, Phoenix.

Breckenridge, Adam Carlyle. 1970. *Congress Against the Court.* Lincoln: Univ. of Nebraska Press.

Brigham, John. 1987. *The Cult of the Court.* Philadelphia: Temple Univ. Press.

Brill, Harry. The Uses and Abuses of Legal Assistance. *Public Interest* 31:38–55.

Brown, Esther Lucile. 1948. *Lawyers, Law Schools, and the Public Service.* New York: Russell Sage Foundation.

Browning, Rufus P. 1968. The Inter-Action of Personality and Political System in Decisions to Run for Office: Some Data and a Simulation Technique. *Journal of Social Issues* 24:93–110.

Brownson, Ann L. 1989. *1989 Congressional Staff Directory.* Mount Vernon, Va.: Staff Directories.

Bryce, James. 1911. *The American Commonwealth.* New York: Macmillan.

Bryden, David. 1984. What Do Law Students Learn? A Pilot Study. *Journal of Legal Education* 34:479–506.

Bucher, Rue, and Joan Stelling. 1977. *Becoming Professional.* Beverly Hills, Calif.: Sage Publications.

Bullock, Charles S. 1976. Motivations for U.S. Congressional Committee Preferences: Freshmen of the 92d Congress. *Legislative Studies Quarterly* 1:201–212.

Cahn, Edgar S., and Jean Camper Cahn. 1970. Power to the People or the Profession? The Public Interest in Public Interest Law. *Yale Law Journal* 79:1005–1048.

Cain, Maureen. 1994. The Symbol Traders. In *Lawyers in a Postmodern World,* ed. Cain and Harrington.

Cain, Maureen, and Christine B. Harrington, eds. 1994. *Lawyers in a Postmodern World: Translation and Transgression.* New York: New York Univ. Press.

Caldeira, Gregory A. 1983. On the Reputation of State Supreme Courts. *Political Behavior* 5:83–108.

———. 1988. Legal Precedent: Structures of Communication between State Supreme Courts. *Social Networks* 10:29–55.

Caldeira, Gregory A., and Samuel C. Patterson. 1987. Political Friendship in the Legislature. *Journal of Politics* 49:953–975.

———. 1988. Contours of Friendship and Respect in the Legislature. *American Politics Quarterly* 16:466–485.

Caldeira, Gregory A., John A. Clark, and Samuel C. Patterson. 1993. Political Respect in the Legislature. *Legislative Studies Quarterly* 18:3–28.

Calhoun, Emily. 1984. Thinking Like a Lawyer. *Journal of Legal Education* 34:507–514.

Cameron, Charles M., Albert D. Cover, and Jeffrey A. Segal. 1990. Senate Voting on Supreme Court Nominees: A Neoinstitutional Model. *American Political Science Review* 84:525–534.

Canon, Bradley C., and Lawrence Baum. 1981. Patterns of Adoption of Tort Law Innovations: An Application of Diffusion Theory to Judicial Doctrines. *American Political Science Review* 75:975–987.

Canon, David T. 1989. Political Amateurism in the United States Congress. In *Congress Reconsidered,* edited by Lawrence C. Dodd and Bruce I. Oppenheimer. 4th ed. Washington, D.C.: Congressional Quarterly Press.

———. 1990. *Actors, Athletes, and Astronauts: Political Amateurs in the United States Congress.* Chicago: Univ. of Chicago Press.

Caplan, Lincoln. 1987. *The Tenth Justice: The Solicitor General and the Rule of Law.* New York: Vintage Books.

Carlin, Jerome. 1962. *Lawyers on Their Own: A Study of Individual Practitioners in Chicago.* New Brunswick, N.J.: Rutgers Univ. Press.

———. 1966. *Lawyers' Ethics: A Survey of the New York Bar.* New York: Russell Sage Foundation.

Carpinello, George. 1989. Should Practicing Lawyers be Legislators? *Hastings Law Journal* 41:87–129.

———. 1991. Should Lawyers be Legislators? *State Government News,* May 1991, 12–14.

Carrington, Paul, and James Conley. 1977. The Alienation of Law Students. *Michigan Law Review* 75:887–899.

Carter, Lief H. 1988. *Reason in Law,* 3d ed. New York: HarperCollins.

Casper, Jonathan D. 1972. *Lawyers before the Warren Court: Civil Liberties and Civil Rights 1957–66.* Urbana: Univ. of Illinois Press.

———. 1976. The Supreme Court and National Policy Making. *American Political Science Review* 70:50–63.

Center for Leadership Studies. 1991. *The Massachusetts Political Almanac.* Centerville, Mass.: Center for Leadership Studies.

Characteristics of Congress. 1991. *Congressional Quarterly Weekly Report,* 12 Jan. 1991, 118–30.

Clausen, Aage R. 1973. *How Congressmen Decide: A Policy Focus.* New York: St. Martin's Press.

Clayton, Cornell W. 1992. *The Politics of Justice: The Attorney General and the Making of Legal Policy.* Armonk, N.Y.: M. E. Sharpe.

Clifford, Clark, with Richard Holbrooke. 1991. *Counsel to the President: A Memoir.* New York: Random House.

Cohen, Michael. 1969. Lawyers and Political Careers. *Law & Society Review* 3:563–574.

Cohodas, Nadine. 1980. Kennedy and Rodino: How Two Very Different Chairmen Run Their Panels. *Congressional Quarterly Weekly Report,* 2 Feb. 1980, 267–271.

———. 1982. House Judiciary Committee Bottles Up the Tough Ones. *Congressional Quarterly Weekly Report,* 17 Apr. 1982, 863–64.

———. 1986. House Judiciary Looks to Post-Rodino Era. *Congressional Quarterly Weekly Report,* 7 June 1986, 1307.

Coll, Steve. 1994. Economic Change, Social Upheaval. *Washington Post,* 7 Aug. 1994, p. A1.

Congressional Quarterly, Inc. 1983. *How Congress Works.* Washington, D.C.: Congressional Quarterly.

———. 1989. *Congressional Quarterly Almanac, 1988.* Washington, D.C.: Congressional Quarterly.

———. 1990. *Congressional Quarterly Almanac, 1989.* Washington, D.C.: Congressional Quarterly.

Cooper, Joseph. 1970. *The Origins of the Standing Committees and the Development of the Modern House.* Houston: Rice Univ. Press.

Cooper, Joseph, and David W. Brady. 1981. Toward a Diachronic Analysis of Congress. *American Political Science Review* 75:988–1006.

Cortner, Richard C. 1968. Strategies and Tactics of Litigants in Constitutional Cases. *Journal of Public Law* 17:287–307.

Council of State Governments. 1988. *The Book of States, 1988–89.* Vol. 27. Lexington, Ky.: Council of State Governments.

Craig, Barbara Hinkson. 1988. *Chadha: The Story of an Epic Constitutional Struggle.* New York: Oxford Univ. Press.

Cranford, John R. 1992. Characteristics of Congress—The New Class: More Diverse, Less Lawyerly, Younger. *Congressional Quarterly Weekly Report,* 7 Nov. 1992, 7–10.

Cronin, Thomas E. 1989. *Direct Democracy.* Cambridge: Harvard Univ. Press.

Cross, Frank B. 1992. The First Thing We Do, Let's Kill All the Economists: An Empirical Evaluation of the Effect of Lawyers on the United States Economy and Political System. *Texas Law Review* 70:645–683.

Crossette, Barbara. 1991. Castro, in Talk with U.S. Senator, Calls Fuel Crisis "the Biggest Test." *New York Times,* 5 Dec. 1991, p. A14.

Culp, Maurice S. 1929. A Survey of the Proposals to Limit or Deny the Power of Judicial Review by the Supreme Court of the United States. *Indiana Law Journal* 4:386–474.

Curran, Barbara A. 1986. American Lawyers in the 1980's: A Profession in Transition. *Law & Society Review* 20:19–52.

Dahl, Robert A. 1958. Decision-making in a Democracy: The Supreme Court as a National Policy-Maker. *Journal of Public Law,* 279–295.

———. 1961. The Behavioral Approach in Political Science: Epitaph for a Monument to a Successful Protest. *American Political Science Review* 55:763–772.

———. 1984. *Modern Political Analysis.* 4th ed. Englewood Cliffs, N.J.: Prentice-Hall.

Dalton, Cornelius, John Wirkkala, and Anne Thomas. 1984. *Leading the Way: A History of the Massachusetts General Court 1629–1980.* Boston: Office of the Massachusetts Secretary of State.

D'Amato, Anthony. 1987. The Decline and Fall of Law Teaching in the Age of Student Consumerism. *Journal of Legal Education* 37:461–494.

Daniels, Stephen. 1988. A Tangled Tale: Studying State Supreme Courts. *Law & Society Review* 22:833–868.

Darcy, R., Susan Welch, and Janet Clark. 1987. *Women, Elections, and Representation.* New York: Longman.

Darrell, Norris, and Paul A. Wolkin. 1980. The American Law Institute. *New York State Bar Journal* 52:99–101, 139–143.

Davidson, Roger H. 1988. What Judges Ought to Know about Lawmaking in Congress. In *Judges and Legislators,* ed. Katzmann.

———. 1990. Congress as a Representative Institution. In *The U.S. Congress and the German Bundestag: Comparisons of Democratic Processes,* edited by Uwe Thaysen, Roger H. Davidson, and Robert Gerald Livingston. Boulder, Colo.: Westview Press.

———. 1991. Legislative Research: Mirror of a Discipline. In *Political Science: Looking to the Future.* Vol. 4, *American Institutions,* edited by William Crotty. Evanston, Ill.: Northwestern Univ. Press.

Davidson, Roger H., and Walter J. Oleszek. 1990. *Congress and Its Members.* 3d ed. Washington, D.C.: Congressional Quarterly.

Davidson, Roger H., Walter J. Oleszek, and Thomas Kephart. 1988. One Bill, Many Committees: Multiple Referrals in the U.S. House of Representatives. *Legislative Studies Quarterly* 13:3–28.

Davis, Kenneth Culp. 1971. *Discretionary Justice: A Preliminary Inquiry.* Champaign: Univ. of Illinois Press.

Denvir, John. 1976. Towards A Political Theory of Public Interest Litigation. *North Carolina Law Review* 54:1133–1160.

Derge, David R. 1959. The Lawyer as Decision-Maker in the American State Legislature. *Journal of Politics* 21:408–433.

———. 1962. The Lawyer in the Indiana General Assembly. *Midwest Journal of Political Science* 6:19–53.

Dexter, Lewis Anthony. 1969a. *The Sociology and Politics of Congress.* Chicago: Rand McNally.

———. 1969b. *How Organizations Are Represented in Washington.* Indianapolis: Bobbs-Merrill.

Di Palma, Giuseppe, and Maurizio Cotta. 1986. Cadres, Peones, and Entrepreneurs: Professional Identities in a Divided Parliament. In *Parliaments and Parliamentarians in Democratic Politics,* edited by Ezra N. Suleiman. New York: Holmes and Meier.

Dodd, Lawrence C., and Bruce I. Oppenheimer. 1989. Consolidating Power in the House: The Rise of a New Oligarchy. In *Congress Reconsidered,* edited by Lawrence C. Dodd and Bruce I. Oppenheimer. 4th ed. Washington, D.C.: Congressional Quarterly.

Dowd, Maureen. 1993. A Lawyerly Search for a Good Lawyer. *New York Times,* 13 Feb. 1993, p. 8.

Drozdiak, William. 1994. New Global Markets Mean Grim Trade-Offs: Europe's Welfare Benefits Hang in Balance. *Washington Post,* 8 Aug. 1994, p. A1.

Duncan, Phil, ed. 1989. *Politics in America 1990: The 101st Congress.* Washington, D.C.: Congressional Quarterly.

———. 1991a. Freshman Class Adds Some Spice to Congressional Blend. *Congressional Quarterly Weekly Report,* 12 Jan. 1991, 87–117.

———. 1991b. *Politics in America 1992.* Washington, D.C.: Congressional Quarterly.

———. 1993. *Politics in America 1994: The 103rd Congress.* Washington, D.C.: Congressional Quarterly.

Durkheim, Emile. 1933. *The Division of Labor in Society.* New York: Free Press.

———. 1957. *Professional Ethics and Civil Responsibility.* London: Routledge and Kegan Paul.

Dye, Thomas R. 1993. The Friends of Bill and Hillary. *PS: Political Science and Politics* 26:693–695.

Dyer, James A. 1976. Do Lawyers Vote Differently? A Study of Voting on No-Fault Insurance. *Journal of Politics* 38:452–456.

Easton, David. 1953. *The Political System.* New York: A. A. Knopf.

———. 1965. *A Framework for Political Analysis.* Englewood Cliffs, N.J.: Prentice-Hall.

———. 1967. The Current Meaning of Behavioralism. In *Contemporary Political Analysis,* edited by James C. Charlesworth. New York: Free Press.

———. 1992. Tenets of Post-Behavioralism. In *Approaches to the Study of Politics,* edited by Bernard Susser. New York: Macmillan.

Edinger, Lewis J., and Donald D. Searing. 1967. Social Background in Elite Analysis: A Methodological Inquiry. *American Political Science Review* 61:428–445.

Edman, Irwin, ed. 1956. *The Philosophy of Plato.* Translation by Benjamin Jowett. New York: Modern Library.

Ehrenhalt, Alan, ed. 1983. *Politics in America: Members of Congress in Washington and At Home.* Washington, D.C.: Congressional Quarterly.

———. 1991. *The United States of Ambition: Politicians, Power, and the Pursuit of Office.* New York: Random House.

Ehrmann, Henry W. 1976. *Comparative Legal Cultures.* Englewood Cliffs, N.J.: Prentice-Hall.

Elazar, Daniel. 1966. *American Federalism: A View from the States.* New York: Crowell.

Elkins, James R. 1985. Rites of Passage: Law Students Telling Their Lives. *Journal of Legal Education* 35:27–55.

Elliott, Shelden D. 1958. Court-Curbing Proposals in Congress. *Notre Dame Lawyer* 33:597–616.

Emmert, Craig F. 1992. An Integrated Case-Related Model of Judicial Decision Making: Explaining State Supreme Court Decisions in Judicial Review Cases. *Journal of Politics* 54:543–552.

Emmert, Craig F., and Carol Ann Traut. 1992. State Supreme Courts, State Constitutions, and Judicial Policymaking. *Justice System Journal* 16:37–48.

Engle, David M. 1984. The Oven-Bird's Song: Insiders, Outsiders, and Personal Injuries in an American Community. *Law & Society Review* 18:549–579.

Engstrom, Richard L., and Patrick F. O'Connor. 1980. Lawyer-Legislators and Support for State Legislative Reform. *Journal of Politics* 42:267–276.

Epp, Charles R. 1992a. Do Lawyers Impair Economic Growth? *Law & Social Inquiry* 17:585–623.

———. 1992b. Toward New Research on Lawyers and the Economy. *Law & Social Inquiry* 17:695–711.

———. 1992c. Let's Not Kill All the Lawyers. *Wall Street Journal,* 9 July 1992, p. A13.

Epstein, Lee. 1985. *Conservatives in Court.* Knoxville: Univ. of Tennessee Press.

———. 1991. Courts and Interest Groups. In *American Courts,* ed. Gates and Johnson.

Epstein, Lee, Thomas G. Walker, and William J. Dixon. 1989. The Supreme Court and Criminal Justice Disputes: A Neo-Institutional Perspective. *American Journal of Political Science* 33:825–841.

Epstein, Leon. 1967. *Political Parties in Western Democracies.* New York: Praeger.

———. 1981. Political Parties: Organization. In *Democracy at the Polls: A Comparative Study of Competitive National Elections,* edited by David E. Butler, Howard Rae Penniman, and Austin Ranney. Washington, D.C.: American Enterprise Institute.

Erlanger, Howard S. 1978a. Lawyers and Neighborhood Legal Services: Social Backgrounds and the Impetus for Reform. *Law & Society Review* 12:253–274.

———. 1978b. Young Lawyers and Work in the Public Interest. *American Bar Foundation Research Journal* (Winter): 83–104.

Erlanger, Howard S., and Douglas A. Klegon. 1978. Socialization Effects of Professional School: The Law School Experience and Student Orientations to Public Interest Concerns. *Law & Society Review* 12:11–35.

Eron, Leonard, and Robert Redmount. 1957. The Effect of Legal Education on Attitudes. *Journal of Legal Education* 9:431–443.

Eskridge, William N. 1991. Overriding Supreme Court Statutory Interpretation Decisions. *Yale Law Journal* 101:331–455.

Eulau, Heinz. 1963. *The Behavioral Persuasion in Politics.* New York: Random House.

Eulau, Heinz, and John D. Sprague. 1964. *Lawyers in Politics: A Study in Professional Convergence.* Indianapolis: Bobbs-Merrill.

Feinman, Jay M. 1985. The Failure of Legal Education and the Promise of CLS. *Cardozo Law Review* 6:739–764.

Felice, John D., and John C. Kilwein. 1993. High Court- Legislative Relations: A View from the Ohio Statehouse. *Judicature* 77:42–48.

Fenno, Richard F. 1966. *The Power of the Purse: Appropriations Politics in Congress.* Boston: Little, Brown.

———. 1973. *Congressmen in Committees.* Boston: Little Brown.

———. 1978. *Home Style: House Members in Their Districts.* Boston: Little Brown.

Fineman, Howard, and Ann McDaniel. 1992. Bush: What Bounce? *Newsweek,* 31 Aug. 1992, 26–31.

Fino, Susan P. 1987. *The Role of State Supreme Courts in the New Judicial Federalism.* Westport, Conn.: Greenwood Press.

Fiorina, Morris P. 1989. *Congress: Keystone of the Washington Establishment.* 2d ed. New Haven, Conn.: Yale Univ. Press.

———. 1990. The Presidency and Congress: An Electoral Connection? In *The Presidency and the Political System,* edited by Michael Nelson. 3d ed. Washington, D.C.: Congressional Quarterly.

Fisher, Louis. 1985. Constitutional Interpretation by Members of Congress. *North Carolina Law Review* 63:707–747.

———. 1986. Congress and the Fourth Amendment. *Georgia Law Review* 21:107–170.

———. 1987. *The Politics of Shared Power: Congress and the Executive.* 2d ed. Washington, D.C.: Congressional Quarterly.

———. 1988. *Constitutional Dialogues: Interpretation as Political Process.* Princeton, N.J.: Princeton Univ. Press.

Footlick, Jerrold K. 1977. Too Much Law? *Newsweek,* 10 Jan. 1977, 44.

Fowler, Linda L., and Robert D. McClure. 1989. *Political Ambition: Who Decides to Run for Congress.* New Haven, Conn.: Yale Univ. Press.

Fox, Harrison W., Jr., and Susan Webb Hammond. 1977. *Congressional Staff: The Invisible Force in American Lawmaking.* New York: Free Press.

France, Steve. 1991. Public Interest Law: Retooling for the '90s. *Washington Lawyer,* May–June 1991, 40–45.

Freeman, Donald M. 1991. The Making of a Discipline. In *Political Science: Looking to the Future.* Vol. 1, *The Theory and Practice of Political Science,* edited by William Crotty. Evanston, Ill.: Northwestern Univ. Press.

Friedenthal, Jack H. 1991. Too Many Lawyers? *George Washington University Magazine,* Nov. 1991, 2.

Friedman, Lawrence M. 1985. *A History of American Law.* 2d ed. New York: Simon and Schuster.

———. 1989. Lawyers in Cross-Cultural Perspective. In *Lawyers in Society: Comparative Theories,* ed. Abel and Lewis.

Friedman, Lawrence M., Robert A. Kagan, Bliss Cartwright, and Stanton Wheeler. 1981. State Supreme Courts: A Century of Style and Citation. *Stanford Law Review* 33:773–818.

Frisby, Michael K. 1992. Kerrey Voices Hope of a South Dakota Turnaround. *Boston Globe,* 24 Feb. 1992, p. 10.

Galanter, Marc. 1974. Why the "Haves" Come Out Ahead. *Law & Society Review* 9:95–160.

———. 1983. Reading the Landscape of Disputes: What We Know and Don't Know (and Think We Know) about Our Allegedly Contentious and Litigious Society. *UCLA Law Review* 31:4–71.

Galanter, Marc, and Thomas Palay. 1991. *The Tournament of Lawyers: The Growth and Transformation of the Big Law Firm.* Chicago: Univ. of Chicago Press.

Gandhi, J. S. 1988. Past and Present: A Sociological Portrait of the Indian Legal Profession. In *Lawyers in Society: The Common Law World,* ed. Abel and Lewis.

Gates, John B. 1991. Theory, Methods, and the New Institutionalism in Judicial Research. In *American Courts,* ed. Gates and Johnson.

Gates, John B., and Charles A. Johnson, eds. *The American Courts: A Critical Assessment.* Washington, D.C.: Congressional Quarterly.

Gee, E. C., and Donald Jackson. 1977. Bridging the Gap: Legal Education and Lawyer Competency. *Brigham Young University Law Review* 1977:695–990.

Geison, Gerald L., ed. 1983. *Professions and Professional Ideologies in America.* Chapel Hill: Univ. of North Carolina Press.

Gertzog, Irwin. 1984. *Congressional Women: Their Recruitment, Treatment, and Behavior.* New York: Praeger.

Gilligan, Carol. 1982. *In a Different Voice: Psychological Theory and Women's Development.* Cambridge: Harvard Univ. Press.

Glendon, Mary Ann, Michael W. Gordon, and Christopher Osakwe. 1982. *Comparative Legal Traditions in a Nutshell.* St. Paul, Minnesota: West Publishing.

Glick, Henry R. 1971. *Supreme Courts in State Politics.* New York: Basic Books.

———. 1982. Supreme Courts in State Judicial Administration. In *State Supreme Courts,* ed. Porter and Tarr.

———. 1991. Policy Making and State Supreme Courts. In *American Courts,* ed. Gates and Johnson.

Gold, David. 1961. Lawyers in Politics: An Empirical Exploration of Biographical Data on State Legislators. *Pacific Sociological Review* 4:84–86.

Goldfarb, Ronald. 1968. A Fifth Estate—Washington Lawyers. *New York Times Magazine,* 5 May 1968, 37–58.

Goldfarb, Sally F., and Edward A. Adams. 1991. *Inside the Law Schools.* 5th ed. New York: Plume Books.

Goldman, Sheldon. 1985. Reaganizing the Judiciary: The First Term Appointments. *Judicature* 68:313–16.

———. 1987. Reagan's Second Term Appointments. *Judicature* 70:326–339.

———. 1991. Federal Judicial Recruitment. In *American Courts,* ed. Gates and Johnson.

Goldstein, Abraham. S. 1968. The Unfulfilled Promise of Legal Education. In *Law in Changing America,* edited by Geoffrey G. Hazzard. Englewood Cliffs, N.J.: Prentice-Hall.

Goodman, Ellen. 1992. Where are the Women? *Boston Globe,* 9 Feb. 1992, p. 19.

Goodwin, George. 1970. *The Little Legislatures.* Amherst: Univ. of Massachusetts Press.

Gordon, James Wice. 1980. Lawyers in Politics: Mid-Nineteenth Century Kentucky as a Case Study. Ph.D. diss., Univ. of Kentucky, Lexington.

Goulden, Joseph C. 1971. *The Super-Lawyers: The Small and Powerful World of the Great Washington Law Firms.* New York: Weybright and Talley.

Granfield, Robert. 1991. Making It by Faking It: Working-Class Students in an Elite Academic Environment. *Journal of Contemporary Ethnography* 20:331–51.

Green, Justin J., John R. Schmidhauser, Larry L Berg, and David Brady. 1973. Lawyers in Congress: A New Look at Some Old Assumptions. *Western Political Quarterly* 26:440–52.

Green, Mark J. 1978. *The Other Government: The Unseen Power of Washington Lawyers.* New York: W. W. Norton.

Greenhouse, Carol J. 1988. Courting Difference: Issues of Interpretation and Comparison in the Study of Legal Ideologies. *Law & Society Review* 22:688–707.

———. 1989. Interpreting American Litigiousness. In *History and Power in the Study of Law: New Directions in Legal Anthropology,* edited by June Starr and Jane F. Collier. Ithaca, N.Y.: Cornell Univ. Press.

Greider, William. 1987. *Secrets of the Temple: How the Federal Reserve Runs the Country.* New York: Simon and Schuster.

Haber, Samuel. 1991. *The Quest for Authority and Honor in the American Professions, 1750–1900.* Chicago: Univ. of Chicago Press.

Hacker, Andrew. 1964. Are There Too Many Lawyers in Congress? *New York Times Magazine,* 5 Jan. 1964, 14, 74–75.

Hager, George. 1994. House Approves Energy Panel's Bill on Insurance "Redlining." *Congressional Quarterly Weekly Report,* 23 July 1994, 2010.

Hain, Paul L., and James E. Pierson. 1975. Lawyers and Politics Revisited: Structural Advantage of Lawyer-Politicians. *American Journal of Political Science* 19:41–52.

Hall, Melinda Gann, and Paul Brace. 1989. Order in the Courts: A Neo-Institutional Approach to Judicial Consensus. *Western Political Quarterly* 42:391–407.

———. 1992. Toward an Integrated Model of Judicial Voting Behavior. *American Politics Quarterly* 20:147–168.

Hall Oswald. 1948. The Stages of a Medical Career. *Journal of Sociology* 53:327–336.

Hall, Richard L. 1987. Participation and Purpose in Committee Decision Making. *American Political Science Review* 81:105–127.

Hall, Richard L., and Bernard Grofman. 1990. The Committee Assignment Process and the Conditional Nature of Committee Bias. *American Political Science Review* 84:1149–1166.

Halliday, Terence Charles. 1979. *Parameters of Professional Influence: Policies and Policies of the Chicago Bar Association, 1945–70*. Ph.D. diss., Department of Sociology, Univ. of Chicago.

———. 1987. *Beyond Monopoly: Lawyers, State Crises, and Professional Empowerment*. Chicago: Univ. of Chicago Press.

Halper, Thomas. 1970. Supreme Court Response to Congressional Threats: Strategy and Tactics. *Drake Law Review* 19:292–325.

Halpern, Charles R. 1976. The Public Interest Bar: An Audit. In *Verdicts on Lawyers*, ed. Nader and Green.

Halpern, Charles R., and John M. Cunningham. 1971. Reflections on the New Public Interest Law: Theory and Practice at the Center for Law and Social Policy. *Georgetown Law Journal* 59:1095–1126.

Halpern, Stephen C., and Charles M. Lamb, eds. 1982. *Supreme Court Activism and Restraint*. Lexington, Mass.: Lexington Books.

Hand, Samuel B., William C. Hill, and Lyman J. Gould. 1981. The New England Judiciary: Courts in Transition. In *New England Politics*, edited by Josephine F. Milburn and Victoria Schuck. Cambridge, Mass.: Schenkman Publishing.

Handberg, Roger, and Harold F. Hill Jr. 1980. Court Curbing, Court Reversals, and Judicial Review: The Supreme Court Versus Congress. *Law & Society Review* 14:309–22.

Handler, Joel F. 1978. *Social Movements and the Legal System: A Theory of Law Reform and Social Change*. New York: Academic Press.

Handler, Joel, Ellen J. Hollingsworth, and Howard S. Erlanger. 1978. *Lawyers and the Pursuit of Legal Rights*. New York: Academic Press.

Harrigan, John J. 1993. *Empty Dreams, Empty Promises: Class and Bias in American Politics*. New York: Macmillan.

Harringer, Katy J. 1992. *Independent Justice: The Federal Special Prosecutor in American Politics*. Lawrence: Univ. of Kansas Press.

Harrington, Christine B. 1985. *Shadow Justice: The Ideology and Institutionalization of Alternatives to Court*. Westport, Conn.: Greenwood Press.

———. 1994. Outlining a Theory of Legal Practice. In *Lawyers in a Postmodern World,* ed. Cain and Harrington.

Harrington, Christine B., and Sally Engle Merry. 1988. Ideological Production: The Making of Community Mediation. *Law & Society Review* 22:709–735.

Hartz, Louis. 1955. *The Liberal Tradition in America.* New York: Harvest.

Harvard Law Review, 1986. *Critical Legal Studies: Articles, Notes, and Book Reviews Selected from the Pages of the Harvard Law Review.* Cambridge: Harvard Law Review Association.

Harwood, Richard. 1992. Along the Cultural Divide. *Washington Post,* 21 Aug. 1992, p. A25.

Hedegaard, James. 1979. The Impact of Legal Education: An In- Depth Examination of Career Relevant Interests, Attitudes and Personality Traits among First-Year Law Students. *American Bar Foundation Research Journal* (1979): 793–868.

Hedlund, Ronald D. 1985. Organizational Attributes of Legislative Institutions: Structure, Rules, Norms, Resources. In *Handbook of Legislative Research,* edited by Gerhard Loewenberg, Samuel C. Patterson, and Malcolm E. Jewell. Cambridge: Harvard Univ. Press.

Hegland, Kenney. 1983. *Introduction to the Study and Practice of Law.* West's Law in a Nutshell Series. Minneapolis: West Publishing.

Heinz, John P., and Edward O. Laumann. 1978. The Legal Profession: Client Interests, Professional Roles, and Social Hierarchies. *Michigan Law Review* 76:1111–1142.

———. 1982. *Chicago Lawyers: The Social Structure of the Bar.* New York: Russell Sage Foundation.

Heiser, Peter E. 1982. The Opinion Writing Function of Attorneys General. *Idaho Law Review* 18:9–41.

Henschen, Beth M. 1983. Congressional Response to the Statutory Interpretations of the Supreme Court. *American Politics Quarterly* 11:441–459.

———. 1985. Judicial Use of Legislative History and Intent in Statutory Interpretation. *Legislative Studies Quarterly* 10:353–371.

Henschen, Beth M., and Edward I. Sidlow. 1989. The Supreme Court and the Congressional Agenda-Setting Process. *Journal of Law & Politics* 5:685–724.

Herrmann, Mark E. 1992. Note: Looking Down from the Hill: Factors Determining the Success of Congressional Efforts to Reverse Supreme Court Interpretations of the Constitution, *William and Mary Law Review* 33:543–610.

Hibbing, John R. 1991. *Congressional Careers: Contours of Life in the U.S. House of Representatives.* Chapel Hill: Univ. of North Carolina Press.

Himmelstein, James. 1978. Reassessing Law Schooling. *New York University Law Review* 53:514–60.

Hinckley, Barbara. 1975. Policy Content, Committee Membership, and Behavior. *American Journal of Political Science* 19:543–557.

———. 1988. *Stability and Change in Congress.* 4th ed. New York: Harper and Row.

Hojnacki, Marie, and Lawrence Baum. 1992. "New Style" Judicial Campaigns and the Voters: Economic Issues and Union Members in Ohio. *Western Political Quarterly* 45:921–48.

Horowitz, Donald L. 1977a. *The Jurocracy: Government Lawyers, Agency Programs, and Judicial Decisions.* Lexington, Mass.: Lexington Books.

———. 1977b. *The Courts and Social Policy.* Washington, D.C.: Brookings Institution.

———. 1977c. The Courts as Guardians of the Public Interest. *Public Administration Review* (Mar./Apr.): 148–54.

House Democrats Kill Proposal for Contribution Loophole. 1990. *Congressional Quarterly Weekly Report,* 8 Dec. 1990, 4068.

Hughes, Everett Cherrington. 1958. *Men and Their Work.* Westport, Conn.: Greenwood Press.

Huitt, Ralph K. 1957. The Morse Committee Assignment Controversy: A Study in Senate Norms. *American Political Science Review* 51:313–329.

———. 1961. The Outsider in the Senate: An Alternative Role. *American Political Science Review* 55:566–575.

Hunt, Alan. 1985. The Ideology of Law: Advances and Problems in Recent Applications of the Concept of Ideology to the Analysis of Law. *Law & Society Review* 19:11–37.

Hurst, James Willard. 1950. *The Growth of American Law: The Law Makers.* Boston: Little Brown.

———. 1956. *Law and the Condition of Freedom in the Nineteenth-Century United States.* Madison: Univ. of Wisconsin Press.

Hutchinson, Allan, ed. 1989. *Critical Legal Studies.* Totowa, N.J.: Rowman and Littlefield.

Hyneman, Charles S. 1959. Who Makes Our Laws? In *Legislative Behavior,* edited by John C. Wahlke and Heinz Eulau. Glencoe, Ill.: Free Press.

Idelson, Holly. 1993a. Baird's Wrenching Withdrawal Mars the Inaugural Week. *Congressional Quarterly Weekly Report,* 23 Jan. 1993, 179–81.

———. 1993b. Still More Baby Sitter Problems in Attorney General Search. *Congressional Quarterly Weekly Report,* 6 Feb. 1993, 271.

Insurance Information Institute. 1979. *Occupational Profile of State Legislatures.* New York: Insurance Information Institute.

Irons, Peter. 1982. *The New Deal Lawyers.* Princeton, N.J.: Princeton Univ. Press.

Isaak, Alan C. 1985. *Scope and Methods of Political Science: An Introduction to the Methodology of Political Inquiry.* 4th ed. Homewood, Ill.: Dorsey Press.

Jacob, Herbert. 1978. *Justice in America: Courts, Lawyers, and the Judicial Process.* 3d ed. Boston: Little Brown.

———. 1990. Courts: The Least Visible Branch. In *Politics in the American States: A Comparative Analysis,* edited by Virginia Gray, Herbert Jacob, and Robert B. Albritton. 5th ed. Glenview, Ill.: Scott, Foresman; Little Brown.

Jacobson, Gary C. 1992. *The Politics of Congressional Elections.* 3d ed. New York: HarperCollins.

Jacobson, Gary C., and Samuel Kernell. 1983. *Strategy and Choice in Congressional Elections.* 2d ed. New Haven, Conn.: Yale Univ. Press.

Jenrette, John W. 1977. The Care and Feeding of a U.S. Congressman. *Trial,* Apr. 1977, 27–28.

Jewell, Malcolm E. 1982. *Representation in State Legislatures.* Lexington: Univ. of Kentucky Press.

Jewell, Malcolm E., and Samuel C. Patterson. 1986. *The Legislative Process in the United States.* 4th ed. New York: Random House.

Johnson, Charles A., and Bradley C. Canon. 1984. *Judicial Policies: Implementation and Impact.* Washington, D.C.: Congressional Quarterly.

Johnson, Earl. 1974. *Justice and Reform.* New York: Russell Sage Foundation.

Jones, Harry W. 1952. Bill Drafting Services in Congress and the State Legislatures. *Harvard Law Review* 65:441–451.

Kaack, Heino. 1990. The Social Composition of the Bundestag. In *The U.S. Congress and the German Bundestag: Comparisons of Democratic Processes,* edited by Uwe Thaysen, Roger H. Davidson, and Robert Gerald Livingston. Boulder, Colo.: Westview Press.

Kagan, Robert A., and Robert E. Rosen. 1985. On the Social Significance of Large Law Firm Practice. *Stanford Law Review* 37:399–443.

Kahlenberg, Richard. 1992. *Broken Contract: A Memoir of Harvard Law School.* New York: Hill and Wang.

Kairys, David, ed. 1990. *The Politics of Law: A Progressive Critique.* 2d ed. New York: Pantheon Books.

Kammerer, Gladys M. 1951. The Record of Congress in Committee Staffing. *American Political Science Review* 95:1126–1136.

Karst, Kenneth. 1984. Women's Constitution. *Duke Law Journal* (1984): 447–508.

Kastenmeier, Robert W., and Michael J. Remington. 1988. A Judicious Legislator's Lexicon to the Federal Judiciary. In *Judges and Legislators,* ed. Katzmann.

Katsh, M. Ethan. 1993. *Taking Sides: Clashing Views on Controversial Legal Issues.* 5th ed. Guilford, Conn.: Dushkin.

Katz, Jack. 1982. *Poor People's Lawyers in Transition.* New Brunswick, N.J.: Rutgers Univ. Press.

Katzmann, Robert A. 1981. *Regulatory Bureaucracy: The Federal Trade Commission and Antitrust Policy.* Cambridge, Mass.: MIT Press.

———. 1988. *Judges and Legislators: Toward Institutional Comity.* Washington, D.C.: Brookings Institution.

———. 1992. Bridging the Statutory Gulf Between Courts and Congress: A Challenge for Positive Political Theory. *Georgetown Law Journal* 80:653–669.

Kay, Susan Ann. 1978. Socializing the Future Elite: The Nonimpact of a Law School. *Social Science Quarterly* 59:347–354.

Kearney, Mary Kate, and Mary Beth Beazley. 1991. Teaching Students How to Think Like Lawyers: Integrating Socratic Method with the Writing Process. *Temple Law Review* 64:885–908.

Keefe, William J., and Morris S. Ogul. 1989. *The American Legislative Process: Congress and the States.* 7th ed. Englewood Cliffs, N.J.: Prentice-Hall.

Kelly, Michael J. 1994. *Lives of Lawyers: Journeys in the Organizations of Practice.* Ann Arbor: Univ. of Michigan Press.

Kelman, Mark. 1987. *A Guide to Critical Legal Studies.* Cambridge: Harvard Univ. Press.

Kelton, Nancy. 1991. Lawyers and Love, Hormonally Speaking. *New York Times,* 5 Aug. 1991, p. A13.

Kemp, Kathleen A. 1986. Lawyers, Politics, and Economic Regulation. *Social Science Quarterly* 67:267–282.

Kennedy, Duncan. 1990. Legal Education as Training for Hierarchy. In *Politics of Law,* ed. Kairys.

Key. V. O. 1961. *Public Opinion and American Democracy.* New York: Alfred A. Knopf.

Kim, Chong Lim. 1973. Consensus on Legislative Roles Among Japanese Prefectural Assemblymen. In *Legislatures in a Comparative Perspective,* edited by Allan Kornberg. New York: David McKay.

Kingdon, John W. 1989. *Congressmen's Voting Decisions.* 3d ed. Ann Arbor: Univ. of Michigan Press.

Kluger, Richard. 1976. *Simple Justice*. New York: Alfred A. Knopf.

———. 1977. *Simple Justice: The History of Brown v. Board of Education and Black America's Struggle for Equality*. New York: Vintage Books.

Knoke, David. 1986. Associations and Interest Groups. *Annual Review of Sociology* 12:1–21.

Kofmehl, Kenneth. 1962. *Professional Staffs of Congress*. West Lafayette, Ind.: Purdue Univ. Press.

Kohlmeier, Louis M. 1969. *The Regulators: Watchdog Agencies and the Public Interest*. New York: Harper and Row.

Kolko, Gabriel. 1963. *The Triumph of Conservatism*. New York: Free Press.

Kraft, Joseph. 1964. The Washington Lawyers. *Harper's,* Apr. 1964, 102–8.

Laband, David N., and John P. Sophocleus. 1988. The Social Cost of Rent-Seeking: First Estimates. *Public Choice* 58:269–276.

Labaton, Stephen. 1993. Clinton's White House Echoes Bush's on Gay Ban. *New York Times,* 14 Sept. 1993, p. A21.

Larson, Magali Sarfatti. 1977. *The Rise of Professionalism: A Sociological Analysis*. Berkeley and Los Angeles: Univ. of California Press.

Lasswell, Harold D. 1954. The Selective Effect of Personality on Political Participation. In *Studies in the Scope and Method of the Authoritarian Personality,* edited by Richard Christie and Marie Jahoda. Glencoe, Ill.: Free Press.

Lasswell, Harold D., and Myres S. McDougal. 1948. Legal Education and Public Policy. In *The Analysis of Political Behaviour: An Empirical Approach,* edited by Harold D. Lasswell. London: Routledge and Kegan Paul.

Laumann, Edward O., John P. Heinz, Robert L. Nelson, and Robert H. Salisbury. 1985. Washington Lawyers—and Others: The Structure of Washington Representation. *Stanford Law Review* 37:465–502.

Lawrence, Susan E. 1990. *The Poor in Court: The Legal Services Program and Supreme Court Decision Making*. Princeton, N.J.: Princeton Univ. Press.

Lee, Carol F. 1988. The Political Safeguards of Federalism? Congressional Responses to Supreme Court Decisions on State and Local Liability. *Urban Law Journal* 20:301–40.

The Legal Profession. 1992. *Economist,* 18 July 1992, 3–18.

Lefcourt, Robert, ed. 1971. *Law Against the People*. New York: Vintage.

Levi, Edward H. 1963. *An Introduction to Legal Reasoning*. Chicago: Univ. of Chicago Press.

Levine, Felice J. 1990. Goose Bumps and "The Search for Signs of Intelligent Life" in Sociolegal Studies; After Twenty-Five Years. *Law & Society Review* 24:7–33.

Levitan, Donald, and Elwyn E. Mariner. 1980. *Your Massachusetts Government.* 9th ed. Newton Centre, Mass.: Government Research Publications.

Lewis, Philip S. C. 1986. A Comparative Perspective on Legal Professions in the 1980's. *Law & Society Review* 20:79–92.

———. 1988. Introduction. In *Lawyers in Society: The Common Law World,* ed. Abel and Lewis.

———. 1989. Comparison and Change in the Study of Legal Professions. In *Lawyers in Society: Comparative Theories,* ed. Abel and Lewis.

Lijphard, Arend. 1981. Political Parties: Ideologies and Programs. In *Democracy at the Polls: A Comparative Study of Competitive National Elections,* edited by David E. Butler, Howard Rae Penniman, and Austin Ranney. Washington, D.C.: American Enterprise Institute.

Lipset, Seymour M. 1981. *Political Man: The Social Bases of Politics.* Baltimore: Johns Hopkins Univ. Press.

Loewenberg, Gerhald, and Samuel C. Patterson. 1988. *Comparing Legislatures.* 2d ed. Landham, Md.: Univ. Press of America.

Loomis, Burdett. 1988. *The New American Politician: Ambition, Entrepreneurship and the Changing Face of Political Life.* New York: Basic Books.

Lopez, Gerald P. 1992. *Rebellious Lawyering: One Chicano's Vision of Progressive Law Practice.* Boulder, Colo.: Westview Press.

Lortie, Dan C. 1959. Laymen to Lawmen: Law School, Careers, and Professional Socialization. *Harvard Educational Review* 29:352–369.

Loth, Renee. 1991. Weld's Hunt for Judges. *Boston Globe,* 7 July 1991, p. A19.

Lowi, Theodore J. 1979. *The End of Liberalism.* 2d ed. New York: W. W. Norton.

Lytle, Clifford M. 1963. Congressional Response to Supreme Court Decisions in the Aftermath of the School Desegregation Cases. *Journal of Public Law* 12:290–312.

MacKinnon, Catharine. 1987. *Feminism Unmodified.* Cambridge: Harvard Univ. Press.

———. 1989. *Toward a Feminist Theory of the State.* Cambridge: Harvard Univ. Press.

Magee, Stephen P. 1992a. The Optimum Number of Lawyers: Cross-national Estimates. Speech delivered at the Law School, 28 Feb. 1992., University of Wisconsin, Madison.

———. 1992b. The Optimum Number of Lawyers: A Reply to Epp. *Law & Social Inquiry* 17:667–84.

———. 1992c. How Many Lawyers Ruin an Economy. *Wall Street Journal,* 24 Sept. 1992, p. A17.

Magee, Stephen P., William A. Brock, and Leslie Young. 1989. The Invisible Foot and the Waste of Nations. In *Black Hole Tariffs and Endogenous Policy Theory: Political Economy in General Equilibrium.* Cambridge: Cambridge Univ. Press.

Malbin, Michael J. 1979. *Unelected Representatives: Congressional Staff and the Future of Representative Government.* New York: Basic Books.

Manley, John F. 1970. *The Politics of Finance: The House Committee on Ways and Means.* Boston: Little, Brown.

March, James G., and Johan P. Olsen. 1984. The New Institutionalism: Organizational Factors in Political Life. *American Political Science Review* 78:734–49.

———. 1989. *Rediscovering Institutions: The Organizational Basis of Politics.* New York: Free Press.

Marcus, Ruth. 1992. Republicans Aim Barbs at Hillary Clinton. *Washington Post,* 19 Aug. 1992, p. A21.

Margolick, David. 1983. The Trouble with American Law Schools. *New York Times Magazine,* 22 May 1983, 22.

———. 1992. Another Public Drama Puts Yale Alumni Out Front. *New York Times,* 20 Mar. 1992, p. B16.

Marshall, Thomas R. 1989. Policymaking and the Modern Court: When Do Supreme Court Rulings Prevail? *Western Political Quarterly* 42:493–507.

Matthews, Donald R. 1954. *The Social Backgrounds of Political Decision-Makers.* Garden City, N.Y.: Doubleday.

———. 1959. The Folkways of the United States Senate: Conformity to Group Norms and Legislative Effectiveness. *American Political Science Review* 53:1064–89.

———. 1960. *U.S. Senators and Their World.* Chapel Hill: Univ. of North Carolina Press.

———. 1985. Legislative Recruitment and Legislative Careers. In *Handbook of Legislative Research,* edited by Gerhard Loewenberg, Samuel C. Patterson, and Malcolm E. Jewell. Cambridge: Harvard Univ. Press.

Mayhew, David R. 1974. *Congress: The Electoral Connection.* New Haven, Conn.: Yale Univ. Press.

McCann, Michael W. 1986. *Taking Reform Seriously: Perspectives on Public Interest Liberalism.* Ithaca, N.Y.: Cornell Univ. Press.

McCormack, Mark H. 1987. *The Terrible Truth about Lawyers: How Lawyers Really Work and How to Deal with Them Successfully.* New York: Beech Tree Books.

McCubbins, Mathew D., and Terry Sullivan. 1987. Institutional Aspects of Decision Processes. In *Congress: Structure and Policy,* edited by Mathew D. McCubbins and Terry Sullivan. Cambridge: Cambridge Univ. Press.

McGuire, Kevin T. 1993a. Lawyers and the U.S. Supreme Court: The Washington Community and Legal Elites. *American Journal of Political Science* 37:365–390.

———. 1993b. *The Supreme Court Bar: Legal Elites in the Washington Community.* Charlottesville: Univ. Press of Virginia.

McHugh, Edward T. 1994. Governor's Council May Defy Description. *Worcester (Mass.) Telegram and Gazette,* 28 Aug. 1994, p. C2.

McIntyre, Lisa J. 1987. *The Public Defender: The Practice of Law in the Shadows of Repute.* Chicago: Univ. of Chicago Press.

McKeen, Sid. 1992. Gobbledygook, Bafflegab Obfuscate Our Language. *Worcester (Mass.) Telegram and Gazette,* 29 Mar. 1992, p. C3.

Meador, Daniel J. 1980. *The President, the Attorney General, and the Department of Justice.* Charlottesville: White Burkett Miller Center of Public Affairs at the Univ. of Virginia.

Melone, Albert P. 1979. *Lawyers, Public Policy and Interest Group Politics.* Washington, D.C.: Univ. Press of America.

———. 1980. Rejection of the Lawyer-Dominance Proposition: The Need for Additional Research. *Western Political Quarterly* 33:225–32.

Mellors, Colin. 1978. *The British MP: A Socio-economic Study of the House of Commons.* London: Saxon House.

Meltsner, Michael. 1973. *Cruel and Unusual: The Supreme Court and Capital Punishment.* New York: Random House.

Menkel-Meadow, Carrie. 1985. Portia in a Different Voice: Speculations on a Woman's Lawyering Process. *Berkeley Women's Law Journal* 1:39–63.

———. 1989. Feminization of the Legal Profession: The Comparative Sociology of Women Lawyers. In *Lawyers in Society: Comparative Theories,* ed. Abel and Lewis.

Merryman, John. 1969. *The Civil Law Tradition.* Palto Alto, Calif.: Stanford Univ. Press.

Mezey, Michael L. 1979. *Comparative Legislatures.* Durham, N.C.: Duke Univ. Press.

Mikva, Abner J. 1983. How Well Does Congress Support and Defend the Constitution? *North Carolina Law Review* 61:587–611.

Mikva, Abner J., and Jeff Bleich. 1991. When Congress Overrules the Court. *California Law Review* 79:729–50.

Miliband, Ralph. 1969. *The State in Capitalist Society.* New York: Basic Books.

Miller, Geoffrey P. 1989. From Compromise to Confrontation: Separation of Powers in the Reagan Era. *George Washington Law Review* 57:401–26.

Miller, Mark C. 1992. Congressional Committees and the Federal Courts: A Neo-Institutional Perspective. *Western Political Quarterly* 45:949–70.

———. 1993a. Lawyers in Congress: What Difference Does It Make? *Congress and the Presidency* 20:1–24.

———. 1993b. Lawmaker Attitudes toward Court Reform in Massachusetts. *Judicature* 77:34–40.

———. 1993c. Courts, Agencies, and Congressional Committees: A Neo-Institutional Perspective. *Review of Politics* 55:471–489.

———. 1993d. Congress and the Constitution: A Tale of Two Committees. *Constitutional Law Journal* 3:317–362.

Miller, William. 1951. American Lawyers in Business and in Politics. *Yale Law Journal* 60:66–76.

Mills, C. Wright. 1951. *White Collar: The American Middle Classes*. New York: Oxford Univ. Press.

———. 1956. *The Power Elite*. New York: Oxford Univ. Press.

Minow, Martha. 1990. *Making All the Difference: Inclusion, Exclusion, and American Law*. Ithaca, N.Y.: Cornell Univ. Press.

———. 1991. Partial Justice: Law and Minorities. In *Fate of Law*, ed. Sarat and Kearns.

Moll, Richard W. 1990. *The Lure of the Law: Why People Become Lawyers, and What the Profession Does to Them*. New York: Penguin Books.

Moon, J. Donald. 1991. Pluralism and Progress in the Study of Politics. In *Political Science: Looking to the Future*. Vol. 1, *The Theory and Practice of Political Science*, edited by William Crotty. Evanston, Ill.: Northwestern Univ. Press.

Moore, Beverly C., Jr. 1972. The Lawyer's Response: The Public Interest Law Firm. In *With Justice for Some*, ed. Wasserstein and Green.

Moore, Wilbert E., and Gerald W. Rosenblum. 1970. *The Professional: Roles and Rules*. New York: Russell Sage Foundation.

Morgan, Donald. 1966. *Congress and the Constitution: A Study of Responsibility*. Cambridge: Harvard Univ. Press.

Morris, Thomas R. 1987. States before the U.S. Supreme Court: State Attorneys General as Amicus Curiae. *Judicature* 70:298–305.

Murphy, Kevin M., Andrei Schleifer, and Robert Vishny. 1991. The Allocation of Talent: Implications for Growth. *Quarterly Journal of Economics* 106:503–30.

Murphy, Walter F. 1962. *Congress and the Court*. Chicago: Univ. of Chicago Press.

———. 1986. Who Shall Interpret? The Quest for the Ultimate Constitutional Interpreter, *Review of Politics* 48:401–23.

Murphy, Walter F., and C. Herman Pritchett. 1961. *Courts, Judges, and Politics: An Introduction to the Judicial Process.* New York: Random House.

Murrin, John M. 1971. The Legal Transformation: The Bench and Bar of Eighteenth-Century Massachusetts. In *Colonial America,* edited by Stanley N. Katz. Boston: Little Brown.

Nader, Ralph. 1969. Crumbling of the Old Order: Law Schools and Law Firms. *New Republic,* 15 Nov. 1969, 20.

Nader, Ralph, and Mark Green, eds. 1976. *Verdicts on Lawyers.* New York: Thomas Y. Crowell.

Nagel, Stuart S. 1969. Court Curbing Periods in American History. In *Impact of Supreme Court Decisions,* ed. Becker.

Nardulli, Peter, ed. 1991. *The Constitution and American Political Development: An Institutional Perspective.* Urbana: Univ. of Illinois Press.

Neely, Richard. 1983. *Why Courts Don't Work.* New York: McGraw-Hill.

Nelson, Robert L., and John P. Heinz. 1988. Lawyers and the Structure of Influence in Washington. *Law & Society Review* 22:237–300.

Nelson, Robert L., John P. Heinz, Edward O. Laumann, and Robert H. Salisbury. 1987. Private Representation in Washington: Surveying the Structure of Influence. *American Bar Foundation Research Journal* (1987): 141–200.

Nelson, Robert L., David M. Trubek, and Rayman L. Solomon, eds. 1992. *Lawyers' Ideals / Lawyers' Practices: Transformations in the American Legal Profession.* Ithaca, N.Y.: Cornell Univ. Press.

Nelson, Robert L., and David M. Trubek. 1992. New Problems and New Paradigms in Studies of the Legal Profession. In *Lawyers' Ideals / Lawyers' Practices,* ed. Nelson, Trubek, and Solomon.

Neustadt, Richard E. 1990. *Presidential Power and the Modern Presidents.* New York: Free Press.

Nichols, Egbert Ray, ed. 1935. *Congress or the Supreme Court: Which Shall Rule America?* New York: Noble and Noble.

Note: Congressional Reversal of Supreme Court Decisions: 1945–57. 1958. *Harvard Law Review* 71:1324–37.

Note: Tension Between Judicial and Legislative Powers as Reflected in Confrontations Between Congress and the Courts. 1979. *Georgia Law Review* 13:1513–57.

O'Brien, David M. 1986. *Storm Center: The Supreme Court in American Politics.* New York: W. W. Norton.

———. 1988. The Reagan Judges: His Most Enduring Legacy? In *The Reagan Legacy: Promise and Performance,* edited by Charles O. Jones. Chatham, N.J.: Chatham House.

O'Connor, Karen, and Lee Epstein. 1983a. Beyond Legislative Lobbying: Women's Rights Groups and the Supreme Court. *Judicature* 67:134–43.

———. 1983b. The Rise of Conservative Interest Group Litigation. *Journal of Politics* 45:479–89.

———. 1984. Rebalancing the Scales of Justice: Assessment of Public Interest Law. *Harvard Journal of Law and Public Policy* 7:483–505.

———. 1989. *Public Interest Law Groups.* New York: Greenwood Press.

O'Connor, Karen, and Gregg Ivers. 1987. Friends as Foes: The Amicus Curiae Participation and Effectiveness of the Americans for Effective Law Enforcement in Criminal Cases, 1969–1982. *Law and Policy* 9:161–78.

O'Connor, Patrick F., Justin J. Green, Richard L. Engstrom, and Chong Lim Kim. 1978. The Political Behavior of Lawyers in the Louisiana House of Representatives. *Louisiana Law Review* 39:43–79.

Olson, Susan M. 1984. *Clients and Lawyers: Securing the Rights of Disabled Persons.* Westport, Conn.: Greenwood Press.

Ornstein, Norman J., Thomas E. Mann, and Michael J. Malbin. 1990. *Vital Statistics on Congress 1989–1990.* Washington, D.C.: Congressional Quarterly.

———. 1992. *Vital Statistics on Congress 1991–92.* Washington, D.C.: Congressional Quarterly.

Pacelle, Richard L. 1991. *The Transformation of the Supreme Court's Agenda: From the New Deal to the Reagan Administration.* Boulder, Colo.: Westview Press.

Palmer, Robert. 1984. The Confrontation of the Legislative and Executive Branches: An Examination of the Constitutional Balance of Powers and the Role of the Attorney General. *Pepperdine Law Review* 11:331–89.

Parker, Glenn R., and Suzanne L. Parker. 1985. *Factions in House Committees.* Knoxville: Univ. of Tennessee Press.

Patterson, Samuel C. 1959. Patterns of Interpersonal Relations in a State Legislative Group: The Wisconsin Assembly. *Public Opinion Quarterly* 23:101–9.

———. 1983. Legislators and the Legislatures in the American States. In *Politics in the American States: A Comparative Analysis,* edited by Virginia Gray, Herbert Jacob, and Kenneth N. Vines. 4th ed. Boston: Little, Brown.

Peabody, Robert L., Susan Webb Hammond, Jean Torcom, Lynne P. Brown, Carolyn Thompson, and Robin Kolodny. 1990. Interviewing Political Elites. *PS: Political Science and Politics* 23 (Sept.): 451–55.

Pedersen, Mogens N. 1972. Lawyers in Politics: The Danish Folketing and United States Legislatures. In *Comparative Legislative Behavior: Frontiers of Research,* edited by Samuel C. Patterson and John C. Wahlke. New York: John Wiley and Sons.

Perez Perdomo, Rogelio. 1988. The Venezuelan Legal Profession: Lawyers in an Inegalitarian Society. In *Lawyers in Society: The Civil Law World,* ed. Abel and Lewis.

Perkins, Lynette P. 1980. Influences of Members' Goals on Their Committee Behavior: The U.S. House Judiciary Committee. *Legislative Studies Quarterly* 5:373–93.

———. 1981. Member Recruitment to a Mixed Goal Committee: The House Judiciary Committee. *Journal of Politics* 43:348–64.

Peterson, Mark A. 1990. *Legislating Together: The White House and Capitol Hill from Eisenhower to Reagan.* Cambridge: Harvard Univ. Press.

Petracca, Mark P., ed. 1992. *The Politics of Interests: Interest Groups Transformed.* Boulder, Colo.: Westview Press.

Pike, David F. 1980. Washington Lawyers: Rise of the Power Brokers. *U.S. News and World Report,* 10 Mar. 1980, 52–56.

Plattner, Andy. 1983. Scrappy House Energy Panel Provides High Pressure Arena for Wrangling Over Regulation. *Congressional Quarterly Weekly Report,* 12 Mar. 1983, 501–8.

Plumlee, John P. 1981. Lawyers as Bureaucrats: The Impact of Legal Training in the Higher Civil Service. *Public Administration Review* 41:220–28.

Podmore, David. 1980. *Solicitors and the Wider Community.* London: Heinemann.

Polsby, Nelson W. 1990. The Social Composition of Congress. In *The U.S. Congress and the German Bundestag: Comparisons of Democratic Processes,* edited by Uwe Thaysen, Roger H. Davidson, and Robert Gerald Livingston. Boulder, Colo.: Westview Press.

Porter, Mary Cornelia, and G. Alan Tarr, eds. 1982. *State Supreme Courts: Policymakers in the Federal System.* Westport, Conn.: Greenwood Press.

Pound, Roscoe. 1906. The Causes of Dissatisfaction with the Administration of Justice. *Reports of the American Bar Association* 29:395–17.

———. 1914. The Lay Tradition as to the Lawyer. *Michigan Law Review* 12:627–38.

Powell, Michael J. 1988. *From Patrician to Professional Elite: The Transformation of the New York City Bar Association.* New York: Russell Sage.

Powell, Walter W., and Paul J. DiMaggio, eds. 1991. *The New Institutionalism in Organizational Analysis*. Chicago: Univ. of Chicago Press.

President's Council on Competitiveness, 1991. *Agenda for Civil Justice Reform in America*. Washington, D.C.: Government Printing Office.

Prewitt, Kenneth. 1970. *The Recruitment of Political Leaders: A Study of Citizen-Politicians*. Indianapolis: Bobbs-Merrill.

Price, David E. 1979. *Policymaking in Congressional Committees: the Impact of Environmental Factors*. Tucson: Univ. of Arizona Press.

———. 1985. Congressional Committees in the Policy Process. In *Congress Reconsidered*, edited by Lawrence C. Dodd and Bruce I. Oppenheimer. 3d ed. Washington, D.C.: Congressional Quarterly.

Priest, Tom, and John Krol. 1986. Lawyers in Corporate Chief Executive Positions: Career Characteristics and "Inner Group" Membership. *International Journal of the Sociology of Law* 14:33–46.

Pritchett, C. Herman. 1961. *Congress versus the Supreme Court: 1957–1960*. Minneapolis: Univ. of Minnesota Press.

Provine, Doris Marie. 1986. *Judging Credentials: Nonlawyer Judges and the Politics of Professionalism*. Chicago: Univ. of Chicago Press.

Quindlen, Anna. 1992. Little Big Women. *New York Times*, 2 Feb. 1992, p. 17.

Quirk, Paul J. 1981. *Industry Influence in Federal Regulatory Agencies*. Princeton, N.J.: Princeton Univ. Press.

Rabin, Robert. 1976. Lawyers for Social Change: Perspectives on Public Interest Law. *Stanford Law Review* 28:207–61.

Ragsdale, Lyn. 1993. *Presidential Politics*. Boston: Houghton Mifflin.

Ralph Nader Congress Project. 1975a. *The Judiciary Committees: A Study of the House and Senate Judiciary Committees*. New York: Grossman.

———. 1975b. *The Commerce Committees: A Study of the House and Senate Commerce Committees*. New York: Grossman.

Ranney, Austin. 1981. Candidate Selection. In *Democracy at the Polls: A Comparative Study of Competitive National Elections*, edited by David E. Butler, Howard Rae Penniman, and Austin Ranney. Washington, D.C.: American Enterprise Institute.

Rathjen, Gregory J. 1976. The Impact of Legal Education on the Beliefs, Attitudes and Values of Law Students. *Tennessee Law Review* 44:85–119.

Rawls, John. 1971. *A Theory of Justice*. Cambridge: Harvard Univ. Press.

Richardson, Frank K. 1983. Law Reviews and the Courts. *Whittier Law Review* 5:385–93.

Riley, David. 1976. The Mystique of Lawyers. In *Verdicts on Lawyers*, ed. Nader and Green.

Ripley, Randall B. 1969. *Power in the Senate.* New York: St. Martin's Press.

———. 1975. *Congress: Process and Policy.* New York: W. W. Norton.

Roberts, Susan L. 1989. Constitutional Deliberation in the Modern Congress. Paper presented at the annual meeting of the Southern Political Science Association, 1989, Memphis.

Rockman, Bert A. 1994. The New Institutionalism and the Old Institutions. In *New Perspectives on American Politics,* edited by Lawrence C. Dodd and Calvin Jillson. Washington, D.C.: Congressional Quarterly.

Rosenthal, Alan. 1981. *Legislative Life: People, Process, and the Performance of States.* New York: Harper and Row.

———. 1989. The Legislative Institution: Transformed and at Risk. In *The State of the States,* edited by Carl E. Van Horn. Washington, D.C.: Congressional Quarterly.

———. 1990. *Governors and Legislators: Contending Power.* Washington, D.C.: Congressional Quarterly.

Ross, J. F. S. 1955. *Elections and Electors.* London: Eyre and Spottiswoode.

Rovner, Julie. 1990. Congress Clears Sweeping Bill to Guard Rights of Disabled. *Congressional Quarterly Weekly Report,* 14 July 1990, 2227–28.

Rueschemeyer, Dietrich. 1973. *Lawyers and Their Society: A Comparative Study of the Legal Profession in Germany and in the United States.* Cambridge: Harvard Univ. Press.

———. 1989. Comparing Legal Professions: A State-Centered Approach. In *Lawyers in Society: Comparative Theories,* ed. Abel and Lewis.

Rydon, Joan. 1987. Lawyers in the Australian Commonwealth Parliament. *Australian Journal of Politics and History* 33:23–38.

Sack, Kevin. 1992. Quayle Says Letter Shows Lawyers "Own" Clinton. *New York Times,* 28 Aug. 1992, p. A16.

Salisbury, Robert H. 1990. The Paradox of Interest Groups in Washington, D.C.: More Groups and Less Clout. In *The New American Political System,* edited by Anthony King. 2d ed. Washington, D.C.: American Enterprise Institute.

Salisbury, Robert H., John P. Heinz, Robert L. Nelson, and Edward O. Laumann. 1992. Triangles, Networks, and Hollow Cores: The Complex Geometry of Washington Interest Representation. In *Politics of Interests,* ed. Petracca.

Salisbury, Robert H., and Kenneth A. Shepsle. 1981a. Congressional Staff Turnover and the Ties-That-Bind. *American Political Science Review* 75:381–96.

———. 1981b. U.S. Congressman as Enterprise. *Legislative Studies Quarterly* 6:559–76.

Salmore, Barbara G., and Stephen A. Salmore. 1989. *Candidates, Parties, and Campaigns: Electoral Politics in America.* 2d ed. Washington, D.C.: Congressional Quarterly Press.

Salokar, Rebecca Mae. 1992a. Lawyers for the Legislature: The Roles of the Senate Legal Counsel and the General Counsel for the House of Representatives. Paper presented at the annual meeting of the Law and Society Association, May 1992, Philadelphia.

———. 1992b. *The Solicitor General: The Politics of Law.* Philadelphia: Temple Univ. Press.

———. 1994. Legal Counsel for Congress: Protecting Institutional Interests. *Congress and the Presidency* 20:131–55.

Sander, Richard H. 1992. Elevating the Debate on Lawyers and Economic Growth. *Law & Social Inquiry* 17:659–66.

Sarat, Austin, Gregory Caldeira, Timothy O'Neill, and Kim Land Scheppele. 1990. Report of Committee on the Status of the Law, Courts, and Judicial Process Organized Section. *American Political Science Association's Law, Courts, and Judicial Process Section Newsletter* 8 (Fall): 1–12.

Sarat, Austin, and William L. F. Felstiner. 1988. Law and Social Relations: Vocabularies of Motive in Lawyer/Client Interaction. *Law & Society Review* 22:737–69.

Sarat, Austin, and Thomas R. Kearns, eds. 1991. *The Fate of Law.* Ann Arbor: Univ. of Michigan Press.

Savoy, Paul N. 1970. Towards a New Politics of Legal Education. *Yale Law Journal* 79:444–504.

Scales, Ann. 1986. The Emergence of a Feminist Jurisprudence. *Yale Law Journal* 95:1373–1403.

Scheingold, Stuart A. 1974. *The Politics of Rights: Lawyers, Public Policy, and Political Change.* New Haven, Conn.: Yale Univ. Press.

———. 1994. The Contradictions of Radical Law Practice. In *Lawyers in a Postmodern World,* ed. Cain and Harrington.

Schleef, Debra J. 1992. Thinking Like a Lawyer: The Process of Professional Socialization of Law Students. Paper presented at the annual meeting of the Law and Society Association, May 1992, Philadelphia.

Schlesinger, Joseph A. 1957. Lawyers and American Politics: A Clarified View. *Midwest Journal of Political Science* 1:26–39.

———. 1958. *How They Became Governor: A Study of Comparative State Politics, 1870–1950.* East Lansing: Governmental Research Bureau, Michigan State Univ..

———. 1966. *Ambition and Politics: Political Careers in the United States.* Chicago: Rand McNally.

Schlozman, Kay Lehman, and John T. Tierney. 1986. *Organized Interests and American Democracy.* New York: Harper and Row.

Schmidhauser, John R. 1987. Alternative Conceptual Frameworks in Comparative Cross-National Legal and Judicial Research. In *Comparative Judicial Systems: Challenging Frontiers in Conceptual and Empirical Analysis,* edited by John R. Schmidhauser. London: Butterworths.

Schmidhauser, John R., Larry L. Berg, and Albert Melone. 1971. The Impact of Judicial Decisions: New Dimensions in Supreme Court—Congressional Relations, 1945–1968. *Washington University Law Quarterly* (1971): 209–51.

Schneider, David M. 1968. *American Kinship: A Cultural Account.* Englewood Cliffs, N.J.: Prentice-Hall.

Schubert, Glendon A. 1960. *Constitutional Politics.* New York: Holt, Rinehart, and Winston.

Searing, Donald D. 1969. The Comparative Study of Elite Socialization. *Comparative Political Studies* 1:471–500.

———. 1991. Roles, Rules, and Rationality in the New Institutionalism. *American Political Science Review* 85:1239–60.

Sedgwick, Jeffrey Leigh. 1992. The Massachusetts General Court and the Commonwealth's Political Crisis. In *The Reform of State Legislatures and the Changing Character of Representation,* edited by Eugene W. Hickok Jr. Lanham, Md.: Univ. Press of America.

Seligman, Joel. 1978. *The High Citadel: The Influence of Harvard Law School.* Boston: Houghton-Mifflin.

Selznick, Philip. 1974. Social Advocacy in the Legal Profession in the United States. *Juridical Review* 1974:113–26.

Seymour, Whitney North. 1975. *United States Attorney: An Inside View of "Justice" in America under the Nixon Administration.* New York: William Morrow.

Shanfield, Stephen, and Andrew Benjamin. 1985. Psychiatric Distress in Law Students. *Journal of Legal Education* 35:65–75.

Shapiro, Martin. 1993. Public Law and Judicial Politics. In *Political Science: The State of the Discipline II,* edited by Ada W. Finifter. Washington, D.C.: American Political Science Association.

Sheldon, Charles H. 1977. Influencing the Selection of Judges: The Variety and Effectiveness of State Bar Activities. *Western Political Quarterly* 30:397–400.

Sheldon, Charles H., and Nicholas P. Lovrich Jr. 1991. State Judicial Recruitment. In *American Courts,* ed. Gates and Johnson.

Shepsle, Kenneth A. 1978. *The Giant Jigsaw Puzzle: Democratic Committee Assignments in the Modern House.* Chicago: Univ. of Chicago Press.

Sheridan, Richard G. 1989. *Governing Ohio: The State Legislature.* Cleveland: Federation for Community Planning.

Shklar, Judith. 1964. *Legalism: An Essay on Law, Morals, and Politics.* Cambridge: Harvard Univ. Press.

Silbey, Susan S. 1985. Ideals and Practices in the Study of Law. *Legal Studies Forum* 9:7–22.

Silbey, Susan S., and Austin Sarat. 1987. Critical Traditions in Law and Society Research. *Law & Society Review* 21:165–74.

Sinclair, Barbara. 1989. Leadership Strategies in the Modern Congress. In *Congressional Politics,* edited by Christopher Deering. Chicago: Dorsey Press.

Sirico, Louis J., Jr., and Jeffrey B. Margulies. 1986. The Citation of Law Reviews by the Supreme Court: An Empirical Study. *UCLA Law Review* 34:131–47.

Sisson, Richard. 1973. Comparative Legislative Institutionalization: A Theoretical Exploration. In *Legislatures in a Comparative Perspective,* edited by Allan Kornberg. New York: David McKay.

Skinner, Quentin, ed. 1985. *The Return of Grand Theory in Human Sciences.* Cambridge: Cambridge Univ. Press.

Slotnick, Elliot E. 1983. Lowering the Bench or Raising It Higher?: Affirmative Action and Judicial Selection During the Carter Administration. *Yale Law and Policy Review* 1:270–98.

———. 1987. The Place of Judicial Review in the American Tradition: The Emergence of an Eclectic Power. *Judicature* 71:68–79.

———. 1988. Review Essay on Judicial Recruitment and Selection. *Justice System Journal* 13:109–24.

Smith, Christopher E. 1991. *Courts and the Poor.* Chicago: Nelson-Hall.

Smith, Hedrick. 1989. *The Power Game: How Washington Works.* New York: Ballantine Books.

Smith, Rogers M. 1988. Political Jurisprudence, the "New Institutionalism," and the Future of Public Law. *American Political Science Review* 82:89–108.

———. 1989. The New Institutionalism and Normative Theory: Reply to Professor Barber. In *Studies in American Political Development,* vol. 3, edited by Karen Orren and Stephen Showronek. New Haven, Conn.: Yale Univ. Press.

Smith, Steven S., and Christopher J. Deering. 1984. *Committees in Congress.* Washington, D.C.: Congressional Quarterly.

————. 1990. *Committees in Congress.* 2d ed. Washington, D.C.: Congressional Quarterly.

Solimine, Michael E., and James L. Walker. 1992. The Next Word: Congressional Response to Supreme Court Statutory Decisions. *Temple Law Review* 65:425–58.

Somit, Albert, and Joseph Tannenhaus. 1967. *The Development of American Political Science: From Burgess to Behavioralism.* Boston: Allyn and Bacon.

Sorauf, Frank J. 1976. *The Wall of Separation: The Constitutional Politics of Church and State.* Princeton, N.J.: Princeton Univ. Press.

Spangler, Eve. 1986. *Lawyers for Hire: Salaried Professionals at Work.* New Haven, Conn.: Yale Univ. Press.

Spector, Malcolm. 1972. The Rise and Fall of a Mobility Route. *Social Problems* 20:173–85.

————. 1973. Secrecy in Job Seeking Among Government Attorneys: Two Contingencies in the Theory of Subculture. *Urban Life and Culture* 2:211–29.

Spohn, Cassia. 1990. The Sentencing Decisions of Black and White Judges: Expected and Unexpected Similarities. *Law & Society Review* 24:1197–1216.

Stanley, Alessandra. 1992. Kerrey on the Run, Pursued by Failure. *New York Times,* 25 Feb. 1992, p. A16.

Stanley, Harold W., and Richard G. Niemi. 1992. *Vital Statistics on American Politics.* 3d ed. Washington, D.C.: Congressional Quarterly.

————. 1994. *Vital Statistics on American Politics.* 4th ed. Washington, D.C.: Congressional Quarterly.

Stark, Steve. 1992. The Yale Connection. *Boston Globe,* 2 Mar. 1992, p. 9.

Stevens, Robert. 1973. Law Schools and Law Students. *Virginia Law Review* 59:551–707.

————. 1983. *Law School: Legal Education in America from the 1859s to the 1980s.* Chapel Hill: Univ. of North Carolina Press.

Strine, Michael. 1994. New Institutionalism in Sociolegal Research: Teaching the New Dog Old Tricks. Paper presented at the annual meeting of the Law and Society Association, 1994, Phoenix.

Stumpf, Harry P. 1965. Congressional Response to Supreme Court Rulings: The Interaction of Law and Politics. *Journal of Public Law* 14:377–95.

Stumpf, Harry P., and John H. Culver. 1992. *The Politics of State Courts.* New York: Longman.

Suchman, Mark C., and Lauren B. Edelman. 1994. Legal-Rational Myths: The New Institutionalism and the Law and Society Tradition. Paper presented at the annual meeting of the Law and Society Association, 1994, Phoenix.

Sugarman, David. 1994. Blurred Boundaries: The Overlapping Worlds of Law, Business, and Politics. In *Lawyers in a Postmodern World,* ed. Cain and Harrington.

Sugarman, Paul R. 1991. *In the Matter of the Boston Municipal Court, Department of the Trial Court.* Report of the Special Master and Commissioner to the Massachusetts Supreme Judicial Court, 4 Feb. 1991.

Suleiman, Ezra N. 1986. Toward the Disciplining of Parties and Legislators: The French Parliamentarian in the Fifth Republic. In *Parliaments and Parliamentarians in Democratic Politics,* edited by Ezra N. Suleiman. New York: Holmes and Meier.

Sutton, John R. 1994. Neoinstitutional Theory and the Concept of Social Control. Paper presented at the annual meeting of the Law and Society Association, 1994, Phoenix.

Swain, Carol. 1993. *Black Faces, Black Interests: The Representation of African-Americans in Congress.* Cambridge: Harvard Univ. Press.

Swardson, Anne. 1993. Canada: No Problem with Gays in Ranks. *Washington Post,* 6 July 1993, p. A8.

Szelenyi, Ivan, and Bill Martin. 1989. The Legal Profession and the Rise and Fall of the New Class. In *Lawyers in Society: Comparative Theories,* ed. Abel and Lewis.

Tarr, G. Alan, and Mary Cornelia Aldis Porter. 1988. *State Supreme Courts in State and Nation.* New Haven, Conn.: Yale Univ. Press.

Teich, Paul. 1986. Research on American Law Teaching: Is There a Case Against the Case System? *Journal of Legal Education* 36:167–88.

Thielens, Wagner, Jr. 1980. *The Socialization of Law Students.* New York: Arno Press.

Thomas, Clive S., and Ronald J. Hrebenar. 1992. Changing Patterns of Interest Group Activity: A Regional Perspective. In *Politics of Interests,* ed. Petracca.

Thomas, Norman C., Joseph A. Pika, and Richard A. Watson. 1993. *The Politics of the Presidency.* 3d ed. Washington, D.C.: Congressional Quarterly.

Thomas, Philip A., ed. 1992. *Tomorrow's Lawyers.* Oxford, England: Blackwell.

Thomas, Sue. 1994. *How Women Legislate.* New York: Oxford Univ. Press.

Thorne, Barrie. 1973. Professional Education in Law. In *Education for the Professions of Medicine, Law, Theology, and Social Welfare,* edited by Everett C. Hughes, Barrie Thorne, Agostine M. DeBaggis, Arnold Gurin, and David Williams. New York: McGraw-Hill.

Tickamyer, Ann R. 1981. Politics as a Vocation. *Pacific Sociological Review* 24:17–44.

Tocqueville, Alex de. 1969. *Democracy in America,* translated by George
    Lawrence and edited by J. P. Mayer. 1841. Reprint, New York: Harper
    and Row.
Torry, Saundra. 1992. ABA Salutes Anita Hill. *Washington Post,* 10 Aug. 1992,
    p. A-8.
Towell, Pat. 1993. Months of Hope, Anger, Anguish Produce Policy Few Ad-
    mire. *Congressional Quarterly Weekly Report,* 24 July 1993, 1966–71.
Truman, David B. 1951. *The Governmental Process.* New York: Knopf.
———. 1955. The Impact of the Revolution in Behavioral Science on Political
    Science. Brookings Lectures. Washington, D.C.: Brookings Institution.
———. 1971. *The Governmental Process.* 2d ed. New York: Knopf.
Turner, Robert L. 1992. A Council Whose Time has Passed. *Boston Globe,* 27
    Feb. 1992, p. 19.
Turow, Scott. 1977. *One L: An Inside Account of Life in the First Year at
    Harvard Law School.* New York: Penguin Books.
Ulmer, S. Sidney. 1986. Are Social Background Models Time-Bound? *American
    Political Science Review* 80:957–67.
U.S. Government. 1989. *1989–1990 Official Congressional Directory,* 101st
    Congress. Washington, D.C.: Government Printing Office.
Vanderbilt, Arthur T. 1979. *Law School: Briefing for a Legal Education.* New
    York: Penguin Books.
Van Horn, Carl E., Donald C. Baumer, and William T. Gormley Jr. 1989. *Poli-
    tics and Public Policy.* Washington, D.C.: Congressional Quarterly.
Van Loon, Eric E. 1970. The Law School Response: How to Sharpen Students'
    Minds by Making Them Narrow. In *With Justice for Some,* ed.
    Wasserstein and Green.
Vidich, Arthur J., and Joseph Bensman. 1960. *Small Town in Mass Society.*
    New York: Doubleday.
Vogel, David. 1989. *Fluctuating Fortunes.* New York: Basic Books.
Vollmer, Howard M., and Donald L. Mills, eds. 1966. *Professionalization.*
    Englewood Cliffs, N.J.: Prentice-Hall.
Vose, Clement E. 1955. NAACP Strategy in the Restrictive Covenant Cases.
    Western Reserve Law Review 6:101–45.
———. 1957. National Consumers' League and the Brandeis Brief. *Midwest
    Journal of Political Science* 1:178–90.
———. 1958. Litigation as a Form of Pressure Group Activity. *Annals of the
    American Academy of Political and Social Science* 319:20–31.
———. 1959. *Caucasians Only.* Berkeley and Los Angeles: Univ. of California
    Press.

———. 1966. Interest Groups, Judicial Review, and Local Government. *Western Political Quarterly* 19:85–100.

———. 1972. *Constitutional Change: Amendment Politics and Supreme Court Litigation Since 1900.* Lexington, Mass.: Lexington Books.

Walker, Jack L. 1983. The Origins and Maintenance of Interest Groups in America. *American Political Science Review* 77:390–406.

Warkow, Seymour, and Joseph Zelan. 1965. *Lawyers in the Making.* Chicago: Aldine Publishing.

Warren, Samuel D., and Louis D. Brandeis. 1890. The Right to Privacy. *Harvard Law Review* 4:193–220.

Warrick, Lyle. 1993. *Judicial Selection in the United States: A Compendium of Provisions.* 2d ed. Chicago: American Judicature Society.

Wasby, Stephen L. 1970. *The Impact of the United States Supreme Court: Some Perspectives.* Homewood, Ill.: Dorsey Press.

———. 1984. How Planned is "Planned Litigation"? *American Bar Foundation Research Journal* (1984): 83–138.

———. 1986. The Multi-Faceted Elephant: Litigator Perspectives on Planned Litigation for Social Change. *Capital University Law Review* 15:145–89.

———. 1988. *The Supreme Court in the Federal Judicial System.* 3d ed. Chicago: Nelson-Hall.

Wasserstein, Bruce, and Mark Green, eds. 1972. *With Justice for Some: An Indictment of the Law by Young Advocates.* Boston: Beacon Press.

Watson, Andrew S. 1968. The Quest for Professional Competence: Psychological Aspects of Legal Education. *University of Cincinnati Law Review* 37:93–166.

Watson, Richard A., and Norman C. Thomas. 1988. *The Politics of the Presidency.* 2d ed. Washington, D.C.: Congressional Quarterly.

Weaver, R. Kent, and Bert A. Rockman, eds. 1993. *Do Institutions Matter? Government Capabilities in the United States and Abroad.* Washington, D.C.: Brookings Institution.

Weaver, Suzanne. 1977. *Decision to Prosecute: Organization and Public Policy in the Antitrust Division.* Cambridge, Mass.: MIT Press.

Weber, Max. 1946. Politics as a Vocation. In *From Max Weber,* edited by H. Gerth and C. Mills. New York: Oxford Univ. Press.

———. 1954. *Law in Economy and Society.* Translated by Edward Shils and Max Rheinstein. Cambridge: Harvard Univ. Press.

Weisbrot, David. 1988. The Australian Legal Profession: From Provincial Family Firms to Multinationals. In *Lawyers in Society: The Common Law World,* ed. Abel and Lewis.

Wenner, Lettie. 1982. *The Environmental Decade in Court.* Bloomington: Univ. of Indiana Press.

Wexler, Stephen. 1970. Practicing Law for Poor People. *Yale Law Journal* 79:1049–67.

White, William S. 1956. *Citadel: The Story of the U.S. Senate.* New York: Harper and Row.

Wice, Paul. 1991. *Judges and Lawyers: The Human Side of Justice.* New York: HarperCollins.

Williamson, Dianne. 1993. Judges Find Reform Law Falls Short. *Worcester (Mass.) Telegram and Gazette,* 17 Jan. 1993, p. B-1.

Wilson, Woodrow. 1973. *Congressional Government.* 1885. Reprint, Gloucester, Mass.: Peter Smith.

Wollan, Laurin A. 1978. Lawyers in Government—"The Most Serviceable Instruments of Authority." *Public Administration Review* 38:105–12.

Wolpe, Bruce C. 1990. *Lobbying Congress: How the System Works.* Washington, D.C.: Congressional Quarterly.

Wong, Doris Sue. 1992a. Leaders Press for Court Reform. *Boston Globe,* 31 Mar. 1992, pp. 21, 23.

———. 1992b. Officials Say Move Now on Court Bill. *Boston Globe,* 15 Apr. 1992, pp. 41, 45.

———. 1992c. Bill on Court Reform Due for Vote Today. *Boston Globe,* 30 June 1992, pp. 17, 24.

Zemans, Frances Kahn, and Victor G. Rosenblum. 1981. *The Making of a Public Profession.* Chicago: American Bar Foundation.

Zuckman, Jill. 1993a. As Family Leave Is Enacted, Some See End to Logjam. *Congressional Quarterly Weekly Report,* 6 Feb. 1993, 267–69.

———. 1993b. Family Leave Law. *Congressional Quarterly Weekly Report,* 13 Feb. 1993, 335.

Index

Academic lawyers, 14, 52–53, 156
Access to elected offices, lawyers, 69–72, 75
Activism, of courts, 98, 100, 101–3, 110
Agencies, federal, 13–14, 35–39, 140; congressional oversight of, 144, 145, 148; lawyers as employees, 29, 35–39, 56; reactions to decisions of, 105; representation before, 30, 44, 53, 56
Ambition, political, 8, 15, 54–55, 67, 69–70, 131, 181n; of committee members, 144; law as political stepping-stone, 2, 4, 38, 67, 69, 75, 123–24, 131; of lawyer-politicians, 86–87, 90–91, 172; strategic politicians, 69–70
American Civil Liberties Union (ACLU), 153, 182n
American Law Institute (ALI), 52
Americans with Disabilities Act (1990), 167–68
Analysis, levels of, 12, 15, 95, 120–21, 139, 162, 170; macroinstitutional, 162–74; quantitative, 4, 8–10, 12, 172–73
Aristocracy, lawyers as, 64–65, 144
Articulation system, judicial selection, 104
Attacks on, courts, 105, 117–21, 159–60; lawyer-politicians, 74–75, 79–82; legal profession, 33, 55
Attention to courts, 81, 83, 114–17, 138, 149, 181n
Attorney General, 36; nominees, 34–35
Auto insurance, 77

Bar associations, 40, 53
Behavior, political, 6, 9–12
Behavioralism, 6, 7–13, 95, 96, 169–70, 173, 175n
Boston lawyers, 80, 108–9, 133, 135, 181n
Boston Municipal Court, 133–34, 181n
Bush, George, 31, 33, 156–57, 159

Cabinet, number of lawyers, 34–35, 179n
Campaigning for office, judges, in Ohio, 101–2, 111; lawyers, 64–69; lawyers' access to elected offices, 69–72; president, 31–35; as professional advertising, 67–68; as protection of financial interests, 68; special skills of lawyers, 66, 69, 169, 172
Careers, political, 122–23, 129–30; primary, legal, 122–23, 128–29
Changes in individuals, during law school, 22–23, 80, 178n; through professional socialization, 18–19, 21, 178n
Clinton, Bill, 31–35
Clinton, Hillary Rodham, 32–33
Commerce Committee. See Energy and Commerce Committee
Committees, congressional, 14, 139; agency oversight, 144, 145, 148; assignments, 184n; characteristics of members, 139–40; consideration of constitutional issues, 150–60; decision-making styles, 139–48; Fenno's

40–43, 55–56, 78, 98, 171, 176n; *see also* Congress, U.S.; Legislators; State legislatures
Litigation, 144, 148, 179n–80n
Lobbyists, 14, 30, 41, 43–46, 56, 85, 179n
Local government officials, 14, 40, 54, 70

Macroinstitutional analysis, 162–74
Massachusetts, attention to courts by legislators, 115–16, 138; Boston lawyers, 80, 108–9, 133, 135; Boston Municipal Court, 133–34, 181n; conflict between lawyers and nonlawyers, 79, 135–38; courts, 98–101, 108–11, 115–17, 133–38, 181n; Governor's Council, 98–99, 108–9; judicial selection, 98–101, 108–11; legislature, 13, 62–63, 78, 79–81, 87, 91–94, 97–98, 99–101, 108–11, 115–17, 132; "Old Boys Network," in legislature, 80, 133; parties, 100–101; part-time legislators, 132; reform, court, 108–11, 126, 132–38
Middle-class, lawyers as representatives of, 72–75, 164
Myth of rights, 24, 47, 164–65, 168

Natural Resources Committee. *See* Interior and Insular Affairs Committee
Neo-institutional analysis, 5–7, 11–13, 95–96, 140, 162, 172–73, 175n
Nominal, lawyers, defined, 122–24, 130–31, 146; legislators, defined, 122–23, 130–31
Norms, of committees, 144, 184n; of institutions, 96, 140, 173, 184n; legal, 65; of professions, 17–19

Ohio, attention to courts by legislators, 114–15, 181n; conflict between courts and legislature, 102–4, 119–20; courts, 101–4, 111–13, 119–20; judicial selection, 101–4, 111; legislature, 13, 62–63, 78, 81, 87, 89, 91–94, 97–98, 101–4, 111–13, 119–20, 132; parties, 89, 101–2, 112–13; part-time legislators, 115, 132

"Old Boys Network," in Massachusetts, 80, 133

Parliamentarian, committee, 144, 147
Personality, of lawyer-politicians, 67, 69–70, 177n–78n; of lawyers, 179n
Political career paths, 88–89
Political culture, American, of committees, 150–60, 182n, 184n; of governmental institutions, 4–6, 10, 12, 15–16, 76, 139–40, 141, 163–64, 169–74, 184n; as legalistic, 65, 75; of states, 61–62
Political entrepreneurs, 71, 88–89, 123
Political experience. *See* Experience
Political office, access of lawyers to, 69–72
Political parties, American, 59–60, 70–71, 75, 172, 180n; compared to other countries, 72, 74, 169, 180n; as middle-class representatives, 72–75; numbers of lawyer-politicians, 59–60, 147; partisan attitudes toward courts, 106–7, 111–13; state organizations, 89, 100, 101–2
Political science discipline, 5–13; behavioralism, 6, 7–13, 95, 96, 169–70, 173, 175n; lawyers in, 53; neo-institutional analysis, 5–7, 11–13, 95–96, 140, 162, 172–73, 175n; traditionalist approach, 6, 7–8, 12, 76, 95–96
Politicians, professional, 4, 69; *see also* Lawyer-politicians
Politics, defined, 2, 56
Postbehavioralism, 6, 7, 11–12
Presidents, 160; campaigning for office, 31–35; lawyer candidates, 31–32; legal counsel, 55–56; number of lawyers, 31
Prestige, of congressional committees, 88–89; of courts, 96, 100, 121
Procedures and processes, lawyer preoccupation with, 12–13, 15–16, 23–28, 39, 66, 71, 83, 121, 144–45, 163–65, 167–74
Professional colonization, 3, 29, 175n
Professions, study of, 2, 17–19